LA'S DEADLIEST SERIAL KILLER
Patrick Wayne Kearney
By Tony Stewart (Survivor)

RIVERSIDE COUNTY SHERIFF
BULLETIN
ICIAL PUBLICATION OF SHERIFF'S DEPARTMENT, COUNTY OF RIVERSIDE, CALIFORNI
BERNARD J. CLARK, SHERIFF

TUESDAY, JUNE 14, 1977

ARREST FOR MURDER

TRICK WAYNE KEARNEY, WMA DOB 9-24-39
5'10", Wt. 146 lb., Hair/Brown, Eyes/Blue

DAVID DOUGLAS HILL, WMA DOB 12-23-42
Ht. 6'2", Wt. 175 lb., Hair/Brown, Eyes
SS # 453-58-4702

Copyright@2018 Tony Stewart

Tony Stewart Publication Bloomington, Indiana
JohnnieDillinger@aol.com

Copyright © 2018 Tony Stewart, All rights reserved

Cover Design by Tony Stewart

Library of Congress cataloging-in-Publication Data Tony Stewart, 2018

LA's Deadliest Serial Killer - Patrick Wayne Kearney Includes bibliographical references
ISBN: 978-1-312-51999-2

First Edition

Printed in the United States of America

No part of this publication may be reproduced, stored in or introduced into a retrieval system, or transmitted, in any form or by any means electronic, mechanical, photocopying, recording or otherwise without prior written permission of both the copyright owner and publisher of this book.

For my talented son, Keith Richard Stewart, a first-rate *Scriptwriter of Horror* and *gifted Animator*. Thank you for your assistance and knowledge of serial killers. May peace and happiness be with you!

        To my brother, Ron Stewart,
Who escaped this serial killer and later won his excruciating battle with cancer.

My Son walk not thou in the way with them; refrain thy foot from their path: For their feet run to evil, and make haste to shed blood.

... Proverbs 1:15,16

CONTENTS

PROLOGUE..6

THE TRASHBAG MURDERER...12

SLAYER STALKS REDONDO BEACH 28

KILLER ON THE ROAD..40

INAUGURATION OF DEATH 49

MURDER OF INNOCENCE...62

DRINKING WITH A KILLER...80

SCRAPBOOK OF MURDER..96

MISCARRIAGE OF JUSTICE..111

INSULT TO HUMANITY (No Trial).......................................126

ANOTHER TWIST – ZODIAC KILLER..................................137

FINAL ANALYSIS...146

WRITINGS OR A SERIAL KILLER.......................................157

SUMMARY OF EVENTS 163

ABOUT THE AUTHOR...168

VITAL INTERVIEWS..172

ACKNOWLEDGMENTS 183

REFERENCES & SOURCES 185

LETTERS FROM VICTIMS 189

UPDATE..191

PROLOGUE

June 30, 2003 - New York Times reported that the leading U.S. serial killers are homosexuals, to-wit: "John Wayne Gacy (33 murders), Patrick Wayne Kearney (32 – 43 murders), Dean Corll, Elmer Wayne Henley, and David Owen Brooks (27 murders each) and Juan Corona (25 murders.) Not mentioned in the article were Bruce David (28 murders), Stephen Kraft (16 murders); William Bonin (14 murders) and Jeffrey Dahmer of Milwaukee with 17 murders."

Note: Kearney is listed in above statement as having the largest number of victims noted in U.S. history, and possibly Mexico. Yet this killer remains unknown to many Americans.

A recreated picture of Patrick Kearney attempting to dump another body, just a few miles south of Borregos Hot Springs, east of Highway 74. Kearney was proud of his work; he bragged to officers that he could butcher, bag and dispose of a victim's body in less than an hour. He told detectives he couldn't remember exactly how many he had killed, before he casually added, "It was over 30 to 40 people." *Author's Collection*

Left to Right: Ron and Tony Stewart, three decades after the brothers were nearly murdered by serial killer Patrick Kearney. *Author's collection*

　　　I personally knew LA's deadliest serial killer Patrick Kearney, and he appeared to be an ordinary man, but his character would turn out to be far from normal. In comparison to good and evil, he was closer to a demon, or perhaps the devil himself. I would learn this fact, first–hand. In all my years as a crime writer, there has only been one murder story that I've never could completely clear from my mind. Told for the first time, this account of tremendous suffering and great loss of life is more horrific than words can possibly describe. People enjoy things that are different, but they also fear indifference, or things they do not understand. Many serial killers do not appear any different than you or I.
　　　In fact, they were often found to be just ordinary people in disguise. By the time a person realizes they have entered the world of a serial killer, it is much too late. In the killer's bloody lair, they no longer appear as people; they have become merely a product of sacrifice. So how do we describe the profile of a serial killer? It has been confirmed by the experts that it is virtually impossible to detect or identify a serial killer by his or her disposition alone. Many killers live ordinary lives and do not generally appear to be dangerous on the exterior. Nevertheless, there are several breeds of these madcap murderers, who kill with unstable motives, but it is the intellectual serial killers that are noted as the most dangerous, and difficult to catch. With a genius level *intelligence quotient* **(I.Q.) of 180, Patrick Wayne Kearney outsmarted police and the criminal judicial system to become one of the deadliest serial killers ever to escape the death penalty.**

County of Los Angeles
Sheriff's Department Headquarters
4700 Ramona Boulevard
Monterey Park, California 91754-2169

(323) 890-5500

077-01313-0383-014

February 7, 2008

Dear Mr. Stewart:

PATRICK KEARNEY

We have received your e-mail dated February 2, 2008, for records regarding the indicated file. Please be advised the records which you seek are privileged pursuant to California Government Code Section 6254(f). It is contrary to the policies and procedures of this Department and the Homicide Bureau to release copies of such reports unless required to do so by an appropriate court order. Please refer to Williams v. Superior Court (1993) 5 Cal. 4th 337 Rivero v. Superior Court 54 Cal. App. 4th 1048 and Haynie v. Superior Court (County of Los Angeles) (2001) Cal. Lexis 6478.

However, pursuant to the provisions of California Government Code Section 6254(f), the following is provided to facilitate your needs.

On January 23, 1977, the body of Nicholas H. Jimenez was discovered in Los Angeles County, Lennox Sheriff Station's jurisdiction. He had been shot in the head, stabbed in the stomach, bound with tape, and placed into a plastic trash bag. During the subsequent investigation, several other previously found victims were linked to the same killer.

The investigation led detectives to the Redondo Beach, California residence of Patrick Kearney. He fled the residence prior to being apprehended; however, he surrendered to authorities approximately one month later and ultimately confessed to killing 21 young men and boys. Among his victims were a five and an 8-year-old boy; however, most were young teenagers whom Kearney admitted to sodomizing after killing them. Kearney confessed to killing most of his victims by shooting them in the head with a small caliber weapon while they were asleep or somehow distracted. He stated he did this "because they did not bleed much when shot there."

A Tradition of Service Since 1850

Above: Letter from the Los Angeles County Sheriff's Department, regarding the author's request for *Trash Bag Murderer* files, clearly indicates that a court order would be needed to obtain copies of official police transcripts, even though this case has been closed for over 30 years. This is a disregard of the First Amendment Law, which states, "The right to privacy does not prohibit any publication of matter which is of public or general interest."

Tony Stewart   -2-   077-01313-0383-014

Of the 21 victims, five have never been found. This is due to the gruesome method Kearney used to dispose of them. Kearney explained that after killing his victims, he methodically dismembered their bodies using an exacto knife and hacksaw. He then, wrapped the pieces of bodies in plastic bags and discarded them in trash containers on his way to work and on his lunch hour.

These murders were committed from December 1969 to April 1977, with the killing increasing in 1976 and 1977, and they extended from Los Angeles County to the Mexican border.

We regret we are not able to provide any additional information and apologize for any inconvenience this may cause.

Sincerely,

LEROY D. BACA, SHERIFF

James Curtis

James Curtis, Captain
Homicide Bureau

Page two of this letter talks about Kearney's gruesome killing methods, and regret for the inconvenience. This is a refusal to release files associated to the investigation by Los Angeles County Sheriff Leroy D. Baca, and Captain James Curtis, yet several retired homicide detectives have been given liberty to borrow and copy these *Trash Bag Murder* files entitled "Murder Books," for their own personal use. The Sheriff's Department is still protecting serial killer Patrick Kearney, who was charged with 21 counts of murder, which is about half of the actual number of his victims in which he was convicted. Kearney is being treated as though he were the victim.

The story of *LA's Deadliest Serial Killer* is particularly personal to me. I'm not only the author, but also one of only two known survivors of serial killer Patrick Wayne Kearney. Today, Patrick Wayne Kearney aka the *Trash Bag Murderer* remains unknown by many. This is due to the killer's voluntary incarceration without a trial and his eagerness to escape the death penalty. It also remains devastating to all the relatives of victims, who continue to suffer from the scars of everlasting grief that will never entirely heal.

Obtaining information on this case from the L.A. Sheriff's Department was harder than pulling wisdom teeth from the jaws of a live great white shark. Kearney succeeded in destroying thousands of innocent lives during his inhuman bloody rampage that made satanic cult leader Charley Manson look benign in comparison. Kearney's character was like that of fictional killer Dr. Hannibal Lecter from the sensational movie, *Silence of the Lambs*; with the exception that Kearney was the real deal. Unlike Hannibal Lecter, Patrick Kearney was not a cannibal, nor was he a doctor of healing, as he would later claim. However, Kearney did have a genius level of intelligence, which he utilized to avoid capture, for well over a decade, while he continued to murder, seduce, and butcher scores of unfortunate victims. This intelligence presumably distorted his focus of reality, in which Kearney claimed was directly affected by a dysfunctional family and failure to bond during his early childhood.

Whatever the reason, he became a cold-blooded murderer, and a necrophilia that found excitement and pleasure in the seduction of the dead and dying. Kearney confessed to police for killing and draining the blood of over 30 to 40 people. The human body holds approximately ten pints of blood. This means to maintain this flowing river of blood, Kearney had to drain 300 to 400 pints of blood from his victims. This is a horrible thought. Kearney's *Modus Operandi* was usually similar in each case. After premeditatedly selecting his prey of boys and young men; Kearney would lure his victims into his web of horror, and without warning, he would walk up behind his victims and ruthlessly shoot them in the head. Next, to the tempo of a slow waltz, he dragged the dead or dying off to his bathtub, where he would amuse himself by forcibly sodomizing, beating, and mutilating his hemorrhaging fatalities. When the bodies were later recovered on the side of highways, they were neatly wrapped in separate trash bags and drained clean of blood. A qualified pathologist, who examined the remains of several victims, later described the killer as somebody who was familiar with the human anatomy.

Using the study of Victimology, detectives examined the evidence of each individual homicide case and noticed several obvious similarities. The victims generally consisted of vulnerable defenseless children, loners, hitchhikers, runaway teens, and transients passing through the area. These categories became the key characteristics that placed victims in the "High Risk" category, which made them potential targets of this maniac killer.

Contrary to reports, very few of Kearney's victims were homosexuals. If fact, many of the murder victims were so young that they were still virgins, and did not even have a sexual preference yet. Regardless, police jokingly labeled the murders, "The Gay blades," incorrectly suggesting that all the victims were gay. In the nineteen sixties and seventies, homosexuals were still not accepted openly in the public or society, as they are today. This was at a time when homosexuals were hiding their sexuality in the closet, and this is precisely why Riverside Superior Judge Gerald Schulte imposed a gag order on the Trash bag murderer case, during court proceedings. The gag order prevented the press from publicizing the procedures, especially since a few of Kearney's victims were homosexual celebrities, involved in the entertainment business. The names of these entertainers have never been publicized, but we know that Kearney did have sexual contacts with several of them.

It is apparent that criminals have more rights than the people they murder, and it is also evident that families of the deceased are also victims. This is exactly why this monstrous tale has been hushed up for an eternity, while numerous victims are still unaccounted for. Even today, this whispered topic remains a low-profile case, and lingers under veil of secrecy. Many questions have been asked over the years that scream for answers. Did Kearney just get off the hook for murders, in which he was guilty, but never charged? Was his roommate, David Hill involved, and if so, why was he set free? These questions and several others have remained unanswered for over three decades, just as the most important topics in this case have perished into incognito. For the record, this story has never officially been told to this extent of detail or accuracy, until now. The answers to these questions and more are now exposed for the first time.

Patrick Kearney's inner core of crime has been painstakingly studied in this volume. During the journey into the milieu of this ferocious murderer, the evidence illustrates that from his childhood to his surrender in 1977, this serial killer may also be directly linked to several other unsolved cold case murders. These additional murders would not only place Kearney over the top as the deadliest killer in the United States, but in Mexico and other territories as well. But we have not forgotten. This book is dedicated first and foremost to all the victims and relatives who have suffered significantly over the years, which in turn has also affected their health, faith, trust and moral values of society in general.

"From 1962 to 1977, Patrick Wayne Kearney was the most bizarre and deadliest murderer in California's history. Even though he appeared to be friendly on the surface, Kearney secretively manifested a severe homicidal - necrophilia behavior that cost over three dozen people their lives. Personally, I did not perceive any abnormal or peculiar characteristics in his persona; he appeared to be a calm, soft-spoken considerate man, but this compassion turned out to be pure deception to lure victims to their deaths. My brother and I were fortunate, we escaped."

... Tony Stewart - Survivor

THE TRASH BAG MURDERER

"I don't know if we'll ever know the total, because some bodies may be beyond recovery."
Lieut. Edward Douglas – L. A. Sheriff's Department

Serial Killer Patrick Kearney (Right) gives a murderous look as he shuns news Reporters, while his partner David Hill (Left) looks on. Moments before this picture was taken, Kearney surrendered to the Riverside Sheriff's Department in California, confessing to an appalling three-dozen cold-blooded murders. *Authors Collection*

Silence was broken on July 1, 1977, when two men walked into the Riverside Sheriff's Department and pointed at a wanted poster hanging on the wall, boldly announcing, that they were the suspects in question. It was reported that when the two men were asked what they wanted by the deputy seated at the front counter, the shorter man replied, "We're them."

The deputy on duty looked up at the two faces in front of her, and then to the poster they were referring too. Suddenly, her blood ran cold, and she became utterly speechless. She had good reason to be concerned; the wanted poster described both men as wanted for questioning in a series of gruesome murders in five counties. The men standing in front of her were Patrick Kearney and David Hill, both residents of Redondo Beach, California.

In dismay, the hysterical receptionist promptly calls for Riverside officers who immediately rush to her assistance. After Miranda rights are read, both men are placed under arrest and each was held on a $500,000 bond. Newspapers and television cameras flooded the lobby of the Sheriff's Department eager to get an interview with the accused killers. They wouldn't have to wait long; the press would soon learn that Patrick Kearney was a dangerous pedophile that enjoyed raping, and killing defenseless virgin boys, without mercy.

Drawing displays killer Kearney about to dispose of a victim's head and body parts in the trash bend at *Winchell's Donuts House* in Redondo Beach, while David Hill waits patiently in the truck. Although declared innocent, many believe Hill was either involved or knew about the murders first-hand. *Courtesy of Willie Smith*

It seemed like just another lazy sunny day in southern California. Normally my brother, Ron Stewart would be out surfing waves at Hermosa Beach, skate boarding or playing guitar and singing with her girlfriend Sandy Henderson, but on this particular day he was at home watching the news on television. What caught his attention next would send shock waves of horror down his spine. The television announced news of several killings along with the familiar name, Patrick Wayne Kearney of Redondo Beach. Immediately, Ron called me on the telephone in a hysterical voice and said, "Tony, turn the T.V. to Channel (2) News, Hurry!" Immediately I clicked on the old black and white television and turned the channel only to see Patrick Kearney's face covering the small screen. The voice reporting said, "Police say he may have killed as many as thirty-two people and possibly several more along the California coast.

The killer dismembered and stuffed his victims in trash bags." I was in total shock and couldn't believe what I was hearing. The face was that of the same man I had worked for from 1967 to 1970. In those days, I picked up coke bottles for redemption and mowed yards to fill my pockets with enough change to buy snacks and whatever else a young teen may need. Kearney had offered this opportunity as my employer.

As I continued to listen, my hands began to tremble, and my face quickly changed to a pale shade of white. It was as if I had seen an actual monster. Could this be? My mind drifted back, and I realized that I had recently visited Patrick Kearney at his residence during the midnight hours a few months back. Kearney had picked me up while hitchhiking and invited me over to his residence. Not a soul knew I was there. During this visit, Kearney asked to listen to my heartbeat and told me, he used to be a doctor. I thought it was strange, but I agreed to the odd request. I was young at the time and was wondering if his actions were right or wrong?

I watched the news and grasped at the reality that I could have been one of his many victims. Horror and disbelief furthermore raced through my head. "How could this man be a killer? He seemed so harmless." I asked myself, "Why did Kearney let me live, when he killed so many others?" I knew at this very moment, I would one day be telling this story. I spent the next three decades searching for answers. What I discovered would be more devastating and gruesome, than I could have ever possibly imagined.

He was born as Patrick Wayne Kearney, on Sunday, September 24, 1939, in a parenthood bungalow of East Los Angeles. His parents, George, and Eunice Kearney were well-educated and honest citizens, who strived to make a decent life for their family. Eunice was a strict homemaker, while George worked as an officer for the Los Angeles Police Department, commonly known as the L.A.P.D. According to statements made by sources, Kearney's parents were very strict. They made the rules and expected the children to abide by them.

In his childhood years, Patrick Kearney did not seem much different than any of the other kids, with the exception that he appeared wimpy in size and stature. East Los Angeles was a tough area with constant gang violence between the Hispanic and black community. This was a dangerous place to live in the nineteen forties and fifties. The police were persistently breaking up gang related fights and violence that would undermine and disrespect the very foundation of white middle-class communities.

George Kearney would be directly involved in these endless battles against criminals to make the city safe, but the understaffed L.A.P.D. was scarcely equipped to "Protect and serve" a community against the rapidly growing gang population. Young Patrick Kearney survived the violence by staying off the streets after dark. As a young child, he was very much aware of his surrounding environment from the stories his father told at the dinner table. His father had the habit of discussing his hectic workday with his wife as Patrick would overhear or eavesdrop.

In 1944, a nervous five-year-old Kearney began elementary school in Montebello, California. His grades were average, and he was an attentive student, but this would one day change. Only three years later, he developed thoughts of killing in his mind. During the same year, on July 14, a new brother named Michael Erwin Kearney was born in Los

Angeles County. Thirteen months later, his mother Eunice gave birth to her third child, Chester Ross Kearney. He was born on August 28, 1945, also in Los Angeles County. Sometime around 1950, George Kearney decided to move his rapidly growing family to Reseda, near the San Fernando Valley, which was a small farm community located on the outskirts of Los Angeles. Reseda was a tough place to live, due to gang activity in the area. The community consisted of 55 percent Hispanic population, while white families were considered a minority with a 45 percent population. Today, the area consists of 82 percent Hispanic and 6 percent white.

Patrick preferred hanging around the Hispanic kids, because they rarely picked on him, and the minority group accepted him. The family lived on Runnymede Street in a rural single dwelling home bordering the outskirts of town. The residence included a pole barn with chickens and pigs. Many of the families living in the area raised livestock and grew a variety of fruits and vegetables.

Patrick Kearney began attending Reseda Elementary School where sixty percent of children lived within a two-mile radius of the school. Most of the kids either walked or rode bicycles to school. Patrick Kearney was the new kid in school and was also painfully shy. This made him an easy target for the bullies, who often chased him home. He was lucky though, because Reseda Elementary was on Amigo Avenue, and was only about three to six blocks distance from his house. Kearney would try to outsmart the bullies by running across the school playground and straight up to Amigo Avenue. Once he safely reached Amigo Avenue, Kearney could run across a trashy field to Capps Avenue, and then onto Runnymede Street. Unfortunately, this plan did not always work, and they would catch up to him. When caught, he would face the usual mortification of name calling, throwing his shoes over telephone pole wires, ripping his shirt, and sometimes even a slight beating, in which Kearney would run home screaming and crying.

He would later compare his early childhood years to the movie "Carrie," stating that this was how he was treated. The 1976 movie starred Sissy Spacek, as *Carrie White*, a shy teenage girl with telekinetic powers. The story goes that a group of teenagers pulled a prank on Carrie at the High school prom; pouring a bucket of pig's blood from a fresh kill on her head. She retaliated and used her powers to kill half those attending the event. The only comparison between Kearney and Carrie, if any, would be the fact that innocent people were also killed during his bloody vengeance. Kearney was far from the innocent victim, as he so often claimed. His father, George Kearney thought that his son should stand up to these bullies and fight his own battles, but this would not go-over well with Patrick. He was not only a wimp, but also a bit of a "Girly-boy" that always seemed to be on the losing end of the ordeal. He would spend most of his younger years running like a frightened puppy, while dodging the bullies at every turn to escape torment.

In fact, from elementary to his adolescent school years, Kearney did not have many friends or acquaintances. Nor was he a big hit with the girls either. The boys his age looked at Kearney as an undersized weak child with thick glasses. They often called him, "Queer boy or little faggot." Kearney would later claim that the victims he targeted for death, reminded him of those bullies that he deeply despised. However, this is only one of many inconsistencies on Kearney's part, because two of his victims were just small children. One of his victims was an innocent five-year-old boy and the other child was eight years old, far cries from the bullies, he described. They were complete opposites from the bullies that once tormented him.

It was in Reseda on Runnymede Street where George Kearney bought his thirteen-year-old son a .22 caliber rifle. This was the true beginning that would later create and bring out the murderer within. George tried to toughen up his wimpy son by teaching him how to kill pigs and chickens. His father explained to young Kearney that if you shoot a pig just above and behind the left ear; the effect would produce less bleeding from the head, and the bullet would not exit. The projectile would ricochet inside the brain, usually killing the swine instantly. Later, Kearney would try this technique on human beings, just like the pigs he learned to slaughter. His father did not realize it at the time, but he had helped to create a cold-blooded killer. These lessons of slaughtering and butchering animals made Kearney feel a sense of power and control over these helpless unarmed creatures.

Unsupervised, Kearney began slaughtering and torturing animals for his own pleasure and would then flounder in the blood and guts. During these acts of violence, he fanaticized about murdering actual people. He would often place names of bullies on the pigs that he killed and would make them suffer a slow death. Other times after shooting the animals, he would beat and stab them with a brutal passion. Noting his future necrophilia tendencies, we can speculate that Kearney's first early sexual experiments, might have even involved the dead farm animals that he killed.

In his *32-page police confession,* Kearney openly admitted that in his early teens, his very first sexual experience was with the family dog. He over-powered the animal and had his way with him as the dog yelped and growled at his assailant, until anal bleeding occurred. Kearney was nearly bitten during the affair. The defenseless dog would keep his distance from Patrick from this day on. It didn't matter, because Kearney had already decided that his next victim would not be alive to put up a fight. Kearney also admitted that he knew by age eight that he would one day become a vicious killer. It is a scientific proven fact that childhood upbringing often affects our adult years, as it did with Patrick Kearney. Numerous murderers use their childhood experiences as a justification to kill, and Kearney was no different. Kearney kept his feelings bottled up deep inside, secretly hiding a sexual urge that could violently detonate at any given moment.

In the winter of 1953, Patrick Kearney began attending Junior High School at the Diane S. Leichman Special Education Center located at 19034 Gault St. His problems with bullies had not improved, especially since he had to take the bus to school. The bullies sat in the back of the bus where they immediately noticed the wimpy Kearney, just as the kids at other schools did. They began calling him "Fagot" and shot spit wads at the back of his head with straws. Even though Kearney's grades had been somewhat normal in his school studies, he later admitted that he was a mixed-up youngster. He was not diagnosed with any serious mental problems or personality disorders in school records, but he was a far cry from the normal student. When he wasn't daydreaming about cold-blooded murder in the classroom, Kearney enjoyed his favorite studies, which included science, where he looked forward to dissecting frogs, and other species on the school agenda. The frogs that were used as science projects were lucky to be dead during dissections, because Kearney was becoming very creative at the art of torture.

Concerned with the constant dangers of his job, George Kearney decided to seek less stressful employment, and resigned from the L.A.P.D. Next, George took up employment as a salesman for a travel agency, and promptly moved the family to Willcox, Arizona. Midway through seventh grade, Patrick Kearney was transferred to Willcox Middle School on Bisbee Avenue. George figured that since Patrick was living in a new state and would be attending a new school, perhaps things would be different this time. It didn't take long before several students became aware of Kearney's sexual preference, and he was singled out once again. He would become a social outcast and was shunned from normal students that were involved in sports and other academic activities.

An annoyed Kearney continued to foster thoughts of murder, but this time he aimed these hostile feelings directly at several Willcox students. As his murderous instincts began to escalate in his mind, Kearney had to force himself to refrain from killing. There were several places in Box Canyon desert where Kearney could have easily dumped bodies, which would have never been found. This desert area was near the large towering rock formations, where Apache Chief's such as Cochise, and other great Indian warriors, once resided. Willcox is in the Southeastern portion of Arizona and is considered high desert area. It is situated about 80 miles from Tucson, and seventy-five miles from Mexico. Kearney had once commented to police that he could have placed a dead animal on an anthill in the Arizona desert and watches it disappear right before his eyes. While in Willcox, he would become fluent in Spanish and later mastered several other languages, including Chinese, Japanese, some Russian and Arabic. He became fascinated with foreign languages. During these adolescent years, his increasing hunger to kill people also grew at a rapid rate.

Shortly thereafter his family decided to move to the South Bay area in Redondo Beach, California. This residence would be another temporary address, and upon graduating from High School in 1957, the family relocated this time to Houston, Texas. However, Kearney's stay in Texas would be short lived, because he yearned for a life in sunny California, where he grew up. He had changed from the wimpy child to a slender man of 5'7" and 145 pounds. He was ready to move out and start his own life. Once he moved out, Kearney would keep in touch with his mother, his brothers and his grandmother, Libby, but rarely talked to his father. In fact, he would later admit that he tried to avoid his parents entirely. After working several temporary jobs, he saved his money and moved to Long Beach, California.

While in California, he began attending classes at El Camino Community College in Torrance, California. He struggled to juggle work and attend school, and did not complete the courses that he enrolled in. In 1958, at age 19, he decided to join the U.S. Air Force, hoping to see the world. After basic training, he was reluctantly stationed back in Texas. The military would change Kearney. It hardened him to the point that he realized that he had no emotions or feelings towards people in general. This would become a permanent state of mind for Kearney. The army had given Kearney the strength to become who he wanted to be. It was here; during the last nine months of active duty that Kearney would meet his future lover and companion, David Douglas Hill.

Hill, a slender tall 6'2" dishonored Army veteran and noted high school dropout who was born in Lubbock, Texas on Christmas Eve, December 24, 1942. It was a mildly warm seventy-degree winter day, when David Hill took his first breath of air, and became the seventh of nine children. Hill's father was an extremely nervous man who was arrested for intoxication and had committed suicide in prison by hanging himself in a jail cell. Hill's mother became a struggling widow, who did her best to raise the large family at hand. She was a good mother who loved her children, and devoted as much time as possible to them, but couldn't always be there for David Hill. Hill needed special attention. Like his father, Hill was also tremendously nervous and living in a shell of confusion and frustrations.

Hill attended school at Lubbock High where students would recall; "He appeared to be a nervous, quiet and withdrawn individual who rarely spoke unless he knew you through an acquaintance or friend. Even then, he only spoke briefly in a deep low tone voice. This outlandish behavior made him appear very unsociable in public. When someone would offer a friendly "Hello," Hill would not mutter a word; instead, he would quickly walk away to avoid conversation. Hill had several health problems that followed him into his teens and adulthood. He was prescribed antibiotics for bladder and kidney infections, nerve pills, and medicine for ulcers. Hill later described his bisexual school days as saying, "When you find out when you're a kid that you are different from other kids, it kind of fucks you up in the head, you try to hide it or whatever."

At age 18, tired of lazing around the house and being a burden to his mother, Hill decided to join the Army. Not long afterwards, he was diagnosed with an undetermined personality disorder, and received a dishonorable discharge. Soon, he was back living at home in Lubbock, Texas, but it didn't take long before he wore out his welcome and began staying with friends. One of his friends was a high school sweetheart Linda Gayle that he dated, and later married. The two produced a beautiful daughter and named her Julie Anna, but Hill wasn't ready to raise a family. The marriage would be short lived, due to Hill's easygoing nature, and inability to keep steady employment needed to support a family. These repeated patterns of failure, added to the confusion and instability to his life, and made it difficult for him to find himself. Hill didn't finish school, nor did he succeed in completing the military. He couldn't even keep a job for any length of time, and found it hard to fit in. By age twenty-two, Hill had no clue about what he wanted to do in life, until he met Patrick Kearney. Kearney liked Hill, and the two had a lot in common, including the fact that they were both loners and homosexuals.

Kearney initially met Hill through a friend of a friend. He would give them rides in his car to the beach or just around town. In Kearney's eyes, when he looked at Hill, it was love at first sight, and they quickly became close friends. When it came to succeed, Kearney was the contrary of Hill, because he refused to accept failure. When Kearney failed at something, he would try harder, until he achieved his goal. With a genius level I.Q. of 180, Kearney was a man with a brain, and he sought out to use it, but there was also a shadowy side of Kearney's persona that would explode into a murderous rage far worse than the characters Dr. Jekyll and Mr. Hyde.

The nineteen sixties were a time when homosexual lifestyles were not accepted by society, but Kearney and Hill would go against the grain of the social order. The two decided to get a place together. In 1961, Kearney received an honorable discharge from the Air Force, and he talked Hill into moving to sunny Long Beach, California. There, the two rented an apartment in a complex along the beautiful southern *California's* coastlines. As Kearney searched for work, Hill relaxed and enjoyed the warm sunny weather. In the evening, they would cruise the strip and visit locations like the famous *Pike Amusement Park* and *Rainbow Pier*. The Pike had the first wooden roller coaster that extended out over the ocean and included several of other exciting rides and events. Kearney and Hill were having the time of their lives.

California was the place to be in the sixties, with early Rock n' roll music exploding on the scene, and blazing through Hollywood nightclubs, it was like fast spreading wild brush fire. The *Whisky-a-go-go, The Starwood* and several hot spot clubs introduced musical groups such as Dion, Chuck Berry, Righteous Brothers, Johnny Rivers, Roy

Orbison, The Beach Boys, Ricky Nelson and the king of rock n' roll, Elvis Presley. A few years later, Beatles arrived in America and people of all ages just went wild. It was a time of "Flower power," a time of long hair, of love, peace and war. Californians were changing history; it was like the gold rush all over again. Everyone was heading out west to let your hair down and enjoy freedom.

In 1960, John Fitzgerald Kennedy was elected our 35th President of the United States. He was the second youngest president and first catholic leader ever to serve in our nation's history. He was a patriotic and compassionate president, who spoke with influential and meaningful words. When the president would speak, the whole world would listen. "Ask not what your country can do for you, but what you can do for your county," and "Those who make peaceful revolution impossible will make violent revolution inevitable," the president would say.

In Kearney's world, he was growing angry inside, and secretively striving to make his own violence a reality. Kearney was angry with his parents, his life, society and the homophobias, but this wasn't the only thing bothering him. There was also trouble in paradise. Kearney resented the fact that his lover, and close companion, David Hill, was still unemployed and stayed home most of the time doing absolutely nothing. Hill was content with sleeping most of the day and mingling around the dark lonely house and hiding from the world outside. Kearney was supporting Hill financially and trying to get him to find a job, which was a constant struggle. Kearney was furious at Hill's unstable and insensitive decisions. Hill resented his roommate continuously pressuring him to find employment.

In the spring of 1962, Hill left Kearney with a note stating he had gone hitchhiking around the country. During this period, Hill took off and met up with his wife Linda, and the two decided to get back together. At this point, Kearney would become extremely jealous, and the relationship became estranged. The two was not even on speaking terms anymore.

Kearney took to the streets and went on the prowl, searching for some homosexual companionship. He left his apartment on Golden Avenue in Long Beach and rode his motorcycle down Ocean Boulevard, past Lincoln Park. He surveyed the areas, but spotted nothing, except local street gangs that reminded him of the bullies, he once encountered. A couple of gang members looked his way and a nervous Kearney stepped on the gas pedal and sped away on his motorcycle. Next, he cruised down the seaside past Rainbow Pier and down to the YMCA, which was a known homosexual hangout.

His eyes glanced upon some joggers and a few heterosexual couples who were exercising, but nothing sparked his interest. Suddenly, he spotted a couple of young gay boys and stared at them like a hungry wolf searching for meat. One of the boys zoomed in on Kearney's stalking gaze and flipped him off. The teen yelled out, "Fuck you Faggit!" Kearney didn't utter a word. Instead, he started his bike and headed back down South Pine Avenue, towards the Pike Amusement park. He parked his ride outside and walked over to an establishment called the "Plunge," a well-known bathhouse, which also attracted a few homosexuals from time to time. He watched as a few homosexuals were leaving, and he followed them to a nearby restroom. Unaware of two undercover policemen that were watching his every move, Kearney propositioned the two with money.

Kearney was arrested and accused of hanging around with other homosexuals near a bathroom. His bike was impounded, and he would spend the night in jail. This was a charge that Kearney would later claim he was not guilty of. The following morning, Kearney returned to his Golden Avenue apartment in Long Beach and decided to retrieve his motorcycle. Agitated about his recent arrest, Kearney went on the prowl the very next evening. Only this time, he decided, he would not get caught. While in Long Beach, that Kearney would murder three innocent people. Years after the fact, Riverside officers asked Kearney during questioning; "Do you recall where your first one (murder) was?" Kearney responded, "I was living in Long Beach. I lived in a little place down near the Pike in Long Beach." Kearney told officers that he believed two of the victims were either brothers or cousins to someone named Bobby.

He described the first victim as a nineteen-year-old unknown man, from either Louisiana or Oklahoma. Kearney gave the man a ride on his Honda motorcycle. He took the man to a deserted area, near Indio, California. He parked the motorcycle and when the young man turned his back, Kearney walked up from behind and shot him in the head. Next, he dragged the body into the brush to sexually assault him and then he mutilated the body. When Kearney was finished, he ditched the remains in a shallow grave near Indio near State Highway 86, which runs north and south in the southeastern desert region of Southern California. The Highway joins State Route 111 at Coachella in route into Indio, which is located 70 miles east of Riverside and 125 miles east of Los Angeles County and Indio lies 26 miles east of Palm Springs.

Victim number two was about 16 years old, 5'8 and 145 pounds. He had been present when Kearney gave John Doe number one a ride on the motorcycle and was now asking where his relative was. Kearney thoughtfully offered to take the teen to his relation, and the youth climbed on to his bike. Kearney drove him to the same location and the teenager climbed off the motorcycle. Curious, he began looking around for a house or campsite where his friend might be. Confused and bewildered, he began to wonder why Kearney brought him to this area. He would have an answer as he turned his back on Kearney. The killer walked up behind the prey and put a bullet into the back of his head. Just like the first victim, Kearney dragged his dead body off to sexually assault the youth. Victim number three was an 18-year-old named teenager named Mike. He was also taken to Indio, where he met the same fate as the others. Kearney described Mike as a 5'9" and 150-pound transient who was visiting in Long Beach at the time of his death. It should be noted that Kearney was never charged for these murders, and the bodies were never recovered.

In a sense, Kearney completely got away with these three senseless murders. At the time of the murders, Kearney had been attending history courses at Cal State Long Beach University and found some spare time between classes to murder three victims. Hill returned a few months later and knocked at Kearney's door. A moment later, all was forgiven, and Kearney was happy that Hill was back home.

By August of 1963, Kearney was financially stable after finding a good job working as aeronautics engineer for Hughes Aircraft in Culver City and at the El Segundo facility. Soon Kearney would again become frustrated with Hill and his lack of interest to find employment. Kearney would do the unthinkable and leave his job at Hughes on January 25, 1963. Realizing he had made a huge mistake by giving up a good job, Kearney reapplied and was rehired on April 4, 1963. He was quickly promoted to the *Senior Research Assistant* and became a salary employee, earning a whopping twenty-thousand dollars-a-year, without even having a degree. This was a good wage in the nineteen sixties when the average wage was about half of what he was receiving.

At Hughes Aircraft, Kearney's supervisor said; "He was an ideal worker, a model worker." His supervisors would later describe his demeanor as an employee as "clear and prompt." His other duties included deciphering and identifying parts from damaged Russian military aircrafts. Kearney's employers were impressed that Kearney could read, write and speak five to six languages fluently. Regardless, Kearney felt angered that several coworkers were taking advantage of him, even though on the surface, he appeared to be very conservative towards others.

In his public life, Kearney wore a disguise of normalcy, but behind the mask was a real-life unstable character. Behind closed doors; pure evilness reflected from his appearance as he glanced in the bathroom mirror. Within this domain, he would grow more and more aggravated at his unemployed roommate David Hill, who spent his days loafing around the house. While returning home from work one day, Kearney over heard a couple young men in front of his house talking about David Hill. He listened as these young men spoke out loudly about Hill performing oral sex on several of the neighborhood boys. The Kearney residence was becoming popular in the area and this news was quite disturbing to Kearney. He was worried that having sex with minors could bring the police knocking on his door, and this was the last thing Kearney wanted. These incidents would lead to several heated arguments that would spiral into intense fights, until Hill eventually stomped out of the house and left. Many of Hill's friends later became Kearney's victims. Hill would spend several nights away with friends until things eventually cooled down. The relationship would continue to become turbulent and disorderly over the next ten years. It is surprising that Kearney never killed Hill during these disagreements. He had killed several people for far less reasons, if for any reasons at all.

Within a year, Kearney and Hill moved to Culver City, and everything cooled down for a while. Hill began meeting new friends at local bathhouses and would disappear from time to time. On one of these occasions, he left for three to four days to visit his wife, Linda, in Texas. During this time, Hill told Linda, he had gone back to California, but promised to return for her. When he didn't return, Linda went to California looking for him. When she located Hill, he decided to leave Kearney again and reconcile with Linda. This didn't work out because Hill couldn't find a job. As with his previous attempts, Hill most likely did not try too hard to find a job. Oddly, Hill persuaded Kearney to let him and Linda move in with him. Now, Kearney, Hill, and Linda were all living together under the same roof. It did not take long before tribulations began, and there was a lot of tension in the air. As tempers flared, a jealous Kearney attacked Hill during a heated fight and caused him to move out with his wife, Linda. Kearney would later admit that this was when he killed his first victim "George," a San Diego resident. Even though Kearney had already killed, he claimed that the murder took place in 1967, but this was not true. Kearney had conveniently forgotten about the three men he admitted to murdering in Long Beach in 1962. It is also ironic that this victim "George" had the same name as Kearney's father George. Was this just a coincidence? Or was this retaliation against his father and the man died because of his name? We will never know.

We do know that while David Hill was gone, Kearney continued to satisfy his murderous rage. When Hill returned home, he declared his relationship with his wife Linda was permanently over. Linda divorced Hill two years later in 1966. There were several reasons why the marriage failed, but the main reason was most likely because Hill couldn't keep a steady job. It didn't take long before Hill was out running around again. As Hill's roller coaster of events continued, Kearney hit his exploding point. He could transform into an enraged deadly maniac with the ability to maintain a cool and calm personality, which was a dangerous combination. This enhanced his ability to lure his victims in using his soft-spoken tongue, mannerisms, and deceiving trust. Just when Kearney had his victims struck in his sticky web, he would ambush them without warning, suck the remaining life out of them, and wrap them up like a spider does its dead. After he killed his victims at his residence, he would drag them off to the bathroom, where he would undress the corpses and sexually assault them.

Next, he would play doctor, examining and dissecting the bodies, and playing with the corpse like a child with a new toy. Utilizing a hacksaw, Kearney would then cut them into pieces, and study each body part, like a student in school working on a science experiment. He delicately rinsed and washed each severed limb. He drained of all the blood, which he believed would slow the smelling process and eliminate any forensic evidence. It was a clean procedure and he was careful not to leave any fingerprints in the dried blood, which meant no evidence left behind, at least that he was aware of. Not only did Kearney learn how to shoot to kill from his father, (who taught him how to kill pigs) he also learned from studying serial killer Dean Corll. Corll was a homosexual killer and a pedophile. He was from Houston, Texas. Corll had murdered seventeen adolescent boys.

Corll tortured, strangled and shot his victims before wrapping in white trash bags and burying them in swallow graves. Kearney read about Corll's wicked crimes, and then became obsessed with the killer; collecting several newspaper clippings of this torturous murder spree. Corll met a violent death when one of his own murderous crime partners named Elmer Wayne Hensley killed Corll with his own gun. Kearney would surpass his mentor, nearly doubling the number of victims that Corll killed. In fact, Kearney's murders would become a vicious homicidal cycle like no other killer in America's history on record. Kearney, like Corll, may have also had a partner involved in his crimes.

Sometime in June of 1967, Patrick Kearney woke up early Saturday morning at their Culver City residence and invited his companion David Hill to join him on a drive to San Diego and over the border into Mexico. A sleepy-eyed David Hill agreed to go and after taking a quick shower, they were off. It was one of many weekends the two would spend their time driving through the streets of Mexico visiting the bathhouses.

Soon they were driving southward down the San Diego (405) Freeway, until they reach their turn off on the Santa Ana (5) Freeway. Two-and-a-half hours later, they arrived in the city of Chula Vista, near the Mexico border. Next, they decided to drive onto Tijuana to visit the local bathhouses. After spending an enjoyable and fulfilling day having sex, they returned home with the sun setting over the west coast. These weekend visits into Mexico would ultimately become Kearney's training ground for murder. He could easily kill some poor Hispanic children and slip back across the border long before the bodies were found. David Hill Kearney dropped him off the following October at a hotel or a cabana, and then he cruised the back alleys of Tijuana. It was during one of these trips that Kearney met a Spanish fellow who identified himself as "Jorge," also pronounced "Hor-Hey," which is the equivalent to "George" in the English language.

The two begin talking; George had told Kearney that he was presently working in the San Diego area at Caruso's Pizza. George adds that he was temporarily staying with a friend in a nearby apartment and that he often brings money home to his family in Mexico. George says his roommate has been falling behind on his rent, and now they're getting evicted. Kearney appears to be genuinely concerned and has an epiphany. He invited George to come stay with him at his Culver City residence for a few weeks. Kearney assures George that he could find a good job in Culver City. George was ecstatic about the idea, but he would make a grave mistake when he gratefully accepts the offer to stay with Kearney. Later that day, Kearney introduces George to his roommate David Hill. Hill would later deny ever meeting George, even though the three stayed together at the Culver City residence for a few days.

Not long afterwards, Hill bids them goodbye, and Kearney drives him to the airport. Hill boards an airplane bound for Texas to visit his family for Christmas. Hill is gone for two weeks from December 22, until January 2 of 1962. During this time, Kearney and George spend a lot of time together. Kearney eventually becomes annoyed with George, who was supposed to be looking for a job; but instead, he is acting as though he is on vacation at Kearney's expense. Kearney decides he wants to take George back to Mexico before Hill returns, but his visitor isn't ready to leave. Instead, an unmotivated George loafs around, eats and sleeps throughout the end of December.

It wasn't long before Kearney begins to fantasize about sexually assaulting and hurting George. By December, Kearney decided to relieve his frustrations by murdering George. He grabs his .22 caliber rifle and sits on the edge of his bed for several hours trying to build up his confidence to kill George, his friend and lover. He calls out in a calm voice, "George, can you please come in here?" George is sound asleep and doesn't respond. An extremely nervous Kearney grips his rifle tight in his arms as he tells himself, "I can do it." These feelings begin to steadily grow, until Kearney becomes excited. Suddenly, Kearney stands up and quietly marches into Hill's bedroom, where George is still fast asleep. He places the rifle to his shoulder, and like a man about to put a limp horse out of its misery, he takes aim. With his heart pounding a hundred beats per second, he aims the cold barrel "Point blank" directly between George's eyes. A half-awake George opens his eyes to find himself looking down the barrel of Kearney's rifle. However, before he had time to understand what is going on, Kearney pulls the trigger. There was a loud "Boom!" and the smell of gunpowder filled the air. The force of the shot causes George's head to simultaneously jerk away and erupt like a volcano. With blood flowing out everywhere, George's limp body rolls off the bed and onto the floor with a "thump." As George lies there dying, his last fading thoughts were that of confusion, disarray, and fear.
Kearney looks down to see blood rapidly pouring from George's head like red wine spilling straight from the bottle.

In his statement to police Kearney said his heart was beating so hard, he felt as if he was going to experiencing a severe panic attack. He is unprepared about what to do next. He became worried about getting caught. Thoughts began raging through his head, as he asked himself, "Did the neighbors hear the shot? What if Dave comes home early? What if the police come? What did I do?" Frantically, he rushes over and begins looking out every window, searching and surveying the streets of the neighborhood. He runs to the bathroom, and quickly grabs a couple of towels, and then hurries back into the bedroom where George lays dead or dying. He wraps the towel around his victim's head and throws another one on the floor to soak up the blood. Kearney realizes that he had not thought everything through entirely. Even though e had killed before, but the others were outside in a wooded area, not in his own home. He dragged George to the bathroom and placed him in the tub. Then he filled a bucket with hot soapy water and returns to the murder scene to clean the blood on the bed and floor. He sprays Lysol disinfectant in the air to help dilute the smell of gunpowder.

After scrubbing the blood, he returns to the bathroom and begins undressing George. He places the bloody clothes in a trash bag. Next, the killer climbs in the shower and places both hands around the victim's body. He lifts the dead weight with some difficulty, but he is anxious to rape his dead or dying victim. Both nervous and aroused, Kearney begins to sodomise his bloody victim with such force that causes the rectum to bleed rapidly. After he reaches a climax, Kearney calms down and relaxes. Blood is everywhere in the tub and on the tiles as it slowly flows down the drain. He looks down at George and realizes that his bullet is still in the victim's brain. Concerned the bullet may be traced back to his gun; he decides that he must retrieve the bullet from the victim's bloody skull. He grabs a hacksaw, hammer, razor knife and screwdriver from his toolbox. Kearney slices a lemon size hole in the victim's forehead, and then cracks the skull wide open with the hammer and screwdriver. When the opening is large enough to reach inside George's skull, Kearney used his fingers to feel around inside the brain tissue, until he finally locates and retrieves the bullet. It was a bloody mess with brain and bone particles all over his bare hands. After removing the bullet, and cleaning up most of the blood, he became aroused again. Once again, he begins having anal sex on the corpse, until he hears a door slam. David Hill has just returned home. Kearney hears
Hill's voice outside the bathroom door. Hill says, "I'm home, but I'm very tired. I'm going to bed." Kearney responds, "Okay David, I'll see you tomorrow."

By this time, the room is clean and free of blood. Hill later claims that he never realizes what had occurred at the house. Assured that Hill has turned in for the evening, Kearney carries George's body into his bedroom and places it in the closet. Like a man with a huge personal secret, Kearney lies down in his bed, takes a deep breath of air, and recalls what he had done. He feels a feeling of accomplishment. After all he has fulfilled his childhood dream of killing another human being. This evening he sleeps as peaceful as a baby. The next day, Hill tells Kearney that he will be meeting some friends and won't be back until later that evening. After Hill departs, Kearney hurries outside to search for a spot to bury George. He locates an area between two garage structures at the rear of his triplex. After digging two to three feet down beneath the concrete foundation, he returns to George's body in the house. He attempts to lift George, but then he drops him, because of the dead weight. He succeeds a second time and places the body on the bed, where he begins to shave the hair off the body. Kearney breathes heavily, as he decides to dissect the corpse. With a sharp razor knife, he splits open the chest cavity and peels the skin off the body like peeling an orange. He places the skin in a bag and proceeded to remove the inner organs to satisfy his curiosity. He is fascinated as he explores what a human being looks like on the inside.

As he attempts to place the internal organs and other body parts in a large trash bag, he realizes not all the body parts are not going to fit. He decides to use a hacksaw to saw off the head, and then continues by hacking off the arms and legs. First, Kearney places George's torso in the shallow grave outside, and then goes back in the house to retrieve the arms, and legs. He places them on top of the body and goes back in the house to retrieve the head. After placing everything in the shallow grave, he shovels dirt over the remains and buries George without muttering a word. Kearney later tells Hill that George decided to return home to Mexico.

During future visits to San Diego, Kearney stated that he couldn't even drive down the same road near the pizza restaurant where George once worked, because it was much too painful. He claimed killing George made him a nervous wreck thereafter, because he was worried about being caught and going to jail for murder. A month after the killing of George, the manager of the Van Buren Apartments receives several complaints about a horrible smell behind the garage area. She went to investigate, but the woman could not determine where the smell was coming from, but assumes it is a dead animal that died somewhere nearby. She questions Kearney and some of the other renters and this adds to Kearney's extreme nervousness, in which he later claims to experience moments of shaking uncontrollably for several minutes at a time.

Not long afterwards, Kearney persuades Hill to move with him to an apartment just three buildings down the street. He tells the manager he is moving to escape the horrible smell. Whether Hill thought the request was odd or not is not known, but it wouldn't have mattered, since he wasn't paying rent anyway. A year would pass before Kearney realized that he had gotten away with murder. Kearney claimed that he did not kill again in the United States for a few years. However, Hill and Kearney's visits to Tijuana would continue, while bodies littered the streets. These unsolved murders carried Kearney's M.O. (Method of operation). He denied ever killing anyone in Mexico, and his story was not thoroughly checked out by officers, because they were mainly concerned with their *own* jurisdiction.

During an interview with lead Homicide Detective Roger Wilson of the Los Angeles Sheriff's Department, Kearney said he never returned to the scene of his crimes. Kearney lied, because he did return to the house at Culver City residence and found that coyotes had eaten the fresh off George, leaving mostly just the bones. He stated that the pants and wallet with credit card were still where he left them. Looking closer at George's background, he must have been an established individual financially. He had decent job at one time, and was in procession of a credit card, which indicated a good credit rating.

Kearney would later tell detectives that George was heavy into narcotics, but this has never been established. When Kearney was apprehended in July of 1977, he confessed to detectives that he shot George at his home, adding, "I dismembered and skinned the corpse," he said boldly.

Without emotion, Kearney calmly compared the killing and mutilation of a human being, to a fresh caught trout that had been recently filleted. He acted as though murder was just an innocent hobby, adding that he wasn't concerned about the death of George, but he was worried about the bullet in the victim's bloody head that could have been traced back to his gun. Kearney told detectives that George was his first victim and agreed that he was killed around Christmas time of the mid to late sixties. This was another contradiction. Kearney had already confessed to Riverside detectives about the murders that began sometime around 1962 in Long Beach, San Diego and Tijuana, Mexico. This would have been at least five years before George's murder. The unidentified skeletal remains of a man identified only as "George" were officially found buried at Kearney and Hill's residence in Culver City at 4071 Van Buren Place on July 8, 1977. Police would later confirm that the victim was shot between the eyes, sexually assaulted, mutilated and then buried between two garage structures at the rear of the triplex.

When forensics examined the body, they had estimated that Kearney killed George approximately 1968 to 1970. The body had a one-and-one-inch by five-and-one-half cut made on the skull by some type of sharp object, which was most likely, a hacksaw. Lieutenant Ed Douglas of the Los Angeles Sheriff's Department told homicide investigators, "Murderer's Kearney and Hill had shot the victim between the eyes in their apartment." Whether Hill was involved in this murder remains a mystery, even though he has never been indicted on charges. We will need to investigate more on whether Kearney lied to protect David Hill on the killing of George and several others, "I skinned and dismembered the corpse," said Kearney. Without emotion, he spoke calmly about his victim's demise, as though talking about a fresh caught trout that he had previously filleted.

Murder of "George" John Doe.

During an interview with Patrick Kearney by retired Lead Homicide Detective Roger Wilson of the Los Angeles Sheriff's Department, Kearney spoke about how he murdered his roommate George – 1978.

Wilson: Pat, tell us about George. What did you do?
Kearney: Well, I laid his body on a shower curtain on my bed, and then I shaved all the body hair on him.
Wilson: What did you do next?
Kearney: Well, I skinned him. After I skinned him I took a hacksaw to his head. I went in and pulled out the bullet.
Wilson: (The bullet had gone between the eyes all the way through his head and hit the back of the skull, because the back of the skull was fractured where the bullet had hit. I'm sure that a .22 loses velocity quickly and bounces around and that's how he kills them quick) *Wilson:* You skinned him?
Kearney: Yeah,
Wilson: The whole body?
Kearney: Yes,
Wilson: What did you do next?
Kearney: Well, I opened up his chest cavity.
Wilson: What did you do?
Kearney: I pulled everything out and then, just curious.
Wilson: And then?
Kearney: I cut the arms and legs off.
Wilson: How did you do that?
Kearney: I used an Exacto-knife, a number 11 blade, which is the little diagonal blade. Yeah, very sharp as a scalpel.
Wilson: And ah what did you do next?
Kearney: Well, I went out between the garages, and I dug a hole underneath the cement foundation and then placed the torso, and then placed the legs, because I couldn't carry everything at once. I placed the legs on top on the torso and the arms on top of that. Then I took all of

George's possessions, I had even bought him clothes and stuff and I got rid of it and dumped the bloody shower curtain.

Wilson: Kearney gave us all the information on George, and we're still connected to the missing and exploded children. Were still trying to find out who he is.

      In the above statement, Detective Wilson mentions how they are still trying to determine George's identity through missing and exploded children. In the beginning, Riverside and several other counties were working together on the murders, but as soon as the L. A. Sheriff's Department took over the case, it became their sole project. The identify of George could have been determined early on if the L. A. Sheriff's Detectives had communicated with the Riverside Sheriff's Department.

      During his initial interview, Kearney told Riverside detectives that George worked at Caruso's Pizza in San Diego. Caruso's Pizza could have provided an address, phone number, and more important, a last name for George. Over 30 years later, Caruso's Pizza is long gone along with vital information that could have closed the case on George. Police did not investigate Caruso's Pizza where George claimed he was employed. Today, Caruso's Pizza is long gone along with any evidence that may have helped to positively identify the forgotten victim, only known as "George." While talking with *Los Angeles County Detective* Louis Danoff, I was informed that officers were slow at notifying relatives, after the victims were found. This was the case with George.

      In the spring of 1968, Patrick Kearney desperately wanted to move and located a small two-bedroom home in Redondo Beach located at 1906 Robinson Street. They agreed to rent the property from Reid Wilson's Realty with an *option to buy*. That summer, Patrick Kearney moved into the neighborhood and I would meet him through Reid Wilson. It would be a meeting that almost led to my fate, as well as my brother, Ron.

SLAYER STALKS REDONDO BEACH

"From our hideout behind the local bar, no one could see us, but we could see them. It was our secret spot. We could even see Patrick Kearney's house from the parking lot a few feet away."
Tony Stewart

In the 1960's, I lived in Redondo Beach, California. We were a middle to poor class family with two working parents struggling to raise, feed and clothe six children. We had very little food and wore second-hand clothes, but we survived. As kid, we found word picking up trash for local Reid Wilson reality. Mr. Wilson was the same man my father paid his rent to each month. Mr. Wilson had a soft spot for poor kids wanting to earn a little money. We did any type of work we could find, including mowing lawns and collecting coke bottles for redemption at the local store. We had several people in the neighborhood who would set coke bottles outside their door for us. One of these people turned out to be a serial killer named Patrick Kearney. I would later be offered a job mowing his yard each week. Eventually, I would work for Kearney on and off for the next several years.

When my brother and I were not mowing lawns, or picking up trash for Reid Wilson, we were doing odd jobs. On a good day, we could earn up to $10.00 collecting bottles. The wonderful thing was we had regular contributors that would leave bottles outside for us, which was nice, but it was a lot of work. Most stores would not accept bottles, unless they were thoroughly cleaned. Most of coke bottles we picked up were usually dirty and greasy and many were covered in ants, but overall, the money was worth it.

On December 12, 1969, Patrick Kearney purchased his first house on Robinson Street for $20,750.00 from Reid Wilson Realty. This was an entire year's wage for Kearney. He was employed at Hughes Aircraft in Redondo Beach as an engineer. Kearney's killing spree had begun in Long Beach, and Riverside, California and now he was living in Redondo Beach. If he would had stop killing at this point, he probably would have gotten away with murder, but his addiction to kill was too overwhelming. Kearney stayed busy working long hours in the nineteen sixties renovating his new home, which would later become his future habitat for murder.

Within the next few years my younger brother, Ronnie would become exceptionally familiar with the characters of both Kearney and Hill. The pair had chased my brother down Aviation Boulevard in a pickup truck. Ronnie was petrified, but he had escaped several close calls of nearly being kidnapped by Kearney and Hill. It was a horrifying experience, but he kept the incidents to himself for the time being. I was the only person he told, because our parents would not have believed us anyway. In fact, we would have most likely been punished for bringing up such events.

Our parents were very strict and taught us not to get involved in the affairs of others, even if it did affect us personally, we were usually told to keep our mouth shut, which we did. If we had reported the incident to the police, Kearney may have been investigated in the early nineteen seventies, and perhaps lives could have been saved.

The Stewart residence was located at 3000 Aviation Boulevard was just around the corner from Patrick Kearney's residence. *Photo Courtesy of Chris Stewart*

One day after finishing my yard work at Kearney's residence, I went to his side door and knocked to collect my $3.00, but I felt nervous because the next-door neighbor had a couple of vicious German shepherds. These dogs would collide into the fence and bark in an aggressive manner that would scare the daylights out of me. The neighbor's front yard was over my head. It was horizontally level with Kearney's rain gutters at the base of his roof.

So, these shepherds were above me at the fence line, looking down and barking viciously as if in attack mode. A German Shepard had bitten me when I was younger, and it was an experience that left me afraid of dogs. As I look back now, it was Kearney that I should have been afraid of, instead of the dogs. I would learn much later that a police officer lived at this residence next door to Kearney, and these dogs were trained police German shepherds. Even though I was afraid of them, these dogs were probably trying to warn me that I was in danger. German shepherds are smart animals, and they were probably aware of Kearney from the scent of death that radiated from the house.

Moments after knocking on the door, Kearney answered and invited me inside the house. I was always a bashful youngster and would respond by saying, "That's Okay, I'd rather wait outside, I'm not allowed to go into other people's houses. Thanks." This was a rule set by my father. We were never allowed to enter a stranger's house without my father's permission, and he would usually say, "No, you stay out of other people's houses." When I look back now, this was a positive rule that most likely saved my life. If I had gone inside his house, the probability of surviving would have not been good. I most likely would not have lived to see my teenager years or survived to write this book. As you will observe from this thrilling story, both my brother and me would escape Kearney's murderous grip and survive to tell another side of this eerie lurid story. I first met Patrick Kearney in summer of 1967. My family had moved to 3000 Aviation Boulevard in Redondo Beach when I was in fourth grade. We lived in an old style two-story five-bedroom home, located just a block and a half from Kearney's house at 1906 Robinson Street. Our house was the largest on the block, if not the neighborhood. Kids from school thought we were rich, but the reality was that my father had got a deal on the rent. We needed this big house, because we had eight brothers and sisters.

Left to Right: Ron and Tony Stewart, the ONLY two survivors who lived to tell their story.

Left to Right: Bare-footed brothers Tony and Ron Stewart on the front porch of their residence at 3000 Aviation Boulevard, which was just down the Street from Patrick Kearney's house. *Courtesy of Ron Stewart*

Our realtor Read Wilson was a retired police officer who won it big in Las Vegas and invested his money in real estate. He made a fortune and his business prospered with a large monopoly of property and land. Reid Wilson's Real Estate office was only a short walk away from our house. Mr. Wilson and his wife, Fairy, knew we were a poor family and enjoyed having us around the work place. He also owned a whole block of commercial businesses, which included a grocery store, a liquor store, a bar, a flower shop, a restaurant called "Chicken Lickin," a barbershop and several other businesses. He would pay my brother, Ron and I, every weekend to walk around this block of businesses and pick up all the trash littering the grounds.

Each weekend we would grab a large brown paper bag from Bob's Market, and walk around the block barefooted picking up papers, bottles, cigarette butts and whatever was lying around. When we were finished, we would find Mr. Wilson, who napping on the couch in his office. He would walk with us to check our work and at the same time get his daily doctor recommended exercise. If we missed any trash, he would point his finger at it and tell us to "pick it up."

On Saturday's, we would earn a whole dollar. On Sunday, he would pay a dollar each and he reward us to a free lunch at McDonald's. We would all load up in his 1960 four-door Ford Falcon car and drive about three miles to McDonald's located on Artesia Boulevard in Manhattan Beach. Mr. Wilson would buy us a cheeseburger, French fries and a large chocolate milkshake. This was when McDonald's advertised, you could buy a burger, fries and a shake for under a dollar. He was a storyteller and we enjoyed listening to his far-fetched tales, while we worked. He would often tell us how he was a Chicago policeman and he had chased John Dillinger, the top outlaw of the nineteen thirties. His wife would always back anything he said by adding, "Oh yeah, he chased a lot of them." The stories were colorful and exciting, but they were also fictional. We were always hungry kids and there wasn't much food at home, so we enjoyed spending our hard-earned dollar on candy, pop and potato chips. We really enjoyed spending our money on snacks. There was a heavy wooden bench mounted up high behind the local bar called "Popeye's" where we would sit and munch on our treats and watch the drunks stagger out. The drunks could not see us, but we could see them looking down from our bench. It was our secret spot, and from the parking lot nearby, we could even see Patrick Kearney's house. Mr. Wilson not only gave us kids small paying jobs, but he would also pay us for helping to clean up his other properties, after renters vacated the premises.

When we were not working for Mr. Wilson, we would venture out into the neighborhood, and go door-to-door in search of odd jobs to earn money. However, this was a dangerous area for kids to be roaming around without an adult. We were surrounded with perverts that would drive by and flash us, child molesters, rapists and murderers, and several other criminal's types living in the area. During our quest for work, we would meet all kinds of people. Some of the people we crossed paths with were nice, while others would just say, "Get lost and quit bothering us."

One house in the area that left coke bottles out for us was at the home of the notorious Crow brothers. There were four brothers who had been in and out of prison for petty to violent crimes. The Crow's lived around the corner from us on Plant Street. They were a gang of about fifteen strong; they were extremely loud and rowdy people. Gang members were in and out of the house, on a regular basis, and the Redondo Beach Police were constantly watching the residence.

Over the years, several neighbors had called the police to report the loud music, fights, and wild parties. Well-known around the neighborhood, the Crow's looked like hardened ex-cons, fresh out of prison and none of them cared for the police. They were a rough bunch all in their early to mid-twenties. The biggest and meanest guy in the bunch was called *Sugar Crow*. Sugar Crow stood over six feet with several tattoos all over his body and had a scar long across the top of his shaved head. The scar looked like some type of brain surgery wound, which may have been perhaps from a recent street fight or battle. He was a scary looking character, and not a guy to be messing around with. Regardless, all the Crow brothers and their associates may have hated the police, but they seemed nice to the poor kids in the neighborhood. The Crow brother's violence would turn out to be mild compared to butcher Patrick Kearney. However, the brothers would have even sparked fear into the likes of Patrick Kearney, if they had ever met. This was our neighborhood. Patrick Kearney always seemed like a nice guy with an honest face and anyone who knew him would have never assumed he was a killer.

Reid Wilson Realty is building to the right in front of white truck. The market to the left was *S & S Market* where Kearney told the butcher, he admired their knives.

     I remember one day my brother Ron telling me, "Those guys (Kearney and Hill) you are working for were chasing me in a pickup truck." He acted nervous and looked frightened as he told me this story on a couple of occasions. I didn't believe him at the time, because my brother was always kidding around when we were young. Today, I have no doubt that he was telling the truth, because others have confirmed it. In fact, if my brother hadn't been "*Street smart*," Kearney and Hill may have captured and killed him. The day after my brother first told me Kearney and Hill were chasing him, I went over to mow Patrick Kearney's yard, and noticed a pickup truck that matched my brother's description of the vehicle. I thought to myself, "Why would Kearney and Hill chase my brother?" It didn't make any sense to me back then, but now it makes perfect sense. There is no doubt that both Kearney and Hill were trying to kill my brother.

     Hill remains a free man, who has never been charged of any crimes. The first time my brother Ron had a run in with Kearney and Hill, was in 1968, when he was ten-year-old. He was walking home from Lincoln Elementary School when he spotted two men in a pick-up truck racing towards him in a threatening manner. He recognized them both immediately; it was Patrick Kearney and David Hill. Ron became frightened and took off, running hard and fast, cutting across people's yards to escape. The men chased him for a several blocks, until they spotted a neighbor watering his grass, who looked at them suspiciously. Ron was still running full speed and did not look back, until he reached our house at 3000 Aviation Boulevard. I was in the front yard when he came running up. He was out of breath and his face was blood red, and blurted out the words, "Tony, the guys you work for…Patrick Kearney and David Hill were chasing me in their pick-up truck." He looked terrified. The next occurrence was around 1975. Ron Stewart was seventeen years old and he was dating a beautiful young girl named Sandy Henderson.

He had just left her house in Manhattan Beach and was riding his bicycle home. At the time, our family had recently moved to Lawndale, about three miles away from our old house on Aviation Boulevard, which bordered Redondo and Manhattan Beach. Ron turned his bicycle eastbound onto Manhattan Beach Boulevard and immediately noticed Patrick Kearney and David Hill at a stop sign in the same truck that they had chased him in before. Ron tried not to look at them, but they were already observing him like two venomous snakes ready to strike. His worst nightmare was coming true.

They sketched the tires and started chasing him. This time Ron was worried because he lived three miles away. Kearney was driving the truck that was coming up quickly behind Ron. He crossed the four-lane highway, and began riding against the traffic, as Kearney roared right past, with Hill reached out the window, and tried to grab him. Ron watched as Kearney drove ahead of him and made a sharp U-turn, to continue his pursuit. Ron quickly crossed the street again as the cat and mouse game continued.

Every time Kearney would get hot on his trail, Ron would cross the street and peddling away, riding like the wind with the devil hot on his heels. Kearney was determined to catch him, but Ron was more determined to escape. Afraid he would attract attention to witnesses; Kearney eventually backed off and disappeared into the night. Ron wasn't completely convinced that the two men had vanished, so he took side streets, zigzagging all the way home while watching over his shoulders.

My brother's fear of Patrick Kearney and David Hill would be confirmed years later, during a conversation with his High school sweetheart Sandy Henderson. She remembered that Ron was terrified to ride his bike home from her house in Manhattan Beach. "Those guys, Patrick Kearney and David Hill were after him." Sandy recalled her mom, Barbara, telling Ron to load his bike into her station wagon and then she gave him a ride home. He was really scared.

DIAGRAM OF THE NEIGHBORHOOD

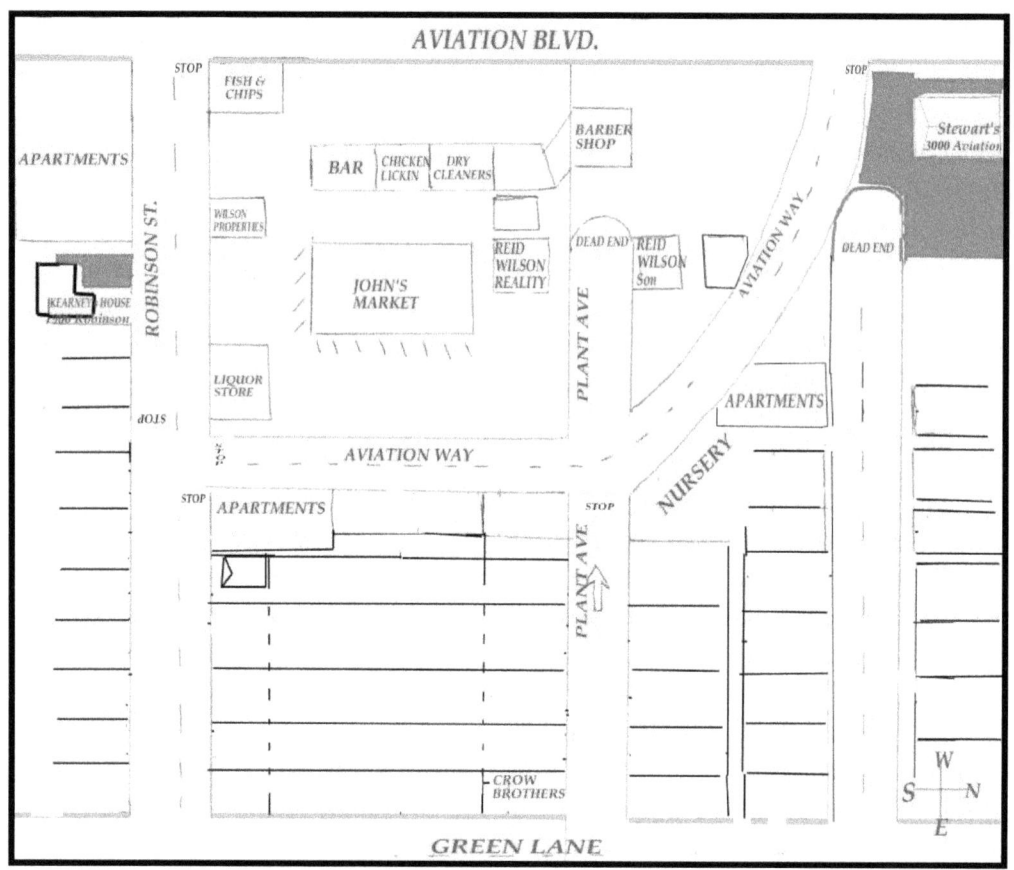

Above sketch: Kearney lived two and a half blocks from the Stewart residence on the right of diagram. "In the mid-sixties, I used to mow Kearney yard for $3.00 a week. He always invited me in his house, but I never went in. It was the right decision."

Tony Stewart

Ron Stewart, as he looked when Patrick Kearney and David Hill chased him.
Photo courtesy of Sandy Henderson

Today, Ron Stewart still asks himself why Hill went free without facing any charges. Ron and I know that both Kearney and Hill were involved. I would also have a close call with death involving Kearney a few years later. In their confessions to police, both Kearney and Hill would later admit that between 1969 to the spring of 1972. The two made several trips to Tijuana, Mexico where they had cruised the streets, just as they did in Los Angeles. Even though Kearney claimed that he never killed anyone during his visits to Tijuana, these habitual patterns have become all too familiar and suggests otherwise.

There were several unsolved murders in the nineteen sixties and seventies, but most of these killings have been written off and blamed on the Tijuana drug cartels. However, some of Tijuana's mutilated victims of the 1970's fit Kearney's exact M.O. If Tijuana and U.S. officials had investigated these murders more thoroughly, they may have learned some shocking facts. Kearney was too smart to confess to murders in Mexico, he knew that doing time in a Tijuana jail would be a genuine nightmare for an American. Mexico was most likely where Kearney began his killing spree.

During the end of June 1971, David Hill left Kearney a hand-written note stating that he had left to visit some friends and would return in a few days. Kearney had made plans to spend the day with Hill, but instead woke up to an empty dark house. He became frustrated and fuming with anger and spent most the day watching television and reading his favorite books about murder. Around dusk, a jaded Kearney grabbed the car keys to his 1972 Ford pickup truck and decided to go for a drive. It was a peaceful summer night without a cloud in the sky. Still angry with Hill, Kearney wanted revenge. Kearney didn't want to take his rage out on Hill, but he did want to vent on someone.

With murder on his mind, he backed the truck out of the driveway, and turned right onto Aviation Boulevard, driving northbound. Searching for victims with plans of slaughtering them is called premeditated First-Degree murder, which usually demands the death penalty in most murder cases, except in this case. Kearney and Hill were never even considered as a candidate. Next, he drove a half mile down the road, he turned right on Manhattan Beach Boulevard and passed Aviation High School, where Kearney admitted driving through on several occasions to check out the guys. It is believed that it was here that Kearney had spotted Robert "Billy" Benniefiel, who he would later murder in 1976. After turning right at the High School, Kearney headed east until he approached Inglewood Avenue.

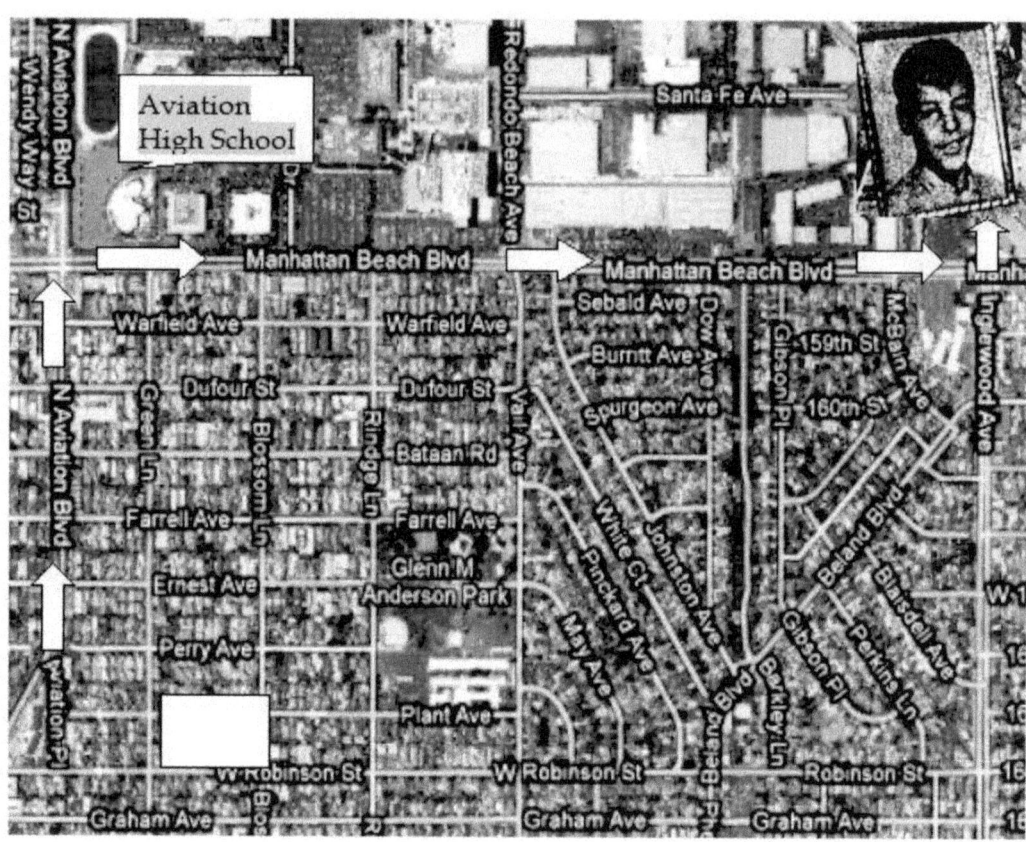

Square box marks Kearney's residence. Map shows Kearney's route that he took from his Robinson Street residence before picking up Demchik. Kearney drove west on Robinson St. and turned right (R) on Aviation Blvd, he made another (R) on Manhattan Beach Blvd, and then (L) on Inglewood Avenue where he spotted Demchik at top right.

Google Earth – Arial Shot

Above photographs: Tony and Ron Stewart attended Aviation High School in the nineteen seventies, where Patrick Kearney admitted driving through on several occasions to "Check out the guys." This is where he may have first spotted student Robert "Billy" Benniefiel, who he later murdered in 1976. *Author's Collection*

KILLER ON THE ROAD

Heartbroken Stephen Demchik (father) talks with a reporter of The Daily Breeze newspaper about the loss of his 13-year-old son, John E. Demchik seen in framed picture (background). He disappeared on June 26, 1971.

Photo credited Daily Breeze newspaper

    The killer made a left turn on the highway and drives north toward the City of Inglewood. As Kearney drives down the avenue, his eyes were busy scanning the streets for possible victims. It would not take long. Upon arriving in the city of Inglewood, Kearney immediately spotted thirteen-year-old John E. Demchik, standing on the corner. He quickly becomes aroused and decides to seize an opportunity to fulfill his lust, and his desire for murder. Like an evil black vulture from hell, zooming in on fresh meat, Kearney rushes over to greet the innocent youth. He pulls over to the curb and in a friendly tone, he asks the teen, "Do you need a ride?" At first Demchik's hesitates, and slowly walks away, but the friendly stranger presses on and refuses to take "No" for an answer. The persistent stranger insists on offering a ride to a venerable Demchik and drives slowly while talking to the youth. "Come on it's getting dark and I could have you home in no time." A nervous

Demchik initially declines Kearney's offer, but eventually accepts the ride, only because it is getting late and he is eager to get home.

The two disappear into the darkness and engage in some friendly conversation. It doesn't take long before a perverted Kearney begins to become aggressively aroused, and is ready for some action. He leans over and turns the heater setting up to high. There was only one vent open and the heat blows directly on Demchik. Several minutes later, Demchik begins to yawn and tells the friendly stranger that he wants to go home, but Kearney has other plans. The teen becomes exhausted until he can barely hold his eyes open. Kearney keeps his eye on the boy, as he reaches in his pocket and pulls out a small .22 caliber handgun. Demchik leans his head on the back of the seat and turns towards the passenger window to get some air. Without warning, Kearney points the gun at Demchik and "Boom!" The bullet penetrates the skull and then bounces around in the victim's head. The small boy slumps over as blood begins bucketing out of his skull. Kearney quickly hits the breaks and pulls the vehicle over and he throws his jacket around Demchik's head and pulls it tight to catch the blood. While Demchik struggles with death, loud gurgling sounds erupt from his chest, like a coffee maker brewing a fresh pot.

Next, he races down Highway (8) until he locates a secluded area, approximately fifteen miles southeast of Calexico. He pulls off the road into the darkness and stops. By the time he arrives at the location, Demchik had bled for several minutes, and had fallen into a deep state of unconsciousness. His pulse is weak, but he is still not dead. Kearney removes the boy's body from the truck and drags him down into a nearby gully. Out of sight from the roadway and rest of the world, Kearney undresses Demchik and sexually assaults the boys bloody limp body. Staring up into the night unhurried, Kearney continued seducing Demchik for several minutes; to fulfill his sick perverted fantasy.

After reaching a satisfied climax, Kearney zips up his pants, and tucks in his shirt. He then tosses Demchik's naked body to the ground like common garage. He looks down and then he takes a moment to admire his victim's dead body under the moonlight. It is far worse than any imaginable crime possible, but to Kearney it is just another beautiful sexual encounter. Without a hint of empathy or remorse for what he had just done, he walks away and leaves the remains for *Mother Nature* to absorb. As the killer vacated the crime scene, his heart is pounding rapidly with adrenalin that rushed through his veins. Proudly he thinks out loud, "I did it, I did it, I killed him, and I screwed him." As he drives away into the star filled night, he reminisces about his recent romance with death and how easy it is to take a small child's life. He didn't think about the family worrying about their loved one. This doesn't matter to Kearney; he realizes how much he loves the power, and the complete control over the dead. Satisfied, he begins the long drive home. Back in Inglewood, Stephen and Norma Demchik tried frantically to call all their son's friends, but they could not seem to locate him anywhere.

While Norma calls the police, Stephen drives around Inglewood in search of their son. The police basically tell the parents to give it twenty-four hours, and their teenage son would eventually show up. The parents knew their own son, and they did not agree with police, but they were helpless. Tensions increased when he did not come home the following day either. Days soon turn into weeks since John's disappearance, as the families suffering intensified with every passing moment. John's father Stephen eventually tells his wife that he is going to search for a better paying job up north, but instead, he spends numerous hours searching for their son. These worries quickly turn into nightmares for the boy's father, Stephen. He has a realistic dream about his son being trapped in a dungeon and is calling out for his help. He could hear his son crying out, "Come and get me!" In the dream, the father asked, "Where are you?" There was never any answer. The family's hell would only get worse. Sadly, the parents would not learn about what happened to their son for six long years, until 1978. It was truly a horrifying experience that no parent should ever have to experience.

The badly decomposed body of John E. Demchik was officially found close to twenty months later. He was found on Friday, February 9, 1973, by the Imperial County Police Department, but it would take years to identify the body. Until this time, Demchik would remain a John Doe.

The difference between this murder and Kearney's other victims is that Demchik's body was not mutilated, whereas others had been found inhumanly disfigured. During the initial examination, the body was not declared a homicide; in fact, the Imperial County Police did not even investigate the incident. The body was so decayed and unrecognizable that police were unaware that they were even dealing with a murder victim. Instead, they mistakenly assumed that it was an illegal Mexican immigrant who crossed the border and died from heat exhaustion. John Demchik's murder was quickly written off as just another victim of the heat and buried in an unmarked grave in the desert. The extreme temperatures during the months of June through September were dreadfully hot, with July and August being the hottest months. Kearney was familiar with the desert environment and knew that a body would disappear rather quickly. He left Demchik's body where the coyotes and buzzards could feast on him. Among the scattered bones, the police department found Demchik's skull and just buried the remains.

Upon closer examination of the skull, it was discovered that a bullet had entered behind Demchik's left ear and bounced around the inside his head like a metal ball in a pinball game. The bullet lodged just behind the right cheek area. In 1978, five years after the body was located; prisoner Patrick Kearney agreed to take detectives Roger Wilson and Al Sett on a rendezvous to the area where he dumped Demchik's body. Wilson and Sett contacted Coroner Lawn Hedinger of Imperial County Sheriff's Department and he agreed to meet with the officers. Kearney led the officers to the spot where he had left the body, but after carefully searching the area, there are no remains found. Kearney told the officers that he is sure this is the spot where he left Demchik's body. Coroner Hedinger pulled Wilson aside to tell him that he found a body, two months ago, about fifty feet from the spot where Kearney claimed he dumped the corpse. He explains that his department thought it was just an illegal Mexican that came across the border, and died from the heat exhaustion, so they just buried the bones. Wilson told Hedinger, "You'll have to dig him up, and you'll probably find a bullet hole behind the left ear."

The coroner explained that his department did not have the funding to deal with a murder of this magnitude. Detective Wilson became annoyed and ordered Hedinger to dig up the body and contact him as soon as he recovers the evidence. Days later, the coroner returns to the scene and locates the skull, but it is the only part of Demchik that is left to recover. The coyotes have devoured and scattered the rest of the remains along the landscape. Officers Wilson and Sett promptly return to Los Angeles and they receive a phone call a few days later from Hedinger. He called to confirm that the skull had a small hole behind the left ear area and added that the bullet was still rattling inside. Wilson asked him to mail the item to Los Angeles Sheriff's Department to examine the skull and confirm the bullet is indeed a .22 caliber. The victim's skull was addressed "Attention Roger Wilson." Since Kearney had already confessed to the murder and he was quickly sentenced without a trial, it was decided that Demchik's remains were not needed for evidence.

In 2008, during my own investigation, I contacted retired Homicide Detective Roger Wilson and we talked about Demchik's murder. While on the phone, Wilson described how the coroner was unconcerned about the identification of the remains. Oddly, there was no investigation, only an assumption by Coroner Lawn Hedinger of Imperial County Sheriff's Department, who simply buried the body where it was found and closed the file. If Kearney had not admitted to the location of this body, the family would have never known what happened to their son. Riverside Sheriff's Department would later claim in official reports that they were the ones responsible for locating Demchik. However, it was Detectives Roger Wilson and Al Sett, it was the Los Angeles Sheriff's Department that located Demchik's remains. It appears everyone wanted the credit for locating the victim.

Imperial County had originally been part of San Diego County; it had been founded on Wednesday, August 7, 1907. The desert climate is hot and dry with highs of 110 degrees or higher in July to August months, while in the low mid 30's in the winter months. San Diego County extends from the Pacific Ocean to the west and to the Colorado River, Arizona border to the east, with Mexico being its southern border. The death of John Demchik continued to haunt the family for years. Norma Demchik was asked to identify her son's clothes, and this took a serious toll on her. The daughter, Norma developed cancer and just didn't want to go on. She died soon after their son was identified, and had become another victim of Patrick Kearney, not directly, but indirectly. Mr. Demchik had lost both his wife and son. His four kids grew up and moved away, but Mr. Demchik stayed in the Inglewood home, where he once lived with his son. When asked how he felt about Patrick Kearney, he simply put it, "That son of a bitch!" Mr. Demchik had every right to feel this way; he had lost his son in a senseless murder.

On October 17, 1973, the U.S. Government imposed a gas rationing. In the state of California, which meant if your license plate ended in an odd number or if you had a vanity plate, you could only buy gas on odd number days. If your number was even, you could only purchase gas on even days. Lines at gas pumps were extremely long, which would lead to mass frustration and anger among the people. During this time, the government also banned the sale of gas on Sunday's with gas station operators limited to ten gallons per customer, which also helped to fuel the anger at gas pumps. Fuel quickly increased from .38 per gallon to $1.00 per gallon. The gas problem began because of an embargo that began on October 17, which was placed upon the United States along with our allies in Western Europe, and Japan, by members of the OAPEC (Organization of Arab Petroleum Exporting Countries). This prevented oil from being sold to the US and its allies. The embargo was in response to protest the US and its allies' for supporting Israel, during a conflict with Syria and Egypt. The embargo was officially lifted on March of 1974, but the US and its allies continued to pay elevated prices for oil for another twelve years, which is even worse today.

Even the 1973 gas embargo, did not even decelerate Kearney's murder binge. The same year victim James Fletcher Barwick would become another fatality to satisfy Kearney's sick sexual appetite. It was a hot 83 degrees, and like most of the others, Barwick had been picked up while hitchhiking on a southern California highway, and is shot in the back of the head. Kearney was out on the town and wanted to have some fun, which meant killing and raping another victim. Detective Wilson stated there was strong evidence that Barwick was most likely raped at the time of his demise, because semen was found in the rectum like most of Kearney's other victims. Seventeen-year-old Barwick was found dead on Saturday, September 22, 1973 off San Pasqual Road, just southeast of Escondido. There is not much known about this murder, except that he was killed, raped, and dumped like discarded garage by Kearney. However, there is a bit of history about the vicinity where Kearney dumped Barwick's body. It was in the same location where the famous bloody battle of San Pasqual took place on Friday, December 6, 1846. Was it just a coincidence that the battle was under the command of a General Stephen Watts Kearny? One must inquire whether Patrick Kearney was actually related to General Kearny or not? The spelling of the name Kearny is different, but many ancestors of the eighteen hundred's often misspelled their last names due to lack of education.

Did Kearney know that General Kearny had fought and died 127 years prior to the murder of James Barwick? If so, the killer may have intentionally picked this location to dump Barwick at the very same spot. The battle of San Pasqual took place in the San Pasqual Valley southeast of Escondido. In 1846, the American army was under the command of General Kearny had fighting to win California from Mexico. Kearny and his 120 troops defending the west had arrived from Missouri through New Mexico. The story goes that Kearny's men were tired and hungry when they were ambushed and defeated by Mexican forces led by General Andres Pico.

James Barwick was also tired, hungry and desperate for a ride when Kearney pulled up in his pickup truck. Kearney had friendly face and trusting voice. Barwick climbed in the truck and the two drove off. He thanked Kearney for stopping and said he had been trying to get a ride for hours, with no luck. Kearney asked Barwick where he is going and he responded, "Anywhere but here." As Barwick relaxes and closes his eyes, Kearney turned on the heater up to "High." He waits for Barwick to fall asleep and then shoots him in the head like the rest of his victims.

The killer pulls the vehicle over to the side of the road to sexually assault his victim in the darkness. Afterward, he dumps the body and just drives off, leaving behind a teenager that will never experience adulthood, or see the future.

The star marks the location where James Barwick's dead body was found on San Pasqual Road, just Southeast of Escondido. When the murder occurred, this area was a deserted field; today it consists of highways, parking lots and tennis courts to the right.

Google Earth – Arial Image

As parents, we all tend to faithfully worry about our offspring's, but no one ever really imagines that a monstrous fiend could invade our neighborhood and hurt our children. There was a cruel reality that existed in Southern California, during the nineteen sixties and seventies, involving an atrocious individual that would horrify families for generations. Kearney's "Raine of terror" would be far worse than the main ingredient of the brain that causes heart-pounding nightmares. Even though Kearney had already killed numerous times, his next murder would certainly be the most tragic. This innocent young child would become his inaugural ceremony of murder. Many have expressed opinion that Kearney should have received the death penalty for this murder alone. Yet, taxpayers continue to feed and clothe this killer, year after year.

It began on Saturday; August 24, 1974, while five-year-old Ronald Dean Smith Jr. was busy playing outside his house. It was another enjoyable sunny day with a temperature of 81 degrees. Smith's parents had divorced the previous year. Smith Jr. was living with his mother in Lennox, California. On this day, Smith's grandmother was babysitting while the mother was at work. A friend stopped by and asked the child if he wanted to go to Lennox Park to play. An excited Smith ran into the house and asked his grandmother if he could go with his friend. The grandmother told young Smith he could go, but only if he promised to be home in a few hours for dinner. The energized youngster agreed, and the two kids ran off with his friend to the park, just a few blocks away. There was no need for the grandmother to be concerned, because Smith had walked safely to Lennox Park on several occasions, besides the neighborhood appeared to be safe.

A half hour after arriving at a park, Smith and his friend had a disagreement, which soon grew to an argument. Even though it was just a kid's spat, the friend took off and went home, leaving Smith all alone. A teary-eyed Smith began walking home around 3:45 p.m. About fifteen minutes earlier, Patrick Kearney had just clocked out from Hughes Aircraft, and was leaving work. He was bored and decided to cruise the area looking for some action. He circled the area, and it wasn't long before Kearney spotted the troubled Smith wondering up and down the streets, walking away from the park. Sadly, this was the day when young Ronald Smith would learn that the tale-tale bogeyman we have heard so much about was indeed real. This bogeyman was Patrick Wayne Kearney, and he was out to do the devils dirty work. Smith would become Kearney's youngest victim on record.

The moment Kearney focused in on the child; he became aroused at the thought of killing and molesting him. He looked at the young child, the way a hunter looks at a soft young doe that he wants to kill, but Kearney was far worse than any hunter. Smith became one those unfortunate kids that was in the wrong place at the wrong time. Kearney approached the child and asked him if he wanted a ride home. With sadness evidently reflecting from the expression on his face, Smith told the stranger, "I'm just going home. It's dinner time." A persistent Kearney insisted that he give the boy a ride on such a hot day. Kearney seemed harmless enough, besides this unfamiliar face offered to buy him a hamburger. Naïve and innocent just like most five-year-old boys, Smith found humbleness in the stranger's friendly tone. Without much consideration, Smith climbed into the stranger's truck and they drove off to McDonald's. Smith was hungry so Kearney ordered him a cheeseburger, French fries and a coke. This would be the child's last meal. He would never live to see the light of another day. The two drove around until Smith finished eating, and then he asked the stranger to take him home. Kearney reacted by pulling the truck to the side of the road in an unpopulated area and wrapped a jacket tightly around the struggling boy's head. The killer slid his hands inside the jacket and the squeezed the helpless boy's nose and mouth securely, until he couldn't breathe. Smith needed air; he was suffocating. He kicked and fought for his life, but Kearney squeezed tighter and overpowered the boy, until he smothered the child to death. Sadly, Smith was murdered just six days short of his sixth birthday.

It was Saturday, October 12, 1974; Smith's decomposed body was found in Riverside County, forty-nine days after Kearney kidnapped the child. The child was dumped like compost on the side of the highway. Smith's decomposed face had abrasions on the nose and chin, and confusions on his lips directly from Kearney's fingernails and pressure from the force applied from his palm.

According to the Forensics Pathologists, prior to his death, Smith had gasped for air and suffered from signs of decreased heart rate and respiration, until complete cessation became a horrible reality. During the fierce struggle, Smith's body had increased the utilization of his oxygen and therefore speeded up the sequence of events that caused his death. In English terms, this basically means that a merciless killer smothered him to death. After cessation of respiration, Smith could not resume breathing spontaneously, without immediate resuscitated, but instead of reviving the child, Kearney watched as he died. Next, Killer Kearney drove the dead child to his Robinson residence, where he could be alone with the corpse. He talked to the boy as if he was alive, before he stripped the child naked and molested his tiny lifeless frame. The following day, he dumped the remains in a wooded area near Lake Elsinore, California.

Smith's body was later found half clothed and hidden beneath an old mattress. The boy's blue gray trousers and his underwear was pulled down around the ankles, indicating that rape and molestation had taken place. There was also semen present in the anal cavity, but without deoxyribonucleic acid (DNA) of today, there was no way to get a match to a suspect. Kearney didn't have any violent criminal records on file to use for a comparison. The deceased child wore a size 26" brown leather belt, black and white high-top tennis shoes, in kid's size 12. The blue tee shirt he was wearing had a small hole in the front and in the back.

Smith's skeletal remains were discovered along Ortega Highway, approximately 8 miles west of Lake Elsinore. A saddened heartbroken mother was asked to make positive identification of her son's clothing. Originally, the coroner determined that Smith had been dead from one to two years, but a subsequent investigation indicated that he had been dead for only a few months. The coroner never officially determined the exact cause of death, but Kearney confessed to detectives that he had strangled the youngster. He later changed his story and said he smothered the poor defenseless child. Either way, the result was the same. The poor child died of suffocation at the hands of a murderer. Sadly, he suffered a painful death.

This is one murder that Kearney did not want to talk about to police, due to the age of the victim, because he feared for his safety. In prison, killing or molesting a child is an automatic death sentence among the other inmates. When it comes to the murder of a child, there seems to be honor and justice even among criminals in prison. The victim died so young. It was a senseless killing of an innocent virgin child, who would never grow to become a teenager. Kearney knew he outweighed the youngster by at least one hundred pounds, and this would be an easy kill. Kearney was honest with officers about the locations of the victim's remains, but he lied about picking up Smith on Saturday during his lunch hour, killing him and deposing the child on the same day. He kept the child for two days. Kearney said he left Hughes Aircraft for lunch and drove to Imperial Highway and along the way; he kidnapped young Ronald Smith in the city of Lennox. Evidence confirms that Kearney clocked out and left his place of employment on Saturday, August 4, after 3:30 p.m. and then kidnapped Smith.

Since Smith's body was found in Riverside County, Kearney most likely took the I105 Freeway east for sixteen miles, merging onto the I-605 south for another 2.5 miles. Next, he drove onto 91-freeway, heading east for thirty-four miles, and turning onto the I15 South towards San Diego. He stayed on the I-15 for 20 miles, getting off on the Main Street exit to Lake Elsinore, to Riverside County.

If Kearney were telling the truth, this would mean he drove the distance of 77.09 miles; which would take an average of one hour, and eighteen minutes in one direction. With this time scale in mind, it is not possible that Kearney murdered Smith on his lunch break from Hughes Aircraft and then returned to work two hours later. Even if he had taken a late lunch break, he couldn't have possibly done everything he claimed in less than two hours, minimum. A letter written to detectives by Kearney, indicated that he was killed the following day as Saturday evening spilled over onto early Sunday, August 25, 1974. Even though he appeared to be honest about the events, there were far too many discrepancies in his statements about Smith.

The family stated that Smith had disappeared about 4:00 that evening, which is about an hour after Kearney would have been getting off work. The truth is that Kearney abducted Smith between 3:45 to 4:30 and took him out for a bite to eat. Afterwards, Kearney took the boy to his home to kill and seduce him. After raping the corpse, a several times, Kearney then dumped the body the following day. This was proved by the coroner's office, due to the condition of the body when found. Even retired Homicide Detective Roger Wilson clarified in his investigation that Kearney did not dump the body the same day, as he claimed.

The brutal truth was that Kearney over-powered the child and murdered him for his own personal sexual gratification. In Kearney's sick perverted mind, his climax was more important than this unfortunate child's life. It was an easy task for a smiling stranger to lure a young innocent boy to his death with false promises, as Kearney did.

The serial killer told officers that he never planned any of his murders, but this was another deception to lure officers away from a premeditated murder case. The moment Kearney laid eyes on Smith, the wheels in his distorted mind started spinning as fast as the turbines of a jet engine. He lusted for a victim, especially a young one, like a diabetic lust for something sweet. Every slaughter committed by Kearney was most certainly a premeditated act of first-degree murder. He would search for victims and then execute them in cold blood. This should have clearly been a capital punishment case, due to the animalistic circumstances involved. Many killers have been executed for far less. The cause of Smith's death was never revealed to the family or the public. During an interview with Detective Roger Wilson, mentioned that he promised killer Patrick Kearney, he would never tell how the child was murdered or the aftermath of the crime. During several interviews, and demands of the author, Wilson reluctantly admitted that Kearney smothered the child and raped him. I asked him, "How could you keep a promise to a killer? The family has the right to know what happened." He responded, "I promised Kearney, I would never tell."

The day that Smith's body was discovered, his father was first suspect accused of his son's murder, which he immediately denied. These accusations by the police only added more pain and stress to an already heartbroken family. Regardless, the father remained a suspect, until Kearney confessed in 1977.

Cameo Bell was the younger sister to Ronald Smith, but she never had the chance to know him. "I myself never got to meet my brother; he was gone by the time I was born. What I do know about him is this; he was five at the time of his death. From the stories I heard his mother was at work when he went to the park, so I believe that his grandmother did give permission. They came to my parents after his body was found in October and accused my father at first."

After Smith was killed, the family became the victims. The family had suffered for many long years, which was a courtesy of killer Patrick Wayne Kearney. Today, the family continues to endure this never-ending loss of their loved one, while Kearney enjoys room service in his cozy cell.

INAUGURATION OF DEATH

"They (L.A. Detectives) told my parents that Ronnie Dean Smith had been fed a hamburger and at some point, he was shot. They didn't say much else. He was 5 at the time of his death."

Cameo Bell _ Sister of Ronald Dean Smith Jr.

Several months after Smith's murder, *twenty-one-year-old* Albert Rivera of Los Angeles, decided to hitch-a-ride to San Diego when Kearney pulled over in his Volkswagen (V.W. Beetle Bug). Kearney had known Rivera for years, but he had not seen him in a while. Kearney claimed he was happy to see Rivera, but the moment he picked his own friend up, he had already decided to kill him. The two chatted about the nice spring weather and he acquired about Rivera's daily life. Albert Rivera had opened up to Kearney and told him everything about his life. Kearney always enjoyed a compassionate conversation with his victims before he killed them. This made him feel closer to his victims and justified the murders in his own mind.

Anxious to kill Rivera and seduce his dead body; Kearney mentioned that he was cold, and then turned on the heater to "High." He pointed all the air vents directly at Rivera and waited for him become exhausted. This method didn't take long. About twenty minutes passed before Rivera began to yawn, and gradually closed his eyes. Kearney wasted no time; he shot Rivera in the head with his twenty-two-caliber pistol and then pulled over to the side of the road.

Kearney wrapped a sweater around Rivera's head, and then hurried back to his Redondo residence to have his way with his victim. The killer arrived at the residence, and first went inside the house to make sure his roommate David Hill wasn't home. He left a dead or dying Rivera in his Volkswagen. As soon as he learned the coast was clear, he backed his vehicle up to the front door, and then dragged Rivera's body through the living room into the bathroom. Next, Kearney placed the remains in the bathtub, and quickly wiped up blood on the car seat. Returning to the bathroom moments later, he began undressing his victim. Kearney yelled at the diseased Rivera, "You Son of a bitch! You bled all over my floor." The killer begins to beat the corpse and then pulls public hairs from Rivera's genitals; while the victim stared back with dead dilate eyes. This excited Kearney and he immediately engaged in sexual intercourse, while the body was still warm. Almost immediately, the victim's rectum began to bleed all over the place. Kearney quickly stuffed the rectum with paper towels to prevent blood from getting on the floor. Kearney then prepared to mutilate the body using his hacksaw and razor sharp exacto-knife.

Prior to his death, Rivera had been staying with a friend on Mathews Avenue in Redondo Beach, which was a little more than 1/2 (half) mile from Kearney's house. His death would officially begin the California "Trash bag" murderer case on Sunday, April 13, 1975.

Police detectives described Rivera as a "Street runner," and a well-known male "Homosexual prostitute." He had been picked up several times on suspicion of selling marijuana and other drugs. Rivera's dead body was located just off Otay Lake road; about 2.8 miles east of Wueste Road in Cula Vista, in California. In his wallet, police discovered that Rivera had an Oregon driver's license with the name Thomas John Faher, and birth date listed as August 26, 1954. Faher immediately became a suspect, but he was later ruled out by an alibi. It appears that Rivera may have stolen Faher's wallet. Faher told police that his wallet had been missing for about three weeks.

During his questioning in 1977, Kearney told police that victim Albert Rivera lived in Tijuana when he was young. He migrated across the border in his teens to search for better wages. Riverside police had announced Rivera and other victims relating to Kearney's M.O., stating, "One thing we noticed on the people we found is that there has never been anybody that was tattooed." Perhaps this is because most of the victims were young children. Two years later while in custody, Kearney had made a comment to police about Rivera by stating, "Uh it wasn't in my planning, except I remember Rivera one time tried to talk me into getting a tattoo, and I purposely didn't let him do it. I first met him in Tijuana when he was just a little boy. I used to give him money and help him out; he managed to come up here to work and live. I met him quite by accident and uh McArthur Park. I didn't recognize him, but I hadn't seen him for a couple of years, and he recognized me. David was away uh for a period of a week or so at a time. I brought Rivera over to stay with us until he found a job or something."

He added, "He um, came from, I met in Los Angeles, again after I hadn't seen him for some time, he was from Mexico, and uh I was, brought him to my house I was going to let him stay there, and uh he kind of turned on me and became very unfriendly and demanding. I thought we had been good friends for years. Uh I picked him up hitchhiking near my place and uh shot him in my VW near the house and I took him there. I did something after I shot him, it was more of curiosity I didn't uh, and it was something I thought I might like." (Pause) "I screwed him."

Kearney did much more than screw his old friend. He put the young man in his grave, after he cut Rivera into several pieces. Kearney claimed he stayed dormant for the next seven months, but during these times, he abided his time by making several trips to

Tijuana, Mexico and sending pen pal letters to young men living in Russia. Although never confirmed, it is believed that Kearney also killed during these many visits out of the country to Tijuana.

Even today many unsolved murders in Mexico fit Kearney's M.O. with the bullet behind the left ear, sexual assaults and mutilations. Kearney still denies killing anyone in Mexico, because the truth could mean the death penalty under Mexico laws. If just one unsolved murder could be brought forth today, Kearney could still face the death penalty even in the United States because murder is one crime that never expires. Kearney remains a pathological liar, serial killer and pedophile of children. There is no amount of time behind bars that will ever bring back the devastation he created. After the brutal murder of his friend Rivera, the murders continued. However, Kearney took the next five months off to concentrate on projects at work and put in some overtime to earn some extra money. Things calmed down on the home front while Kearney and Hill enjoyed relaxing evenings watching television, reading and shopping to decorate the house. Kearney would purchase several cleaning products as well as rugs to replace the bloodstained throw rugs that he tossed out.

There is some controversy on Kearney's next victim Larry Gene Walters. Even though Walters was another confirmed Kearney victim, there was a different serial killer who was active at the time named Randy Kraft. Kraft is often falsely identified as the slayer of Walters. Kraft was born in Long Beach and was murdering young men about the same time as Patrick Kearney. Kraft was also as deadly as Kearney. He preyed on homosexual military men and mutilated his victims using methods that were nearly identical to Kearney's techniques.

According to the evidence, on Monday, November 10, 1975, twenty-one-year-old Larry Walters was hitchhiking along Manhattan Beach Boulevard when he disappeared without a trace. A friend of Walters' stated the last time he had seen Larry Walters; he was thumbing for a ride home. Upon further investigation, police learned that local business owners in the area had reported seeing a light color pickup truck that pulled over to offer a ride to a man fitting Walters' description. The kind stranger that approached Walters with a smile on his face was ready to lend a hand. It wasn't odd to see a hitchhiker out on the street, but what caught their attention was Walters seemed to be hesitating to climb in the vehicle, as he leaned on the passenger side of the truck. Also, they found it peculiar that the stranger kept scanning the streets and looking around nervously. Witnesses did not get a good look at his face, but said they thought the man's actions appeared very suspicious. Once inside the truck, Kearney asked Walters, "Where you are going?" Walters replied, "I'm going to Redondo Beach to a friend's house." Kearney drives off into the night with Walters, who completely disappears and is never to be heard from or seen alive again. Kearney told Walters during the drive that he needed to make a stop by his Redondo residence. Once they arrived, Walters was invited inside the residence where he is told to "Have a seat and relax." Moments later; Kearney walked up behind Walters and shoots him in the head. Boom! Walters crumbles to the grounds and doesn't move. Kearney quickly pockets the gun and drags him across the floor to the bathroom where he begins to undress his victim.

As he begins examining Walters' private parts until he becomes aroused. Anal sex was promptly performed on the comatose body. After reaching a bloody climax, Kearney dismembered Walters with his trusty hacksaw and razor knife. First, he hacked off both feet, to allow the blood to freely deplete from the body. After rinsing each foot thoroughly of blood, he placed the body parts into a trash bag.

Next, he cut off both victims' hands at the wrists, which he found to be difficult because of the he structures of the wrist joint, which is extremely complex. The anatomy of the wrist is the most complex of all the joints in the body. There are fifteen small bones that connect the forearm to the hand, and the wrist itself also contains eight small bones, called carpal bones. With blood flowing steadily down the bathtub drain, he then sawed off the head. He rinsed the head by flushing water through the neck until the red water eventually appeared clear. He examined each body part closely, before placing each piece into separate trash bags. After rinsing the torso, Kearney placed it in a large trash bag that was meticulously wrapped and secured with a heavy microfilm style tape.

In the next few days, Kearney began the disposing of body parts in various locations. He dumped head in a Burger King trashcan, while the hands and feet were discarded into the garbage dumpster at *Winchell's donut House*. He dumped the rest of the torso in a trash bag container that he took to the Palos Verdes' landfill. Homicide Detective Roger Wilson of the Sheriff's department added that Walters was killed on Sunday, November 30, 1975, and put in trash containers that went to the Palos Verdes landfill. None of Walters' body parts have ever been recovered. He disappeared off the face of the earth.

Patrick Kearney committed the senseless murder of Robert "Billy" Benniefiel of Redondo Beach in 1976. Billy's body has never been recovered.

Photographs courtesy of Marcia Born - sister of victim

Another victim whose body has never been recovered is Robert William "Billy" Benniefiel. Billy was a former student attending Aviation High School in Redondo Beach. He was born a premature baby weighing in less than three pounds, on Friday, August 2, 1957 in Louisiana. After his birth, the doctor sent Billy home with some medical advice for his parents to keep him warm and that's exactly what his mother did. The family would later move to Redondo Beach, California where the child would eventually grow to be a healthy muscular 5'-foot 10" teenager, full of energy and ambition. He was considered a late bloomer who worked extra hard to earn his diploma. Billy had struggled with his learning abilities throughout his short adolescent years, but he never gave up. Eventually, it all paid off, and he succeeded in graduating from high school. Around campus at Aviation High School, Billy walked with sort of a lethargic looking posture. Described as sluggish, and a little rough around the edges, but this was normal for a young man, who had struggled to survive from the moment he was born. His family described him as, "Always a challenge. He just did his own thing, like typical teenager stuff with a strong love for music." His sister Marcia Born still has fond memories of her brother singing and goofing around in the garage that was converted into a hang out.

"He really liked the songs *Joy to the World*, and *Horse with no name*. I smile every time I hear them, and then the tears usually flow by the time the song is over. That sort of raw pain never really goes away. There were times I did not like Billy as a little sister; I was probably a nuisance. He did not want hanging around, and so I would get so mad, but he did not deserve to die at Kearney's hands. My grandma always said if we remember people they never really die," said Marcia Born.

Billy was a was an easygoing, laid-back, nineteen years old, who loved the simple things in life, such as riding bicycles, hanging out at the beach, and laying out in the sun. He also enjoyed collecting objects that he could work on such as broken televisions, stereos, or other items that people would just toss out in the trash. These unwanted objects were treasures to Billy. He would tell friends and family, "I can't believe someone could throw this away." The teenager had a gift that allowed him to view the world differently than you or I and would make the absolute best of any given situation. He was one of those rare souls with a big heart that we would unknowingly pass on the streets every so often.

Reports indicate that Billy was reported missing between the periods of September 16 to October 6. In the fall of 1976, Billy set off for a bicycle ride to Hermosa Beach as he had done a hundred times before. However, on this day, it would turn out to be his deadly misfortune. This fatal outcome began during his journey to the beach, as he ran over a nail that punctured his tire and caused a flat. Frustrated, he decided to remove the tire and take it home to repair it. He chained his bicycle to a street sign, and began walking, until he grew tired and decided to "Thumb-a-ride" home. The Police figured that the youth had probably hitchhiked as many teens did in the nineteen seventies, with the exception that this day would be his last. There was even a popular 1970's song by a British group Vanity Fare, entitled "Hitchin a Ride," that made it feel safe to hitch hike. Doomed and blind to the fate that was about to be dealt to him, Billy would become an unwilling participant to his own brutal murder and dissection that followed.

The official police version of what occurred that dreadful day seems to vary from the killer's account. In Kearney's confession, he would tell the gruesome terrifying tale. It was a hot piercing 80-degree day; after puncturing a tire on his bicycle, Billy began walking home. After walking some distance under the sun's sweltering rays, he was beginning to feel drained, when a friendly stranger pulled up and offered him a ride. If his confession was accurate, Billy was not hitchhiking as police assumed, he was simply in the wrong place at the wrong time. Kearney had been cruising the streets in search of another victim, when he spotted Billy walking alone. Aroused by the teenager's tan muscular build and stringy blond hair, Kearney couldn't resist. At first, Billy politely refused the offer for a ride, but Kearney was persistent and overly eager to help.

In his own assertion, Kearney admitted that he initially spotted Billy in Hermosa Beach close to where Pier Avenue, Aviation Boulevard and Pacific Coast Highway all convene. The killer said he picked up the teenager and drove around looking for a bicycle shop with the heater blaring on high. Billy protested about the intense heat blowing on him, but Kearney just apologized, saying it was broken, and wouldn't shut off. It didn't take long until Billy began to tire and doze off. As he yawned into twilight, then Kearney pulled out a .22 caliber pistol and shot Billy just behind and above the left ear. The bullet ricocheted in Billy's brain, killing him almost instantly. He never really knew what was happening to him. It all happened too quickly. The truth is he had made a bad choice by accepting a ride from Kearney, as many other victims had before him.

The moment he stepped into Kearney's car, he has only minutes left to live. Kearney drove Billy to his Robinson residence, where he backed the truck up to the front door and dragged the dead body into the house. After undressing his victim, he admitted plucking pubic hairs from the groin area to distinguish whether he was still alive or not.

He manufactured the theory that if the mortally wounded survived, the victim would respond to this method, after being shot in the head. In all actuality, plucking pubic hairs out the victim was another form of foreplay for Kearney, which would increase his sexual appetite for the victim's deceased cadaver.

This was just another one of Kearney's sexual fanaticizes to add to his sick pleasures. He enjoyed toying with the victim's dead body to gain a feeling of control and dominance. Kearney also admitted that he enjoyed yelling at and beating the corpses on occasion. This was because the victim couldn't fight back, and it made Kearney feel powerful. It was also said that he designed an electrical devise to shock body parts that he would cut off his lifeless victims. It was all a part of the experiment of a madman. Next, Kearney began to violently sodomise the corpse, until he reached an explosive heart pounding climax. After catching his breath, he examined the body more thoroughly.

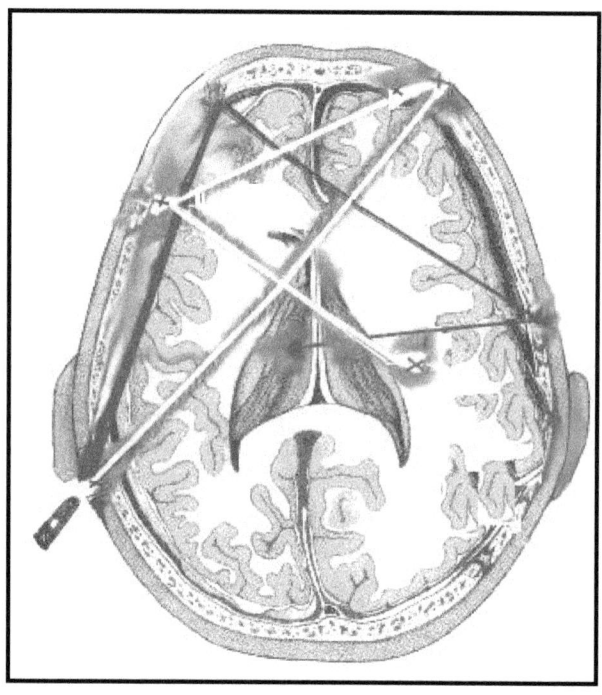

Above: *Sketch of Bullet Entry* (White Line – Bullet path) Killer's .22-caliber bullet perforated into the brain, entering just behind and above the left ear, causing the projectile to tear through the Cerebellum, Pituitary gland, and brain lining, before ricocheting off the interior skull through the Corpus callosum, Hypothalamus severing several arteries, and completely paralyzing the victim, in most cases. Other victims suffered a bullet through the brain stem, which caused difficulty in breathing and cessation of the heart muscle. The *black line* represents another bullet entry path, which is equally as deadly with similar effects. Regardless of the path, all victims suffered trauma and massive bleeding inside the brain and eventually death, with some victims taking several minutes before dying.

Author's Collection

    An hour passed, and Kearney became aroused again, so the sexual games continued. Kearney eventually grew tired of Billy and decided it was time to dismember the teenager, like a butcher processing and packaging beef. This was yet another phrase of his experiment to satisfy his ill pleasures. He placed Billy inside the bathtub on his back and with a sharp razor knife he sliced a bikini cut above the public hair to drain the blood. With a hack sawed and sharp razor, he severed Billy's arteries from the groin area up towards the hip and around through the buttocks, and then back down to the groin. In doing so, Kearney severed the iliac arteries located in the crotch area, this initiated blood to rush out in a constant enduring flow. Next, Billy's hands and feet were both removed and thoroughly rinsed the neck and the decapitated head.

    The killer would meticulously clean and rinse all the blood before wrapping each piece in separate bags. Later that evening, Kearney loaded Billy's body parts in the pickup truck, and covered him up with a sweater. He set out to dispose of the body in the shadows of the night. However, it was foggy, and Kearney immediately spotted several police cruising the area. Kearney became nervous because Billy's dead body was lying on the seat next to him. He noticed the Redondo Beach police racing around following everyone attempting to find any wrongdoers. He later commented, "Police were following everybody around, what they didn't know who was following them and I was sitting there with a body." Kearney later commented that he took Billy's remains to work with him the next day, because it looked less conspicuous. He looked like everyone else driving on the busy streets of Los Angeles.

After work, he dumped Billy's body parts in several different trash bends all over the city. The mystery of what happened to Billy would later come to light with the help of a former neighbor of the Benniefiel family. The neighbor had noticed an article in the Daily Breeze newspaper in which police were requesting help from the public to solve a murder case.

The description of one victim sounded like it was Billy. The killer described the victim's features in the article, as around 5' 10" with stringy blond hair, adding that the body has not been recovered. Marcia Born said that for a year and a half after Billy's disappearance, her family had come to believe he had run away. It wasn't until her neighbor showed the family the newspaper article with Kearney's confession that they made a connection. According to Marcia Born, "Police took a picture (of Robert) to Kearney, and asked, 'Is this one of your victims?' Kearney looked at the photograph, and immediately identified him. "To this day, it eats my other brother up that the picture he took out of his wallet was the one that slime looked at." The end conclusion would prove to be a painful reality for the family, although Billy's death would not be forgotten in vain.

Years later, Billy's mother, Mrs. Benniefiel, formed a very popular and sacred group entitled, "Compassionate friends." It was exclusively for parents who had lost their children or loved ones. The program remains popular even to this day and has expanded over the years to become worldwide. At these meetings, Marcia Born recalls hearing the tearful stories of parents that tragically lost family members. Even though Marcia was supposed to be in bed sound asleep during these meetings, she could hear the sobbing stories echoing through the living room of their small residence. The group had originated at their apartment, but later grew very strong and moved on to larger meeting locations. Ironically, according his sister Marcia Born, Billy's favorite thing to do was hunt for objects from the trash that people would throw out and them bring the stuff home. Born said, "I often think the landfill must be like heaven for him." He was shot to death in the fall of 1976, between September 16, and October 6. Billy's cheerful spirit was taken from him, forced out of his body by this brutal murderer. It was a huge loss of a talented teenager. Robert William "Billy" Benniefiel was never found. Kearney confessed to Benniefiel's murder in 1981, five years after his disappearance, but police have never recovered his body. The killer told officials that he most likely ended up at the South Bay landfill in Torrance Beach, California. Speaking of Benniefiel, Kearney said, <Sic> "One victim that sticks in my mind. I had no idea what his name was, I can describe him, and uh, I think he was from out of town. I'm sure he told me he was a transient from someplace, and he was living some other place, somewhere along Artesta, where a lot of transients they seem to live. I've seen some of them hanging around near an uh taco stand and Chinese food or something on Artesta. I think he came from there and uh he was about 20 years old and he had long blond hair, and pierced earring. I picked him up near the beach and he was carrying a chrome bicycle wheel that I believe he stole." <End Sic>

Kearney's observation of Benniefiel's character was far from correct. It is true that Billy Benniefiel was riding his bike in Hermosa Beach and he got a flat tire. We know that Benniefiel chained his bike to a telephone pole and removed the flat tire. Next, he began walking either towards home or to the bicycle shop to buy a tire patch kit, when Kearney appeared to offer him a ride. However, the real facts are quite different than serial killer Patrick Kearney had assumed. Billy did not steal the bicycle tire, nor was he a transient or a homosexual. He was just a harmless Redondo Beach teenager that lost his life at the hands of a murderous pedophile. He wasn't a celebrity or someone famous, but he was a human being who had his whole life ahead of him, until Kearney stole it. Billy's cheerful smile and peaceful mannerism would never be seen again. Years later, Mrs. Benniefiel would completely forgive Patrick Kearney for taking her son's life, so that she could finally find peace in her own life. She was a very strong-minded person to forgive a killer for murdering her own son. Not all parents would be as forgiving. The brutal murders continued, as the list of fatalities grew longer.

It was Monday, March 1, 1976, with a beautiful forecast of 70 degrees and clear skies, when the Redondo Police Department received a call from the Buchanan family. The concerned voice on the other end of the line was calling to report their missing seventeen-year-old son Kenneth E. Buchanan. The relatives were tremendously worried, because Kenneth Buchanan had not come home or even called. This was not like their son, who always called home, if he was going to be late or needed a ride. After a month of painstaking searching for Buchanan with little results, police concluded that their son was probably staying with friends and would eventually show up at home. The family was told to give it more time, but they were certain that something was seriously wrong. They family exhausted all hopes that their son would return soon after calling his friends and relatives to learn that he was nowhere to be found.

Fate would strike a blow on Wednesday, April 7, 1976, when a dead body that resembled Kenneth Buchanan was recovered. The victim was found by a group of local hikers that were walking along the public road when they spotted what appeared to be a dead body lying in a pool of desiccated blood. The body was located about 16 miles east of Highway 98, lying in a high grassy area.

Upon closer examination, it was discovered that the victim had been shot four times in head. After several tests and the cooperation of the family, police determined the body was indeed that of Kenneth Buchanan. The family and the community were left completely in shock. It did not make any sense. Buchanan did not have any enemies, he was dead, and there was no explanation for his death. It was another pointless killing of a teenager. When arrested in 1977, Patrick Kearney had also admitted to Buchanan's murder. The killer told police that Buchanan was a friend, who would call him on occasions to ask for favors. On one instance, Kearney described how he drove Buchanan to the hospital to be treated for illness, in which he said medical care was needed. Kearney befriended Buchanan and agreed to drive him around, until one day he decided to kill the youth for his own sexual pleasures. When later questioned about why he shot the teenager four times in the head,

Kearney said, "Buchanan wouldn't die so I kept shooting him, so he wouldn't suffer."

What occurred that fatal day was Kearney drove Buchanan to the death site and attempted to kill him, but the cylinder spun and made a clicking sound. At this moment,

Buchanan turned around to see the gun in Kearney's hand. The teen panics and takes off running through the high glass and trees of the desert with Kearney chasing close behind. Kearney pulls the trigger twice, but misses; He succeeds on the third shot and hits Buchanan in the head. The teen collapses to the ground. Aroused, but out of breath, Kearney undresses his victim. Moments later, he begins to sodomise Buchanan, when suddenly the teen awakes and cries out in agony; this disrupts the killer's sexual fantasy. He grows angry and pulls the gun from his pants pocket firing three more bullets into Buchanan's head at close range. Blood is everywhere, while Kearney continues his sexual encounter.

In Kearney's sick perverted mind, he felt that he was a good person because he didn't allow his victim to suffer. The fact that this murderer didn't want the teenager to suffer doesn't make him any less of a cold-blooded killer. After he finishes with Buchanan, he leaves the body for the coyotes, and buzzards.

If police had examined the family phone records at the time of his disappearance, they would have learned that Buchanan had called Patrick Kearney on several occasions. This action may have a given detectives a lead in the case, and perhaps an arrest, which would have ended Kearney's killing spree and saved several lives. In fact, the police should have pulled phone records of previous victims also, but they did not take these disappearances seriously enough.

On Sunday, March 21, 1976, thirteen–year-old Oliver Peter Molitor is reported missing by his family. Again, police tell the parents that Molitor will eventually show up. Nineteen months later, on Friday, December 23, 1977, Los Angeles Sheriff Detectives received a letter from Kearney stating that he killed a boy whom he thought was named Ben.

Detectives didn't have any young victims named Ben, but they did have several unsolved murders. The physical description of Ben fit the victim Oliver Molitor enough to check it out. To connect the dots and confirm a hunch that Ben was Molitor, sheriff detectives confronted Kearney for more details. He recalled that the boy had an uncle, who was a manager of a movie theater in Hermosa Beach. Kearney said he would meet Ben at the Pier Avenue Cove Theater on occasions. Kearney said both the boy and his uncle were gay. At best, he could vaguely remember the details, but said he believed, "It was in the summer of 1976, when he killed and packaged a young boy in several trash bags." Detective's contacted relatives to determine an exact time and date that Molitor went missing. While there, officers also collected some photographs for evidence.

On Tuesday, January 31, 1978, Los Angeles Sheriff Detectives Roger Wilson and Al Sett returned to interview Kearney about the killing of Ben. He wasn't confident of the name, so the investigators suggested the name Oliver who was another missing child. Kearney said, "Yes, I think that is it!" The detectives then showed him some pictures of several missing kids, and he picked out the photograph of Oliver Peter Molitor as being the boy in question. He stated that he remembered murdering Molitor, prior to killing of another victim named Larry Armendariz, which the L.A.P.D. listed as missing on Monday, April 19, 1976.

Kearney said he picked up Molitor hitchhiking at the intersection of Aviation Blvd and Manhattan Beach Boulevard. He believed it was on a Sunday and he was correct. Kearney knew he was going to kill Molitor the moment he picked the boy up. Aroused by the young victim, Kearney invited Molitor into his vehicle, and the two drove off to the killer's house. After arriving at the residence, Molitor relaxed and smoked some marijuana rolled joints. The teen then asked if Kearney had any games that he could play. Kearney suggested the two-play doctor, which lead to having sex several times. Hours later, Kearney grew tired of Molitor and decided to spice up the evening by killing the teen. Kearney later spoke of the boy and the murder, stating that the boy was well built, and had just entered puberty.

"His genitals were not developed; he had very little pubic hair, and was not circumcised," said Kearney. After draining the blood, he chopped the boy into pieces, and then wrapped each body part in separate trash bags. Next, he disposed of the body parts. All the body parts ended up scattered the trash bags in the same manner as several other victims. Detectives contacted Molitor's mother, who stated that her son had not been circumcised and believed it was possible that he had very little pubic hair because of his age. She also believed that the victim was gay and would frequently visit the Hermosa Beach Cove Theater.

Detectives then contacted a Mike McCormick who was the projectionist at the Cove Theater. McCormick stated he knew Molitor and had seen him often at the theater recently. The mother went on to tell detectives that her son had many problems in school and had suddenly changed from receiving an A and B average to D's and F's. He became truant most of the time, until 1976, when he finally dropped out of school entirely.

Police records indicate that Molitor had also been arrested for burglary. Molitor's mother added that her son had several homosexual contacts and he

was leaning heavily in that direction. She added that he had many older homosexual friends, one of which was a motorcycle shop owner in Lawndale who drove a big black limousine and had taken her son to Hollywood on several times. Patrick Kearney confessed to murdering and disposing his body. Molitor's remains were found on March 21, in Manhattan Beach, California.

Above: Palos Verdes landfill in California where several victims found their final destinations. Although workers are not searching for bodies, they were looking for missing "Pieces of hardware" that disappeared from Hughes Aircraft for a secret project.

Courtesy of Marcia Born

MURDER OF INNOCENCE

Eight-year-old Merle "Hondo" Chance was Kearney's second youngest victim.
Courtesy of Neal Chance

The next victim was Merle "Hondo" Chance. Hondo was a cheerful little boy filled to the brim with life, with a nice smile and a big heart. He was a very special child. The family was living at 11945 Jefferson Boulevard in Culver City at the time of his disappearance. Hondo was the youngest of five children and was attending school at Playa Del Rey Elementary School at 12221 Juniette Street also in Culver City.

"He was a mama's boy. My youngest daughter and Hondo were five years apart she was the oldest. At that time, I had two boys and two girls and him. He'd come home from school and bring me a rose or flower. He was just a fun-loving little kid," said Neal Chance, mother of Hondo. Hondo was born March 1, 1969, he celebrated his eighth birthday in 1977, with friends and family, who cheered as Hondo blew out his birthday candles and made a wish. He opened all his presents and a special birthday card containing money inside. He was so excited and knew exactly what he wanted to do with the money.

The child took the money and bought himself a brand-new shiny bicycle that he had been wanting for some time. A cheerful Hondo proudly rode his new bicycle all up and down the streets to "Hughes Hill," which led directly into Hughes Aircraft parking lot. Just one month and six days later, Hondo's wishes, and dreams would be tragically shattered forever. It was another mild spring day with temperature reaching a cool 63 degrees among overcast skies, with a vivacious sun occasionally piercing through the clouds. Hondo arrived home from school and couldn't wait to ride his new stingray bicycle with a banana seat. Before leaving, his mother, Neal, told him to be home for dinner. Hondo went behind the house and found a pack of matches. This was a normal act for a little boy experimenting as all boys do at this age, but sometimes carelessness can lead to destruction. Without thinking, he lit some paper on fire and threw it inside a trashcan in the alley. Moments later, there was a big flame radiating from the trashcan and neighborhood kids quickly put it out. Hondo became worried, because he knew he would be in trouble. He decided to face the music later, so he jumped on his new bike, and quickly raced down the street, leaving his troubles far behind.

The date was Tuesday, April 6, 1977, Patrick Kearney woke up early, showered and dressed for work. David Hill was still was sleeping, so Kearney decided not to wake him. He drove to his place of employment at Hughes Aircraft in Culver City, and walked to the entrance of the building, where a guard asked him to show his security identification card to the camera mounted in front of him. As Patrick Kearney did so, a buzzard sounded allowing him to enter the building. Upon entering, he heard his co-workers talking about how a 70-year-old Howard Hughes had died the previous day on April 5. Kearney was not concerned with the news. If fact, he did even know what the fuss was about, Hughes was an old man. Employees talked about how Howard Hughes died, while traveling from his penthouse in Mexico to the Methodist Hospital in Houston in his private jet. The FBI had to use fingerprints to identify his body since his appearance was significantly changed due to drugs usage. He had also developed an obsessive-compulsive disorder and had developed an intense fear of germs. Hughes body was in very poor condition. X-rays taken at the time indicated that he had broken off hypodermic needles in his arms.

Mr. Hughes is buried at the *Glenwood Cemetery* in Houston, Texas. The autopsy determined that the cause of death was due to kidney failure. He left an estate estimated at $2 billion that was distributed to twenty-two cousins on both sides of his family. Kearney went back to his job as an engineer, where he researched and tested various electronic and avionics systems. He would also identify and describe the uses of top-secret parts recovered from Russian aircrafts from recently crashes. Kearney was very intelligent. Hughes Aircraft depended on him to identify cold war Russian aircraft parts. The Russians had developed horizontal stabilizers, with a 28-degree dihedral used on the wings on jets and later Russian manned space planes. Kearney's job was to assemble and figure out what they were for and how they worked.

Police Ask Public to Help Find Missing 8-Year-Old

Venice division police Sunday turned to the public for help in finding an 8-year-old boy missing since late Wednesday when he left home on his bicycle.

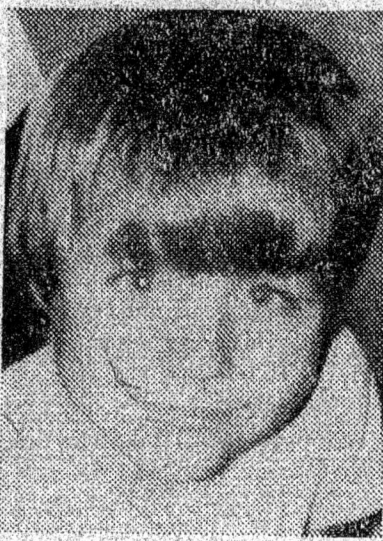

Merle (Hondo) Chance

Officers said Merle (Hondo) Chance was not a habitual runaway, but may have anticipated a parental reprimand for a trash can fire in an alley.

In any event, said Venice Juvenile Investigator Don Hensley, police became concerned and by Saturday officers working overtime were being aided by citizens' band radio owners in the area of the boy's home on Jefferson Blvd. overlooking the Hughes Airport.

The missing boy was described as blond with blue eyes, 4 feet tall and weighing 60 pounds. He wore a brown pullover shirt, brown pants and black boots. He was riding a black Stingray bicycle with a "banana" seat.

Combined efforts from Venice Police, Newspapers and citizen's band radio joined together in search of Hondo Chance.

Daily Breeze Newspaper

On this Tuesday, April 6, Kearney left work a little after 3:00 p.m. As he drove out of Hughes parking lot and approached the intersection, near Hughes Hill, he noticed young Hondo crying out as he struggled to push his bicycle across the street. The back-tire skidding across the blacktop road with the chain jammed between the sprocket and the gear shaft, causing the back wheel to lock up. It was extremely hard to push, especially for a small eight-year-old boy. Kearney immediately became sexually aroused and lusted at the thought of raping and killing another child, as he did Smith a year and a half earlier with victim Ronald Dean Smith Jr. The killer pulled over to the side of the road and shifted his truck into park. The killer stepped out of the driver's seat to offer the child his assistance. Hondo knew he should never get into a stranger's car, but he was more worried about his new bicycle and getting home on time for dinner.

Kearney approached Hondo like a clever wolf drooling over a baby lamb. The killer says, "Hello son, what's wrong with your bicycle?" Hondo replies in a sad tone that his chain is broken, and he needs to get home. A convincingly concerned Kearney offers to drive Hondo to a nearby bicycle shop to get his bike repaired. In a soft-spoken tone of concern, he charms the child like a loyal servant wanting to assist his master. Deliberate and aware that the boy will follow wherever his bike is going, Kearney loads the cycle into the back of his truck, and tells Hondo to get in. As promised, Kearney drives the boy to a local bicycle shop. While waiting for his bike to be repaired, Kearney befriends Hondo, and asks him if he has ever been to Disneyland? Hondo replies, "No."

To gain the boy's trust further, Kearney tells him, "Well, you know what? I'm going to take you to Disneyland sometime." The boy's eyes glisten with excitement and as adrenalin rushes through his body, a smile immediately appears on his face. At this point, the boy is beginning to like the "Nice" stranger. Hondo begins to feel like he has found a new friend. It doesn't take long before the bicycle is fixed and ready to go. Kearney loads it in the back in the truck and the two drive off towards Hondo's home. Overflowing with excitement, Hondo says, "I can't wait to get home, so I can tell my mom you're going to take me to Disneyland."

Suddenly, as the words are leaving the boy's mouth, thoughts of concern begin to race through Kearney's head. He begins to think about what this little boy is going to say to his mother, and then, he panics. He realizes that a stranger offering to take a small boy to an amusement park may not sound appropriate to the mother, or to the police for that matter.

Kearney quickly pulls his truck over to the side of the road. The boy looks up at the stranger and says, "Are you taking me home?" The stranger grabs a sweater on the seat and pulls it tightly over the boy's head and body, and then he slides his hand up underneath the garment. With his fingers, he squeezes the nose with force and covers the boy's mouth tightly with his hand and then smothers the child. The confused child panics, he tenses up, and he struggles uncontrollably, fighting for air, but no avail. Moments later an innocent child is forever gone. He left the world without a clue about why the stranger turned on him and why he had to die. The child's last thoughts were probably a combination of fear, devastating terror, and strenuous efforts to escape the grip of this overpowering detrimental stranger.

This murder arouses Kearney, and he decides to drive to his Redondo residence to sodomise Hondo's small limp frame. Kearney plays with the boy's corpse the entire night, like a prize trophy that he won. The following day, he dumps the child in a ravine off

Angeles Crest Highway. There were trees, brush, and colorful scenery all around; it was a beautiful location for such a sad ending. Hondo's fifteen-year-old sister, Debbie, was the last relative to see him alive. She recalled watching Hondo riding his bike up and down the alley so happy and full of life. This would be her last memory of her brother. He was murdered less than six weeks, after his eighth birthday.

According to the local newspapers, some hikers found a small body in a shallow grave marked by several rocks on May 26, 1977. The body was in a wash near the Monte Cristo Ranger Station, 11 miles north of Altadena in Angeles National Park. There was nothing left but the mostly bones. A short time later, the L.A. County Coroner arrives to pick up the body for a preliminary investigation. Upon examination, the coroner reports that the remains were possibly that of a female, about 6 to 10 years of age, but were unable to determine the cause of death. The body was intact, but it was found naked and almost completely decomposed. Most of the bones that were recovered were dumped in an arroyo and covered with broken branches from surrounding brush. It is noted that there was no soil covering the body. The exact location of the body was fifteen feet down from the Angeles Crest Highway at Marker 24.6, which displays the location in miles from the junction of Highway 14, to the Antelope Valley Freeway.

Weeks later, after a more thorough examination, the body was determined to be that of a male child. The investigation continued as Sheriff's Homicide Division put out a bulletin to identify the body of a young male believed to have been murdered. Los Angeles Police Department responded by stating that they had a missing juvenile out of Culver City area that could possibly match the body found. With this information and weeks of investigation under their belt, it was assumed that the body could possibly be Hondo. The details of the case were transferred to L.A.P.D coroner's office to examine the body more thoroughly and positively confirm the identity, before contacting the family.

After a series of tests were performed and clarified, it was determined that the body was not only a male, but also proved to be the remains of Hondo. Due to the condition of the body, the family was not allowed to view the corpse. However, the body was released to the family for burial, and Hondo was buried in June of 1977. It was a sad closure for a child that never had a chance to experience life.

During the two months of Hondo's disappearance, this would prove to be a very sorrowful time for the family. A pastor in Orange County officiated services at the Hondo's funeral at the family's church. Hondo's murder story was so shocking that it was even published in "True Detective" magazine in late 1977 - 78 issues.

In June of 1977, fourteen months later in a Chino prison cell, Patrick Kearney confessed to killing Hondo, but he requests that officers keep the details quiet. Over 30 years later, the truth is finally revealed. In his statement, the killer confirmed that he had pulled up to an intersection by Hughes Aircraft in Culver City and encountered Hondo crossing the street with his bicycle. On record, Kearney reported that Hondo's bicycle had a broken chain, and the boy was crying out for help. He pulled his truck to the side of the road and offered to take the boy to the bicycle shop for repairs, which he did. While in the shop waiting for the bicycle to be repaired, Kearney had befriended the boy. He wanted to take the boy's spirits to the next level so he promised that one day he would take him to Disneyland and then after the boy became excited, Kearney murdered him.

With a signed confession in place, Detectives Sett and Wilson decided to check out

Kearney's story to confirm the murder details. Detectives then obtained a removal order from the court for Kearney to be transferred back down to L.A. County Jail. St. John and Marvin Enquest of the L.A.P.D joined the investigators. Together, four officers picked up Kearney up in an unmarked car. The group proceeded to the Angeles Crest Highway where Kearney directed them to the exact location where he dumped the body. The officer's drove up Angeles Crest Highway, until they reached several "road closed" barricades that prevented them from driving any further.

A brush fire that had occurred the previous year stripped the land of all vegetation. Next, El Nino had ripped through sending torrential rains that washed the mountains away, sending tons of rocks, sand, and mud sliding down and across the highway. This filled in all the arroyos, a dry creek bed and mountainous terrain that covered the highway and the pavement with four foot of debris. The area resembled a lunar landscape or moonscape. Officers moved several barricades and followed the tire tracks that were still visible, where Cal Trans had been trying to clear the highway for several miles. Kearney advised officers to stop and turn the vehicle around. Then he instructed them to drive back, about a quarter of a mile. Unexpectedly, he yelled out, "Stop the car." The officers climbed out of the vehicle and looked around, but there was nothing but rolling hills of rock, sand stones and mud that had been washed away. They grabbed the "Murder book" out of the car and scanned through the photographs of the crime scene of where the body was found. Kearney jumped from the car and ran to a spot where started to dig with his hands and feet. Detective Roger Wilson asked Kearney, "What are you doing?"

He responded, "I would like to see where the highway marker was." Officers grabbed a *Boy Scout shovel* out of the car and gave it to Kearney. He proceeded to dig down, until he hit a metallic object, which turned out to be a bent mile maker. He attempted to straighten it, until it read, "24.6 L.A. Co." Officer Enquest opened the murder book again and found the sheriff's photo of the crime scene mile marker and it read, "24.6," and could see the background where the body was found. "We all looked at one another in amazement," said Detective Roger Wilson. It was the same marker.

This confirmation satisfied all the investigators who now believed without a doubt, that Kearney was the killer who placed the boy's body at the location. Hondo's bicycle that he purchased with birthday money has never been recovered. It is believed that Kearney gave the bike away in Tijuana Mexico.

INTERVIEW WITH HOMICIDE DETECTIVE ROGER WILSON:

Stewart: You also said you went out to Angeles chest with three other officers where Kearney indicated, "The body was right here," but the area looked like the moon.
Wilson: Yeah.
Stewart: Well, you mentioned that Kearney walked about freely, and he asked you, why you let him walk around so freely. He also asked why your partner wasn't armed.
Wilson: I told him that I was an expert shot, and we only needed one gun, and my partner carried a knife, and we've used Al Sett's knife more than

we've used my gun, and I can pick your eyes out, so don't bother to run.
He stayed real close to me from then on. That was up on Angeles chest
when we found the location of Merle Hondo.
Stewart: What type of gun did you carry on duty?
Wilson: I used a three-inch stainless-steel Smith and Wesson.
Stewart: And what was the caliber?
Wilson: It was a .357; it had .38 a caliber in it, a factory model.

INTERVIEW WITH NEAL CHANCE – MOTHER OF HONDO CHANCE

"Hondo's Birthday was March 1st, and he received money, in which he paid for his own bicycle. We didn't know if his handle bar was broken or what happened to Hondo's bike, but it was the ride down 'Hughes Hill,' which led directly into Hughes Aircraft where he would meet Kearney. He was on his way home and while waiting at a signal light to change, Kearney picked him up. Hondo knew he should never go with strangers, so Kearney had to be real persuasive. "

Neal went to Kearney's second parole hearing, but Kearney didn't show. She never went back again. "He wouldn't come out," said Neal Chance.

Stewart: Can you tell me what Hondo was like as a child?
Neal: We'll he was a mama's boy. My youngest daughter and Hondo were five years apart She was the oldest. At that time, I had two boys, two girls and him (Hondo). He'd come home from school and bring me a rose or flower. He was just a fun-loving little kid.
Stewart: Your sister Rachel said the street that Hondo was picked up on lead into Hughes Aircraft.
Neal: Yes, we lived right across from "Hughes Helicopters. In fact, one time a jet took off and shock my whole house. And he (Kearney) worked over there for fifteen years. Hondo was up there riding on what they called *Hughes Hill*, he was behind *Hughes Helicopters*, riding his bike, and his bike broke and I don't know what happened to it, but there was something wrong with his handle bars or something. Hondo was on his way home and sitting at the light waiting on it to change and Kearney pulled up and saw his bike broken and took him to get it fix. He got his confidence first, because Hondo was told never to get into cars with strangers." He got his confidence and took him to get his bike fixed, and so Hondo got…they didn't tell me what kind of car it was…they just told you it was a vehicle and took him to get it fixed. According to the cops, Kearney told them, he took him to get something to eat, and decided he couldn't let him go home because he was a murderer and was afraid Hondo would come home and tell me. They found him two months later buried at the National forest. They never found his bike.
Stewart: They never found his bicycle?
Neal: "Nope. If they did, they never told me about it.

Stewart: Do you remember the name of the street at the address where you lived at the time?

Neal: I don't remember, but I can get it. I've got all the newspaper clippings. I've got photos of police reports, and the pictures are all put away.

Stewart: Did he get the bicycle he was riding for his birthday?

Neal: He bought himself for his birthday. Somebody had given him some money for his birthday. He got that money and bought himself a bicycle for his birthday on March 1st, and then disappeared on April 6th.

Stewart: When did you actually realize he was missing?

Neal: When my other kids couldn't find him for dinner.

Stewart: Yeah.
What time was that?

Neal: Which was a couple, three hours later.

Stewart: Do you know what time that was around?

Neal: About 4:30 in the afternoon.

Stewart: And so, did they go out looking for him?

Neal: Yeah, they searched until about 6pm. I thought he was at a friend's house or something. We contacted the police and they said give it some time and he will probably be home. You said police set up an operation at a local gas station. And everyone searched for him.

Stewart: What do you think about Kearney?

Neal: I'd like to blow his head off. He is in a cell by himself where no one can hurt him.

Above: The sad reality. Funeral Services for Merle Hondo Chance in June of 1977. Hondo was just a small child, but he had the smile of an angel and a heart of gold. Kearney took all these qualities away, forever.   *Photo Courtesy of Neal Chance*

Kearney's obsession with killing children would continue with the killing of fifteen-year-old Larry Armendariz. He was reported missing on Sunday, April 18, 1976. It was a blazing a hot 80 Degrees, when Armendariz disappeared. Police pleaded their usual case that the teenager probably just ran away or was off with friends. The parents were told, "give it a few days and he'll probably show up." Armendariz' family wasn't so sure. It was not like him to just disappear without even calling home. Police did not have much information on Armendariz, so he remained just another missing kid.

Evidence shows that Kearney picked the fifteen-year-old up and shot him like all the rest, but this victim would never be seen again. Armendariz' dead body was taken to Kearney's home, where he was sexually abused, carefully dismembered and then wrapped up for disposal. His body ended up somewhere in the Palos Verdes landfill, where he has never been recovered to this day. Like so many others, Kearney dumped pieces of the victim's cadaver in trash bends behind restaurants such as *McDonald's*, *Jack in the box*, and *Winchell's Donuts Shop.*

However, on this day, Kearney was nearly apprehended while dumping the body parts of Armendariz. At Winchell's he purchased a dozen donuts and asked the hostess to place them in a large bag. Afterwards, he walked back to car back to where he emptied the bag and placed the head of Armendariz inside. Next, he looked around and then casually walked over to a nearby trash bend. With the head in a Winchell's bag, Kearney attempted to push it down towards the bottom of the trash container, when suddenly the sound of piercing sirens nearby, startled him. Police appeared in the same parking lot with flashing red lights.

Kearney became tremendously nervous and hurried back to his automobile. He felt that any moment he was about to be arrested for murder. Hastily, he tried to back up his car to make an escape, but as he looked in his rear-view mirror, he noticed the sirens and flashing lights had stopped, and both police car doors were now open. Uneasily, he watched as the officers walked unhurried and unsuspicious into Winchell's donuts, to indulge in free donuts and coffee. This was a normal sight to see the L.A.P.D. using their police sirens and flashing lights, speeding down the Boulevard to reach their destination, whether it was for official business or refreshments. Even though it was indeed a waste of taxpayer's money, these acts continue today.

The officers seemed to be more interested in free food, than they were in the suspicious stranger walking quickly away from the trash bend. Winchell's donuts also benefited, by exchanging free donuts for protection, prevented robberies. Kearney later claimed that he was so nervous at Winchell's donuts with the presence of police, that he shook uncontrollably, and thought he was going to have a heart attack right in the parking lot. He later laughed, and would chuckle about the incident, boasting how he had cleverly disposed of a human head, directly in front of the very noses of police.

On this same day, my friend Billy and myself had also spotted the same police car racing by us with sirens screaming and lights flashing. We noticed the police car stopped a short distance ahead. Curious, we raced on our bicycles to see what was going on. We arrived a moment later to see officers walking towards the donut shop, as Kearney as driving off. Kearney looked over at us as he pulled out, and then drove away. He later admitted he found incident amusing.

For years, the Armendariz family prayed and hung onto the slightest hope that their son was still alive. Patrick Kearney shattered all hopes of the family ever seeing their son alive again, after he admitted senselessly murdering the fifteen-year-old boy. The family felt two emotions after learning about the fate of Armendariz, one of relief, and one of grief. The worrying and wondering was over, but the pain and sorrow had just begun to injure. Kearney was a monster, but unlike the ever-popular scary fictional characters like Michael Myers or Jason from horror movies, Kearney made these characters looked tame in comparison. They were fictional characters, whereas he was the real thing, "The worst of the worst."

Twelve-year-old murder victim Micheal McGhee
Courtesy of Elizabeth McGhee

"You know there is not a day that goes by that I don't think about Mike! Your heart just never heals, and you're never the same again." *Betty McGhee*

"Micheal is never out of my mind, also the fact that Redondo Police Department was not very nice at this time; I remember calling, and I asked if there was any news of Mike. I heard the officer say to a woman, 'Its 'Mrs. McGhee calling to see about Mike.' Her answer was, 'Tell her not to call back we will bring him home one way or the other.' I thought that was so cold and unfeeling. I often wondered if she ever had children. My daughter and I usually go to the parole hearings but had to miss the last one due to illness," said Betty McGhee.

The above phone comment was coldly aimed at a worried Elizabeth McGhee, as she acquired about her missing 13-year-old son, Micheal, to the Redondo Beach Police Department. Elizabeth had every reason to be worried, because Micheal McGhee would become another one of Kearney's murder victims.

Last picture of 13-year-old Micheal Craig McGhee
Courtesy of Elizabeth McGhee

Although similar in many ways, each victim had their own horrific and heartbreaking story. The case of Micheal Craig McGhee began on Friday, June 11, 1976, when the police received an urgent phone call regarding the disappearance of a Redondo Beach teenager. It was a warm summer day with temperatures souring to a sweltering 89 degrees in Los Angeles County. Elizabeth McGhee said her missing brother, Micheal, was born on December 5, 1962, and would grow to be a rebellious teenager who had dropped out of school at age 12. Detective Roger Wilson said McGhee was in and out of trouble, and well known by local police for suspicion of crimes ranging from car thief, and sexual offences to burglary. He added that McGhee was a small-time petty criminal, who just couldn't seem to stay out of trouble. In my research, I could not find any criminal records on McGhee.

Going primarily by his supposed criminal record, police figured the teenager was probably up to no good and had not returned home to avoid being questioned about crimes in the area.

What police didn't know was that the teen had met up with Patrick Kearney while hitchhiking and the conclusion would not be good one. McGhee had been walking along Inglewood Avenue near Lennox Boulevard when Kearney pulled over and confronted him. McGhee told Kearney, he was going to Torrance and gracefully accepted a ride. During the journey, Kearney invited McGhee to accompany him on a camping trip to Lake Elsinore (one of Kearney's favorite dead body dumping sites). McGhee replied by saying he couldn't go at the time, but he told Kearney to call him in about a week.

The following week, Kearney did try to call McGhee, but there was no answer. Kearney then decided to drive over to the teen's house. After arriving at the residence, he walked up and knocked on the door.

Moments later, McGhee's sister, 15-year-old Elizabeth "Liz," answered to see an odd man dressed in camouflage clothes. Liz was babysitting her brothers, Micheal, Brian, and sister, Kim, while their mother was working at Host International, located at the Los

Angeles (LAX) airport. The stranger asked to speak with Micheal, but Liz responded that her brother was on restriction for missing school and could not go anywhere. Desperate for a kill, Kearney told her that he had promised to take Micheal camping. Liz told the stranger that her brother could not go anywhere. She called her mother at work, to confirm that Micheal was to stay home. While she was in the kitchen on the phone, Kearney left and walked back to his truck, and was about to drive away, when Micheal raced after him on foot. Liz hung up the telephone and noticed her brother was not in the house. She gathered her brothers and sister, and hurried down the street looking everywhere, but Micheal was nowhere in sight. He had caught up with Kearney and was now hiding in his truck. Micheal watched as his sister searched for him. After she returned to the house, Kearney told Micheal McGhee that he needed to drive by his residence to pick up some camping equipment.

    At the Kearney residence, the killer invited Michael and told him to have a seat. Immediately, Michael began looking around while bragging to Kearney about how he had previous stole a truck and had committed several burglaries in the past year. Kearney wasn't impressed with Michael's pilfering one bit. Michael began scanning the house with his eyes and told Kearney he had some nice stuff.

    Then he asked Kearney if he had any burglar alarms or security systems? Kearney had heard enough. Moments later, he walked up behind the couch and shot Michael McGhee in the back of the head. Kearney dragged Michael off to the bathroom where he beat the victim's dying body, and then raped him repeatedly, before dismembering the corpse. Later that evening, he disposed of the body parts in trash bends all around Redondo Beach. Micheal McGhee's remains would never be found, but like so many victims, he would end up at the Palos Verdes landfill. Eighteen months after the incident, while in custody of Los Angeles Sheriff Homicide Detectives Roger Wilson and Al Sett, Patrick Kearney admitted to details of what had occurred on that tragic warm Friday afternoon.

    <Sic> "We were going to spend the weekend just outing and, he kept talking about how he stole this guy's truck. And then, when I got him in the house, he kept asking me questions." 'Oh, you have all these things around. You don't have any burglar alarms, do you? If you do, where are they?' (Referring to radios and other things about the house). Kearney continued, "He kept asking very pertinent questions. I thought, Yeah, I made a mistake in befriending this kid. Letting him know where I live, and I shot him before we ever went anywhere. I didn't go anywhere for the weekend. I disposed of the body. You aren't going to find him." <End Sic>

    It had been over a year before McGhee's family learned what had happened to Micheal and as painful as the news was, they had already figured that something bad had happened to him. Micheal's mother Elizabeth McGhee said, "It was hard for everybody. I thought my world was coming to an end when my son was murdered. It's never out of your mind. It never goes away. It never will."

    Micheal's sister, Elizabeth (named after her mom), still remembers telling the little guy in glasses, wearing camouflage clothes, "Her brother could not go." If Micheal would have listened to his mom and sister, and stayed home that day, he may still be alive. Micheal McGhee's body has never been recovered. Micheal's older brother, Robert would have trouble dealing with the murder for years to come. He has dealt with the murder of his brother by acting as though the terrible incident never happened. "I just refused to believe it. There was no body. There was no physical evidence. I would rather believe Michael's off in Mexico, goofing off, maybe on the beach somewhere."

All the relatives of victims would need a sense of optimism to give them strength to go on, but sometimes the reality of loss is often too devastating and terrifying to accept. No one ever believes that a family could cross paths with a cold-blooded killer in their town, but the reality is quite common in a large county, especially Los Angeles, California. Crime is usually higher in big cities, but LA has been known as a breeding ground for serial killers.

Next on Kearney's list of horror was John "Woody" Woods. He was a tall, slender 23-years-old man with a red Afro hairdo that fit the nineteen seventies trend. It was Sunday, June 20, 1976, a date that I will always remember well. The previous Saturday evening a bunch of friends were preparing to go to the largest party of the summer in Redondo Beach. There were four of us together that night, but today I'm the only one left alive today to tell the story. The others have all died of unnatural deaths. The evening began with Gene Austin inviting Billy Tibbetts, and myself to attend the big party event. This wasn't an ordinary party, it was said to be the last party of the summer and we were ready to blow off some steam. Gene Austin picked up Billy Tibbetts and me around 7:30 p.m. in his fire engine red Ford van with polished chrome wheels. Gene's van was his pride and joy; it was also our party mobile. Billy jumped in the front passenger seat as he yelled out, "I got shotgun!" I slid opened the side door and jumped in the back on the edge of a fancy velvet oriental rug covering a mattress. Gene grinned and said," You guys ready to party?"

He slid an Allman brother's tape into the cassette player and his voice echoed with excitement, talking loudly about the big party. "Man, this is going to be the party of all parties! I'm not kidding; this is going to be huge!" He shifted into drive and as we drove off, he added, "First, I need to run back by my house to pick up an old high school buddy named Woody. He is going with us." I had never met John Woods, nicknamed "Woody" before this night, but I would never forget the name after this night. Gene and Woody were the oldest of the group; they were both in their early twenties and had been buddies for years.

"We were shocked and stunned as armed detectives ordered to move away from the van and lie face down. They searched us for some our identification, as one of the detectives asked, "What are you doing washing the blood out of your van?" We thought, "Blood?"

…Tony Stewart - *The death of John Woods*

On June 20, 1976, we dropped 23-year-old John "Woody" Woods off at a local bar on Artesia Boulevard in Redondo Beach, and the next day he was found shot to death in San Diego.   *Author's Sketch of victim and Kearney*

Billy was the youngest at age eighteen, and I was nineteen. Lots of people called him "Red," because of his wavy long red hair. Billy had been my best friend since I was tenyears-old. When we arrived at Gene's house, Woody jumped into the back, behind the driver's seat, directly across from me. Introductions were announced, and after a brief "Hello," we were off to Door's Market to purchase some alcohol. We picked up some Budweiser bottles and decided to drive along the beach, down Highway 101, which is also known as Pacific Coast Highway. As we guzzled beer to get primed for the colossal party event, Gene said, "These people are close friends of mine and the party won't really get started until after 10 p.m. He kept saying, "Man, last year they had a huge party, and it was a blast! Ask Woody, he was there."

Woody responded by saying, "Yeah, it was really something!" Woody's red Afro made him look like a product straight out of the nineteen sixties era.

As we drove around with the stereo playing Allman Brother's songs *Midnight Rider* and *Ramblin Man,* Woody began telling me strange stories about Vietnam and all the death involved during the war. This was all he talked about the whole evening as we drove around. "Yeah, in Vietnam American soldiers would throw babies in the air and catch them with the bayonets on the end of their rifles. They had no choice, because the enemy would strap bombs on their babies, and they would explode and kill Americans that were nearby." I really didn't care the least bit for these gory stories about killing babies in cold blood, so I kept trying to change the subject. The music was so loud that Gene and Billy couldn't really hear what Woody was talking about. I yelled out, "Hey Gene, shouldn't we get going to the party?" Gene would just smile and respond, "Man, we have plenty of time, it doesn't really get started until later."

Gene was tapping his hands on the steering wheel to the beat of the music, and dancing around his seat, as he drove. Woody's excited tone moved to a higher level as continued talking about death and war. "Man, I had lots of friends who would kill the Vietnamese and would take their guns, knives and all kinds of shit. The woman used to put razor blades in their pussies to hurt U.S. soldiers who raped them. I'm not shiting you, man. It was badass! I'm not fuckin around. It was some cold-blooded shit." Around 11:00 p.m., we finally arrived at the party to see police everywhere. They were ordering the large crowds of people to disperse and leave the party immediately. The street was completely packed with so people trying to flee the area, and it was crazy. It seemed like there were hundreds of people walking in every direction and police cars were everywhere with their lights flashing. Suddenly, Gene had an epiphany. He suggested that we all hide in the back of his van, until the police and the crowds leave the area. Gene said he knew the people throwing the party and he was sure that they would continue the party again after the police left. So, we all climbed in the back of the van and ducked down. Billy peeked up a few times to see if the police left yet.

For the next twenty-minutes we all hid incognito. Suddenly, when we thought we were home free, bright flashlights shined in the van on us, followed by loud voices. It was the Redondo Beach police and in a serious tone, they demanded that we come out of the van immediately, which we did. The policemen wrote all four of our names on a card, with a threat to arrest us, if we returned to the party. One of the officers said, "It's over, go home!" Gene was so pissed. He kept saying, "We missed the biggest party ever! Fuck! Dammit!" We drove around for about another hour looking for some more parties, without any luck. Finally, Woody grew bored and told Gene to drive him to a bar on Artesta Boulevard. We dropped him off a little before 1:00 a.m.

Billy also asked to be dropped out at his house, and so we took him home. I went back to Gene's house where my car was parked. When we arrived, Gene asked me if I wanted to stay the night at his place, so we could get up early the next day and go surfing at the beach. I agreed, and we ended up playing guitars until we turned in. Gene set his alarm and we woke up at sunrise the next day. Gene dialed 379-8471, which was the number to the local surf report, and we learned that the waves were 1 to 2 feet with poor shape. This was a huge disappointment to a surfer. We lived for the excitement of riding fast hollow waves. Since there was no surf, Gene asked me if I would help him wash his van. He always took pride in keeping his van spotless, from top to bottom, inside and out. I felt obligated to help since he did drive us around searching for parties all night and didn't even ask us to pitch in on the gasoline. We opened up the side and back double doors of the van and pulled everything out. We washed the chrome wheels, bumpers, the grill and the body. Next, Gene began spraying the interior with the hose, while I climbed on the top of the van to wash to the roof.

Suddenly, we both paused as our attention was adverted to the sight four cars that raced up and skid to a stop in front of the house. Several plain clothed detectives jumped out of their cars in a hurry and raced towards us. We stood in awe as these men pulled out guns and began barking orders at us. We both immediately were traumatized and astonished at the same time! We both thought, "What the hell is going on?" We realized right away that these men meant business. One of the suited men yelled out to me, "Get off the vehicle and move away from it, now! Move away from the van! Do it now! Face down on the ground with your hands behind your head! Do it now!" Another detective looked at Gene and asked, "Why are you washing out the inside of the van? Are you trying to wash away all the blood?" We both thought, "Blood?" Gene responded, "Cleaning the Blood? No sir! What's going on officer?"

We were immediately handcuffed, and both searched for weapons and identification. After thoroughly checking out the van and searching us for weapons, detectives then removed the handcuffs. One of the men approached us and said, "According to police reports, you were both with John Woods last night, which makes you guys the last people to see him alive. In a shocked voice, Gene said, "What? Last one to see him alive? Are you saying Woody is dead? What happened?" The officer said, "When did you last see Mr. Woods?" Gene told the detectives, "We dropped him off about a *quarter-to-one* in the morning at a bar over on Artesia Boulevard." The officer said, "So you dropped him off around 12:45 a.m." Gene responded, "Yes, sir." We gave them all the details of the evening that we could remember. The detectives then told us that John Woods was found with a bullet in the head in San Diego at 5:00 in the morning. We were shocked! "Woody was dead?"

The distance from Los Angeles to San Diego was about 130 miles, which would take about two hours by car, or sometimes longer depending on the traffic. Rush hour can get congested, but there wouldn't be much traffic during the midnight to early morning hours.

We dropped him off around 12:50 to 1:00 a.m., and the bar would have been closed by 2:00 a.m. This means that Woody had to be in the killer's car within an hour or sooner to have reached San Diego by 5 a.m., when police found the body. After hearing about Woody's death, we figured he must have met someone in the bar who offered him a ride, and this someone had to be the murderer. I found it odd that police did not even ask us the name of the bar. Perhaps the bartender would have shed some light on his murder by identifying whomever Woody left with that night. Since Woody was on foot he would have accepted a ride home by a stranger, especially after a long night of drinking.

Remembering our conversation, Woody probably told the stranger the same bloody stories about Vietnam that he told me earlier in the evening. Sharing his gory stories may have even intrigued the murderer and may have led to his death. These murder stories may have excited Kearney. There was another newspaper report in which police stated, "Woody was murdered in his Hollywood apartment and then dumped in San Diego." When we look at the time schedule involved, there is only one way that the killer could have possibly driven Woody from Redondo Beach to Hollywood, California, twenty-five miles away, and then onto San Diego. The only possible explanation would be that Woody left the bar shortly after arriving so the killer would have enough time to drive him to Hollywood, kill him, and then drive to San Diego where he was found. The journey would have taken two and a half hours to reach San Diego by 5:00 a.m. Initially, I assumed the detectives that arrived at Gene's house were the L.A.P.D., but after talking with Homicide Detective Roger Wilson, I now believe that the officers were Riverside detectives. Regardless, the result would be the same, Woody was dead, and I would never forget him or the crazy stories he told me that fatal evening.

On Saturday, July 7, 1977, Kearney would identify a photograph of John Woods as the man he killed in a Hollywood apartment. The photograph was sent to John St. John of the Los Angeles Police Department to identify the victim. He identified the photograph of John Woods. He also identified a knife that he used during the murder that was later recovered from Kearney's house. Kearney admitted shooting Woody and then using the knife to puncture the throat and then cut him just above the groin area. A couple months after his arrest, Kearney's murder list appeared on national news, and John Woods name was listed as one of his victims.

When I look back now, the thought never crossed my mind that Kearney could be a murderer. Even today, he seemed to be too much of a wimp to be a killer. I thought Kearney was a bit strange, but I never felt any fear around him. He seemed old fashion with his short hair, thick glasses, dress shirts, and appeared to be harmless. John Woods also made the mistake of believing Kearney was harmless. It cost him his life.

DRINKING WITH A SERIAL KILLER

"While we talked, Patrick Kearney reached into this black doctor's type bag, near the television and pulled out a stethoscope. He told me he used to be a doctor and asked if he could listen to my heartbeat."

Tony Stewart - survivor of Serial Killer Patrick Kearney

Above: Tony Stewart at age 19; when he was invited to Kearney's residence around midnight to drink beer at the very same house where the killer murdered several victims. Stewart would become one of the only survivors who lived to tell his story.
Authors Collection

In the summer of 1973, my family bought a house and moved to Lawndale, California, about five miles away from Kearney. I did not encounter Patrick Kearney again for the next five years, when I was nineteen years old in the summer of 1976. The streets seemed peaceful and quiet except for a few cars passing with music blaring with teenagers yelling blowing off steam. It was one of those infrequent boring nights in Redondo Beach, when there were absolutely no parties; no one hanging out and zilch happening. Bored of doing nothing, I found myself starring up into the skies smoking a cigarette and watching the starlight objects floating around.

I was hoping that maybe a spaceship might land and speed up the tempo of this sluggish night. I thought about my day; it was exciting, I went surfing, skateboarding and then hung out listening to music with my friends. The day was long, and we eventually just ran out of things to do. It was starting to get late, so I decided to call it a night. I turned the key in the ignition to start my 1964 Chevy Impala, and heard "Click, click, click." "Great," I thought, the battery was dead. I didn't have any jumper cables and no one in sight to help.

Reluctantly, I began walking home. I looked at my watch and it was about 11:30 p.m., I had a five-mile walk ahead of me. On my way, I decided to stop at Door's Market in Redondo Beach to try to spot a quart of beer. Door's Market was a good place to ask people to buy you beer when you are a minor, because you could stand behind the store without being spotted by police. Anyway, I tried for a half-hour and didn't have any luck, so I continued walking home. I walked down Artesia Boulevard until my legs began getting sore, so I decided to thumb a ride.

After about fifteen minutes, a pick-up truck pulled over and I jumped in. The driver had a pair shaped face, thick glasses, and dark eyes with bushy eyebrows. He looked very familiar, but I couldn't seem to place his name. While I was busy contemplating his identity, he asked, "Don't I know you?" Before I could answer, he spoke out, "Tony?" The voice sounded familiar, and then it came to me like a lightning flashing in my brain. I said, "You're Patrick, I used to mow your yard." He replied, "That's right. How have you been?" I told him "Good, I was on my way home and was trying to spot a quart of beer, but I couldn't find anyone 21 years old to buy it. "I mentioned the beer in hopes that he would offer to buy it for me. It worked, and he said, "I'll buy you a quart of beer." In an excited tone, I said, "Really?"

He stopped at a 7-11 store located on Manhattan Beach Boulevard and Prairie Avenue, which was only three blocks from my house. I was planning to drink the beer at home, but Kearney had other ideas. I handed him a $5.00-dollar bill and watched as he went to the freezer and picked out a quart of Budweiser. He walked to the counter and he paid for it, and then he walked out the door with a brown paper bag. As he handed me the bag, he said, "Okay, I bought you the beer, but you'll have to drink it at my house, because you are a minor, and I don't want you getting in any trouble." I said, "Okay," but I thought to myself, "I'd rather drink it at home, but since he did give me a ride and was nice enough to buy me the beer; I guess I should drink it at his house."

It was a little after midnight, when we arrived at his house on Robinson Street. This was the same house where I did yard work for close to five years. After he told me to have seat on the sofa in the living room and relax, then he disappeared into the kitchen, which was directly behind me. From this position, my back was facing him. I sat down and cracked open the quart of beer. As I took a big drink, Kearney asked, "Would you like a glass for your beer?" I replied, "No, but thank you. The bottle will be fine." I glanced around the room to see a coffee table in front of me, but no coasters. Then I looked over my shoulders to see where Kearney went, and noticed the kitchen has no doors, just an open doorway. I continued looking about the dimly lit room with dark blue carpet and thought to myself, "The house is too dark for my taste." As I took another swig from the bottle, I noticed there was a love seat to my left, and directly behind it about ten feet away was a hallway leading to a bedroom (Kearney's room). To the left of the hallway was the entrance to the bathroom, with another bedroom (Hill's Bedroom) down the hallway on the right. Then, Kearney yelled out from the kitchen, "It is good to see you, after all these years." I don't know what he was doing in the kitchen, but I was distracted by sounds of chattering silverware, and some dishes.

Directly across from me is a small television on a shelf or stereotype stand. While in the kitchen he kept talking to me. "So, are you working?" I yelled back, "No, but I'm looking for a job. I was working at TRW Semiconductors where they made parts for the Apollo space crafts, until I got laid off." Momentarily, Kearney seemed interested in the electronics job, perhaps because he was an engineer at Hughes Aircraft. A few minutes later, he came back into the living room, and asked how I've been doing all these years? He seemed to want to know everything about me as he continued asking questions.

While talking, he walked across the room towards the television (directly in front of me) and reached into what looked like a black doctor's type bag and pulled out a stethoscope. He told me he used to be a doctor and asked if he could listen to my heartbeat. I thought it was an odd request, but calmly, I said, "Sure, okay." Even though it was a peculiar request, I figured, "Well, he did buy me some beer. "I took another big drink and looked down as he placed the instrument on my chest and began moving it around trying to locate my heart. I thought it was strange that he couldn't find my heartbeat, after he said he used to be a doctor. Then things even became weirder when he asked; "Could you lift up your shirt? I can't hear anything."

I remained calm and said, "yeah, sure, "and then lifted my shirt up for him. He continued to move the cold instrument around my chest area and then suddenly he began to lower it down towards my belly button. I did not feel comfortable with this and reacted by telling him, "I really need to get going." I remember thinking to myself, "If this guy gets too weird, I may have to punch him." I told him that my parents might lock the doors, if I'm out too late, and I didn't have my key. As the words were leaving my mouth, the front door knob began to jiggle. The door swung opened and within seconds, his roommate Dave Hill appeared. A nervous Patrick Kearney quickly jumped back as if he was caught red handed doing something wrong. Apparently, Kearney didn't want his roommate and lover to know what he was doing. He promptly pulled the instrument from around his neck and placed it behind his back. Regardless, even though it all happened so quickly, David Hill had seen the stethoscope in his lover's hand.

Nervously, Kearney nearly stuttering as he spoke, "Dave, do you remember Tony? He used to mow are yard. Say, hello." In a deep voice, Dave said, "Hi" as he continued walking straight towards the bedroom, with Kearney following closely behind him. At this moment, I spoke out loudly and repeated my remark that I needed to get going. I wanted to make sure Dave and Kearney could both hear me.

Kearney then looked back at me and said, "Okay, let me get the keys to my truck." Then I heard Kearney promise Dave, "I'm going to drive him straight home and I'll be right back." It was as if he was trying to thoroughly convenience Hill to believe him that he would be back shortly. Hill didn't seem to care either way, and did not even respond. I always thought Hill was a strange character who rarely talked. On the way home, I was talking to Pat, and telling him how it was good to see him again. Strangely, he was not talking or even muttering a word. It was almost like he was in a trance or mentally preoccupied. I continued talking up a storm as we drove, thanking him for the beer and the ride home, but he didn't say a word...it was creepy! It had been a strange evening so when he got close to Alonda Park; I lied to him and said, "You can stop here, I live right across the Street from the park." I lived about three blocks further away, but I decided I didn't want him to know where I lived. He pulled the truck over to the curb and I climbed out. As I walked around the front of the truck towards the driver's side to cross the street, he finally spoke, "Tony, why don't you come over tomorrow morning around 10:00 for another visit."

I replied, "Yeah, okay, I'll see you tomorrow." This was another lie. I had no intention of going by his house ever again. I didn't trust him anymore because I felt there something strange about him. After the stethoscope incident, I didn't feel comfortable around him anymore. I felt sure he was a homosexual, and I wanted no part of that lifestyle. I don't have anything against gay people, but I have always felt that two men should not be together, and it is my right to object to these relationships. I don't accept it, but if I don't have to see it, it doesn't bother me. I remember Pat Kearney had a weird look in his eyes that I will never forget. After saying goodbye, I began walking across the street and watched as Kearney turned the truck around the opposite direction and drove away. I looked back over my shoulder as I began running full speed. Suddenly, I noticed him make a U-turn and was coming back in my direction. I pondered at the thought that perhaps he had seen me running and out of curiosity, turned around to make sure I was all right.

I made it around the corner and quickly jumped behind a fence of a neighbor's house. I watched as his headlights shined its away around the corner, nearly shinning directly on me him for a moment. He slowly drove by, searching for my whereabouts, but he didn't see me anywhere. Again, I thought it was strange that he would turn around and look for me after I had already said, "goodbye." I didn't realize it until a couple of months later, but if his roommate hadn't come home when he did, I might have surely been murdered. Three months after the incident, I was at my girlfriend's house in Redondo Beach, when my brother called me and said, "Hurry, turn on the channel news, right now!" I turned on the TV and nearly was astonished to see Patrick Kearney's face. I didn't believe what I was seeing, but it was Patrick Kearney, and his face was covering the whole television screen, with a reporter was stating that he killed over thirty-two boys and young men. I became shaky and almost fainted. Immediately I began thinking about the night I was at his house and how he acted towards me. I thought, "My God! I was alone in the middle of the night at his house, drinking beer with a serial killer." I would have nightmares for weeks after hearing this news and would relive every detail of that night over and over in my mind. It really spooked me. I remember reading the newspaper the next day, and it gave all the gruesome details about the murderer.

Today, I often think back and can still see Kearney's face. I can remember the look in his eyes and the tone of his voice, like it was only yesterday. I remember it was the summer of July 1976, and I had just turned nineteen years old. This was my first year out of High school and the only thing on my mind was surfing, playing guitar, parties and beautiful women. Nothing else seemed to matter except having as much fun as possible and living life on the edge. I was living in Lawndale, California at the time with my dad, my new stepmother, Marilyn, two sisters and two brothers.

After years of abuse from my first stepmother Bobby and an alcoholic father, I had turned to drugs and street life to escape the daily reality that I lived. However, there were other means of escape that interested me and helped ease the aches and pains of society. Surfing and living the beach life was a great way to ease stress and break away from humanity for a while. Rock and roll was also in the air and I was breathing in every bit of it. I bought a second-hand acoustic guitar, and soon became musically in tune with the world around me. I never felt freer and more liberated, nevertheless I was also young and naïve. I wouldn't have realized it at the time, but my life would soon be in grave danger the moment I met Patrick Kearney. Newspapers rarely publicized the activity of serial killers in L.A., especially in the nineteen seventies, and our generations would become easy targets. In fact, if things had turned out differently, I would not be here today writing this story.

My brother and I often wondered why David Hill was set free, when we both knew Hill was somehow involved with Kearney's crimes. So why didn't David Hill go to prison? One reason is that Kearney was worried what jail would do to Hill. During an interview with police, Kearney said he was worried about Hill going to jail, because he may attempt commit suicide. Kearney told police all the details about Hill's father and how he hung himself in a Texas prison, years earlier.

Kearney protected Hill because he cared about him, besides he needed someone on the outside that he could trust to keep in touch. For thirty years, Hill and Kearney may have kept this dark secret. I wish David Hill could have answered one question under oath, while connected to a lie detector, "Was he involved in any of these murders, and if not, then why was he chasing my brother with Patrick Kearney many years ago." We are certain that he was involved either directly or by accessory to murder. There is no doubt about Hill's involvement, yet five counties let him go free, and he immediately fled back to Texas.

Another question that has always puzzled me is the night when I was at Kearney's house and Hill came home. I believe that if Hill would not have returned home when he did, then I would have surely become a victim. We know that Hill was with Kearney when he chased my brother, so why didn't he help Kearney kill me that night? There can only be one answer. Hill had to of known about the killings, and whether he was directly involved or not, one thing was certain. Hill was probably tired of the murders and the fact that many of the victims were his friends. When Hill came home that night to see Kearney, and me, he acted as if he was upset. He did not mutter a word, until Kearney told him to speak. Even then, he acted as though he didn't want to talk. I believe at this point, he was disgusted with all the murders, and didn't want anything more to do with it.

Regardless of what Hill thought about the murders, a month after I was nearly murdered by Kearney, he was back at it again. Another victim known only as John Doe was found on Sunday, August 22, 1976. This victim would be later discovered to be Larry Espy, a white male, estimated to be from age of about seventeen-years-old. He was hitchhiking in the south bay area in-route to the beach when Kearney picked him up. Kearney gave him a ride to his murderous Robinson residence, where the two talked. While watching television, Espy's life ended when Kearney walked up behind him and shot "Point blank" into the back of his head. Like the rest of his victims, Kearney then dragged Espy off to the bathroom to fool around with his body, until he became sexual satisfied. Then he cut him up the body to dispose of the corpse like a used throw-away condom or blow-up sex doll.

Patrick Kearney and David Hill's residence on Robinson Street, where he murdered, sodomized, and mutilated his victims – Note the strange array of light or ghostly orbs beaming down from the heavens. It is a light breaking through the clouds or a sign from the victims?
Author's Collection

After Kearney used Espy's dead body to reach a climax, he slaughtered and gutted the victim like an animal going to market. He then placed Espy into the trash bags like the others. The mutilated remains of Espy were discovered near San Juan Capistrano by a San Juan camp group of scouts lead by the Nelson family. It began when the scoutmaster pulled over onto the side of the road by the Ortega Mountains, near the Cleveland National Forest. The Charley–do-gooder group included six adults and eleven kids. They were out on a journey to learn about nature. On this day, the scouts would all learn a about the deadly reality that lurks within the terrains of Mother Nature. The scoutmaster instructed his young scouts to pick up any trash they can find and place them in trash bags. After about an hour, the scouts were instructed to gather several trash bags and bring the litter down to the bottom of the dry riverbed at a trash pickup location.

Another strange photograph of Kearney's death house, where scores of victims were cold bloodily shot, sexually abused, and butchered dead and alive. Note the tornado-like shape shining through the trees in an orange shade. The picture was taken with an ordinary camera and no special effects were used. Could be another sign from victims screaming for justice?

Author's Collection

A few of the scouts complained that one of the trash bags was much too heavy to lift. So, the Scoutmaster grabbed the heavy trash bag and attempted to pull it down the hillside with the other scouts watching. This particular trash bag had softened up after lying in the scorching sun for days, and the heavy contents also added to the bags weaken state.

As the Scoutmaster struggled to pull and lift, suddenly the bag broke open and its contents of warm body fluids and internal organs spilled out all over the man. It was a shocking and horrifying sight. The body parts of Larry Espy had been there for some time and were very ripe, and the smell was literally breath taking. The moment the bag ripped open, and the filling poured out, the scouts were left dumbfounded and speechless. Flies and other insects immediately stormed in on the body the moment the smell mixed with the air.

Orange County Police were contacted to investigate a possible murder. Once the police arrived on the scene, their main problem to contend with was trying to keep the scouts away from the body. Apparently, the body sparked the imagination of the children, who sought it fascinating to explore the bloody remains of a real corpse. One of the kids yelled out, "Wow look, there's an arm over there." Another scout pointed to what looked like a foot. The investigation quickly reached a dead end, until Homicide Detectives Al Seth and Roger Wilson of the Los Angeles Sheriff's Department were called in.

While detectives investigated the remains, Riverside County Sheriff's Department called to report a similar case found in January of 1975. The officers arranged a meeting to compare notes and realized that all the victims were killed in the same manner, but very evidence was left at the murder scenes. By the following November, six additional bodies had been found in Los Angeles, Orange, Riverside and San Diego Counties. Police knew they had a serial killer to contend with, however, capturing this killer would be a difficult task. After reviewing the victim's police record, detectives learned that Espy was considered a bad kid, who had been in and out of trouble. Espy's parents never even bothered to file a missing person report, after their son disappeared. The parents ended up divorcing and moving out of the area and could not be located. There was no forwarding address or other information, so police never made contact with the parents.

"The unidentified body was immediately named John Doe, of the missing head, feet and hands and there was no way to identify the victim at the time. Orange County had jurisdiction of this homicide and their investigation would reach a dead end, until Kearney later admitted to the crime when he talked to Al and myself. This kid was such a bad kid that the parents never filed a missing on him and then they divorced and moved from the area. This info came to us after we convicted Kearney and some articles came out in newspapers and magazines. We never made contact with any family members as I recall. As best as we can say is that nobody cared for the boy," said Homicide Detective Roger Wilson.

Meanwhile, the count continued to grow with bodies littering the major Highways. Mark Andrew Orach was a 20-year-old, 5'11" 165-pound, white male from of Ottawa; Canada. He was the next to be found. Orach had ventured out on the open road and began hitchhiking from Vancouver, Canada to Mexico. Orach told his family and friends that he wanted to travel around and see the country. It was going to be a fascinating journey for a young lad. His first stop was going to be America, a neighboring land that he had always dreamed of seeing. It would be here on America soil where he would only find death. Sadly, his fate would become a certainty about 1000 miles from Orach's home, and his life would be cut short, only ten days after he set out on his adventurous journey. He was murdered and his body was found on Wednesday, October 6, 1976, in Orange County. Orach's body was found in the same location as another "John Doe" victim, later to be identified as Larry Espy. He was location on Sunday, August 22, 1976. The two victims were both found in Ottawa alongside Ortega Highway, (Hwy 74) in Orange County, one and a half miles east of the San Juan Fire Station. The bodies lay alongside the Ortega Highway between San Juan Capistrano and Lake Elsinore. Both the victims were killed in the same manner. They were both fatally shot in the head by a .22 caliber weapon and found nude.

After killing Mark Orach, Patrick Kearney took off the victim's clothes and dragged his body down a jagged path of rock and dirt. He sodomized the victim and disposed of his clothes in various trash containers. The coroner stated that there was semen found in the anal cavity, but none in the oral cavity. Orach remained unidentified, until his murderer Patrick Kearney confessed to investigators the victim's name. He added that he had picked up Orach in the South Bay area, while he was hitchhiking near the San Diego Freeway. Orach had told Kearney that he was from Canada and was in route to Baja, California, but his destiny would only lead to his murder, in a ditch on the side of the road. He had ventured to America with hopes of adventure and excitement, only to become a victim of a serial killer.

Six days after Larry Espy's body was discovered, the diseased body of 20-year-old Wilford Lawrence Faherty was found on Saturday, *August 28, 1976*, on Otay Lakes Road in Southeast San Diego County. Initially, police thought the murder was drug related, since reports indicated that Faherty was a known drug dealer. Evidence would later reveal that this was not a drug related murder; it would later be discovered as another *Trash Bag* murder.

Police estimated that the victim was shot four times in the head sometime between April and August. Patrick Kearney had been out for another midnight drive when he spotted Faherty hitch hiking, and immediately pulled over to offer him a ride. Faherty jumped in Kearney's truck without hesitation. He had been a veteran hitchhiker for years and had met a lot of exciting and strange L.A. people along the way, but he never had any serious problems. The two engaged in some friendly conversation right away, as Kearney stepped on the gas pedal and drove off. An intoxicated Faherty laughed as told Kearney that he had been out drinking with friends and was on his way home. After a short chat, Kearney invited Faherty to go for a short drive before taking him home. Faherty wanting to get home reluctantly agrees, and the two drove southbound towards San Diego. After driving several miles in complete darkness, Faherty tells Kearney that he needs to urinate and asks if could locate a restroom. With no rest areas in sight, Kearney pulled to the side of the road at an isolated area, and Faherty jumps out to relieve himself.

As the two exited the vehicle, Faherty makes a fatal mistake as he turns his back on Kearney. This mistake would cost him his life. Kearney walked up directly behind him, and pulled out a .22 caliber derringer, but when he tried to pull the trigger, the cylinder spun out of alignment. The gun made a clicking sound as the cylinder spun that caught Faherty's attention. As he turned around to see what was going on, Kearney tried to realign the cylinder. Faherty realized that something wasn't quite right and broke into a run. Kearney chases after him, as Faherty races through the tall grass and scattered trees. The killer fires two shots, but misses. However, the third bullet hits the teen in the head, and he collapses to the ground. The bullet ripped through the back of his head, but the bullet did not kill him. Kearney tore Faherty clothes off and began to sodomise his body, when the victim regained consciousness and screamed in severe agony. As Kearney realizes Faherty wasn't dead, he stops briefly, and grabs his gun from his pants pocket. He fires three more bullets at close range distance into Faherty's brain, until the teen finally stops moving. Kearney takes a quick look around, and then continues to sodomize his victim in the murkiness of the night. He leaves the body for the coyotes and the buzzards to feed on and drives off into the night.

On August 30, two days after the murder, Patrick Kearney contacted the Redondo Beach police to report a burglary at his residence. The official police report indicated that Kearney reported several guns and other items stolen which included, a .357 magnum colt trooper, a two-inch .38 smith and Wesson with two-inch barrels, a .22 H&R pistol with a two inch barrel, a .410 shotgun, two pairs of handcuffs, and two two-way portable "Walkie talkie" radios. A routine check on other weapons purchased by Patrick Kearney and David Hill revealed that in addition to those weapons reported missing, they still had in their possession, three .22 caliber derringers, and an H&R caliber revolver.

A few weeks later, police received a call that shots had been fired in the back yard of the Kearney residence at 1906 Robinson Street. David Hill had been shooting cans in the backyard with a .22 derringer. Shortly after the incidents, Patrick Kearney arrived home. Ten minutes later, police arrived at the residence, and were knocking on the door to question Hill and Kearney about the shooting. Both denied the incident, stating that they did not shoot any weapons. They added that they don't like guns, nor do they own any guns. The officers on the scene were puzzled; they reminded the two men of the burglary they had reported in an official document, in which several guns had been stolen from the residence. The officers also told them that they had prior information that a witness had watched David Hill shoot at cans in the backyard, and even kill a cat on one occasion. This information was acquired during the murder investigation, while questioning a man about Hill and Kearney. At the time, the two were not yet suspects.

After confronting the two men about the incident, and the fact that the officers had prior knowledge from a source that they had been target practicing in the backyard, they reluctantly admitted guilt. They promptly admitted to having a pellet gun, and small blue steel .22-caliber six-shot revolver Rossi Pocket vest. A nervous Hill and Kearney promised there would not be any further shooting. They were let off with a stern warning about shooting weapons within city limits, with a strict warning that if officers should have to return, extreme measures would be taken, which included possible jail time. Kearney was extremely furious at Hill for carelessly bringing police to their front door, but the incident was soon forgotten. It wasn't long before Kearney was back on the streets looking for another victim. This search wouldn't take long.

Randall "Randy" Lawrence Moore was a sixteen-year-old, who was hitchhiking from Phoenix, Arizona to San Diego, California. Moore was just outside of San Diego near Highway (8) when Patrick Kearney picked him up and his good fortune soon became horrifying. He was a street-smart teenager that didn't trust Kearney. He had good reason to be concerned, because the moment he stepped into the vehicle, Kearney made a pass at Moore. The teenager reacted by pulling a knife and warning Kearney, "Look, I really need the lift, but I don't like faggots. So, keep your fucking hands to yourself!" This angered Kearney. He drove a short distance and then pulled out a gun and shot Moore in the head. Kearney drove to the desert where he removed the knife that Moore carried for protection and stabbed the victim and cursed at him several times. He then seduced the teenager and dumped the body in a shallow grave. Moore's body was found on Sunday, October 10, 1976 near Highway 80, just east of El Cajon, on the same day he was murdered. The teenager collapsed. Kearney would later say that Moore was a transient that said he was traveling from Fresco, and south to San Diego.

One month later, nineteen-year-old Timothy B. Ingham from Merced, California was walking along the highway with his backpack trying to "thumb a ride" at the on ramp of the San Diego freeway at Hawthorne Boulevard. Patrick Kearney spotted Ingham and picked him his Volkswagen bug. The teenager told Kearney that he was on his way to San Diego to meet some friends. As they sped off, Kearney told Ingham that he was cold as he had previous victims. Next, he turned the heater on high and faced all the vents directly on Ingham. Sometime during the drive Ingham began to doze off. The killer let him rest as they proceeded to drive south to Calexico, and then eastbound on Highway 79 towards Indio.

When they reached the intersection of Highway 79 and 86, he looked over at Ingram who was now sound asleep. This was going to be an easy kill. Kearney pulled out a .22 revolver and shot a sleepy-eyed Ingham one time behind the left ear. Then he continued driving unhurried, until they reached a remote area near Borrego Springs. Kearney dragged Ingham from the car and began beating the body. The killer removed all the victim's clothing, and then dragged him out of the vehicle into the open desert, where he sodomized the body. Afterward, he attempted to toss the body down a steep ravine, but the remains got hung up on the ledge above a wash. Kearney crawled down to a point where he tried to kick the body the rest of the way down. Next, he took the clothing and backpack that Ingham had been carrying and gave them to friends in Mexico. He was killed between September 15, and September 24.

After disposing the remains, Kearney continued to drive south across the border. On Friday, September 24, 1976, Ingham was found along Ortega Highway about a quarter mile west of Borrego Springs in San Diego County, which was a few miles south of Hot Springs and east of Highway 74. According to detectives, "He had been shot once in the head, and was found lying in a wash in an advanced state of decomposition. This was mainly due to the wooded area where he was found. Animals such as coyotes and buzzards appeared to have been gnawing on his flesh. It appeared there was no effort made to hide the remains, and due to the extreme purification and maggot activity, there was no evidence of semen in the body found by the coroner."

Kearney was later shown photographs of several missing people that police thought fit his M.O. and may have been some of his victims. He immediately picked out Ingham's photograph. Kearney stated that he had killed Ingham, while the youth was hitchhiking near the San Diego Freeway. Upon further investigation, Homicide Detective's Al Sett and Roger Wilson discovered that Ingham had left his home in Merced, California on September 15, 1976, to hitchhike to Alexandria, Louisiana. In his confession, Kearney stated that he picked Ingham up in the City of Lawndale. Kearney proceeded in driving south towards San Diego, and while in route, he shot the victim one time behind the left ear. The killer continued driving until he reached a remote area near Borrego Springs. Kearney stated that at this time he was driving a VW bug.

In his jail cell, an excited Kearney told detectives the details of several murders. He was shown photographs of missing people that might have been some of his victims. Right away he picked out Ingham's photograph and informed detectives that he had killed this kid. Ingham's biggest mistake was getting into Patrick Kearney's car, which turned out to be fatal. Today, tumbleweeds blow across the landscapes where Ingham's body once lied. The region is dry and all that remains is the memory of nineteen-year-old Timothy B. Ingham murdered over three decades ago.

Kearney's next victim was older than his usual murders. There is not much known about David Allen, except that he was age 27, and was enlisted in the United States Marine Corps. He was stationed at Camp Pendleton in San Diego, California. We do know that in the fall of 1976, he had taken a leave of absence from the armed forces to spend some quality time with his wife and three children. About a week later, Allen was out on Interstate 15, hitchhiking back to his Marine base in San Diego. After about a half hour or so, a friendly stranger pulled over in a pick-up truck to offer him a ride. Allen tossed his army green canvas duffle bag in the back of the truck and climbed into the cab. As the two drove off on this mild day with temperatures in the mid-sixties, they engaged in some welcoming conversation. Allen thanked the queer looking man for stopping to pick him up by saying, "I really appreciate the ride, my name is David." Kearney responded, "My name is Pat. Where are you going?"

He continued by saying that he was a U.S. marine on his way back to Camp Pendleton returning from a leave. Kearney told Allen that he had also served in the army in the nineteen-sixties in El Paso, Texas. Allen told Kearney that he felt more comfortable talking to an army comrade rather than a civilian. Adding that civilians who had never been in the service didn't really understand what it was like. Although Kearney maintained a pleasant tone during their conversation, he began to boil inside. It was the army that helped Kearney realize that he had no sympathy for human life anymore, and these feelings were returning at this very moment. He asked Allen if he had his weapon on him and what was the issued caliber that the military was using. Allen replied, "I carry a .45 ACP (Automatic Colt Pistol) with a 4 1/4" barrel and full-size grips, it's really nice." Then he smiled and said, "Don't worry it's in my duffle bag in the back of the truck. Do you wanna see it." Kearney told Allen that he had not needed weapons since his discharged in the nineteen sixties. Then, he turned on the radio and the two drive on. Eventually Kearney said, "I need to take a leak." Then he pulls over by a rocky hillside on the side of the road. Allen says, "Hell, I've gotta go too." As both men climb out of the truck and Kearney pulls a gun from his pants pocket. Allen finds a spot nearby and begins busy doing his business, while Kearney quietly creeps up behind him and shoots the marine in the head. Allen immediately collapses and falls to the ground, but to Kearney's amazement, he doesn't die. Instead, he screams out for help as he rolls around on the ground in severe pain. Kearney shoots the soldier three more times in the head at point blank range, until Allen stops moving. Patrick Kearney then pulls off the dead man's pants and brutally rapes and beats the soldier's corpse. About twenty minutes after the assault began, Kearney drags the soldier's bloody battered body on the side of the road like a piece of rotted garbage. Kearney leaves the scene and only stops to dump the soldier's duffle bag in a trash dumpster. He takes the soldiers gun to admire, but he disposes it the next day so the murder can't be traced back to him. Allen's body was recovered the following day on an isolated road in the Fallbrook, California area, which is about two miles west of Interstate 15, and twelve miles east of Camp Pendleton.

Fallbrook is a community of northern San Diego County, known for its avocado orchards. The marine's body was found naked and there is no identification found on him, so police did not have a clue who the who the man was. His commanders soon list him as AWOL, "Absent without official leave." It would be a few weeks until positive identification could be made, and Camp Pendleton was notified. He would be buried with full honors. However, his murder would remain unsolved until Kearney confessed in 1977. Allen's commanders were shocked. He was a dedicated husband, father and was a U.S. Marine serving to protect our country with of honor and dignity. He did not deserve to die in the humiliating way he was killed. By this time, Kearney was killing on an average of one victim per month. It was becoming a bloody messy affair in large volume. Twenty-four-year-old Arturo Romos Marquez of Oxnard would become another Kearney fatality.

He was born on October 15, 1952 in Oxnard, California. Kearney had just met Arturo, but he had already been acquainted with Arturo's friend Nicolas Hernandez Jimenez "Nicky" for a couple of weeks. He met them both at the Midtown Spa and invited them out to dinner. Later that night, Kearney dropped off Nicky, and then drove Arturo to a location near San Bernardino, where he was killed. After Arturo Marquez was reported missing by his family, police set out to question some of his friends. They contacted Carlos Sandoval of 1851 LaPuerta in Oxnard, California, who stated that on February 26, 1977 at approximately 7:30 p.m., he gave Arturo a ride to an area in downtown Los Angeles. Arturo told Sandoval he was going to meet a friend named Carlos Narvaes. Sandoval told police that Arturo drove off in Narvaes' late model international pickup truck and was going to Santa Monica Boulevard in Westwood. When questioned, Narvaes told police that he dropped Arturo off so he could catch a bus back to Los Angeles. This was the last time any of his friends would see him again. What his friends didn't know was that Marquez was on his way to meet Patrick Kearney at the Midtown Spa and would be killed soon afterwards.

Kearney's confession was established on Thursday, March 3, 1977, and he agreed to take police to the location of Marquez's body. At 9:30 a.m., police arrived at the murder site that was noted as approximately 500 feet (167 yards) east of Sunset Avenue. Police found bloodstains at the scene where Kearney had shot Marquez in the head. A short distance from the area police detectives discovered the disturbing reality, the location where Kearney cut and eviscerated Marquez, removing all his entrails and intestines. It was also confirmed by police that Marquez' body had been dragged on his stomach, face down on an incline and then hidden in some nearby bushes. Patrick Kearney had performed this maneuver by tucking the victim's feet tightly beneath his belt at the waistband of his pants and dragging him by his legs.

<sic> "I think the purpose in going there was to make friends. I think, I, I got side tracked. His personality changed, it bothered me. I don't think that entirely what did it, though he was probably going to be a liability or a problem you know. You know, living with me, inviting him in the house, it would be a problem if David came back, you know. He bled a whole lot, all over his clothes. I wrapped a jacket around his head to try to keep it clean. Funny enough, Arturo was the only one; he bled more on the seat. Most of them didn't, they were sitting up with only drops of blood on the floor. He was dragged face down," said Kearney. <End sic>

In the above statement, Kearney uses the word "Funny" when describing his victim bleeding on the seat of his vehicle. There was nothing funny about someone bleeding to death. Also, he was more worried about David Hill returning home, than he was about taking the life of a human being. Was Kearney afraid of Hill?

On Tuesday, July 26, 1977, Riverside Sheriff's contacted Michael Bertocchi from the Department of Justice in Sacramento to request documents in reference to the envelopes and typewriter samples submitted by Larry Miller of the Banning Station in the Arturo Marquez homicide. After receiving the samples, and the report on the findings, everything was placed into evidence in Riverside Sheriff's Department for further investigation. The following day on July 27, Riverside Sheriff's Department and Deputy District Attorney Dan Bacalski traveled to the El Segundo Police Department to coincide and share new evidence in the case. They also met with Deputy Homicide Detective Roger Wilson of the Los Angeles Sheriff's Department to compare notes. Evidence included bullets and casings that had been test fired from a Rossi vest pocket .22-caliber revolver similar to the weapon used by Kearney. This was turned over to detective Wilson. The revolver had been found in David Hill's bedroom, hidden beneath his mattress.

Three of these bullets had also been tested by Fay Springer, at the Justice of Department Laboratory in Riverside for ballistics to determine whether the cases were relative to the L.A. cases. The results turned out to be negative, indicating the weapon was not used in Marquez' murder. Following the murder of Arturo Marquez in March, Kearney had set his sights on Nicky Hernandez. Nicky was described as a male prostitute of Redondo Beach. He was known as "Nicky – Wonder buns," because supposedly his buttocks were shaped just like a woman. Police found nude pictures of Nicolas with buns showing and said if you put your thumb over his face, he really did look just like a female. Nicky had sexually serviced both Kearney and Hill on numerous occasions and was well liked in the homosexual community. Whether it was a case of Kearney's jealousy of his lover David Hill being involved in sexual activities with Nicky or something else is not clear. What is clear is that Kearney eventually grew tired of Nicky hanging around the house and murdered him in cold blood. Kearney later confessed to shooting Nicky twice in the head. He said the first shot went through the back of his head but didn't kill him, and he noticed Nicky was suffering. So, he fired again sending a bullet through side of his head, which finished him off. He was found thoroughly wrapped in with a micro-type tape and trash bags.

Nicky was found on Monday, January 24, 1977, when a manual laborer practically stumbled over two heavy-duty commercial type plastic trash bag liners. The bags were found in the Lennox Boulevard tunnel, underneath the (405) San Diego Freeway underpass. Inside the trash bags was the corpse of 28-year-old Nicolas Hernandez-Jimenez of Los Angeles. Like his other victims, Kearney had mutilated the body and drained all the blood from the victim.

Los Angeles Sheriff Homicide Detective Al Sett was sent to investigate and reported findings to the district attorney, "The body was wrapped in a fetal position, using heavy duty nylon fiber tape, and the remains were placed in two heavy-duty commercial plastic trash can liners."

"This defendant has certainly perpetrated series of ghastly and grisly crimes. I can only hope the community release board will never release Mr. Kearney. He appears to be an insult to humanity."
Superior Judge Breckenridge

A recreated moment scenario of Kearney, as he brutally murders another young boy in above picture. The killer is seen here creeping up behind another victim at his Redondo Beach residence.
Author's Collection

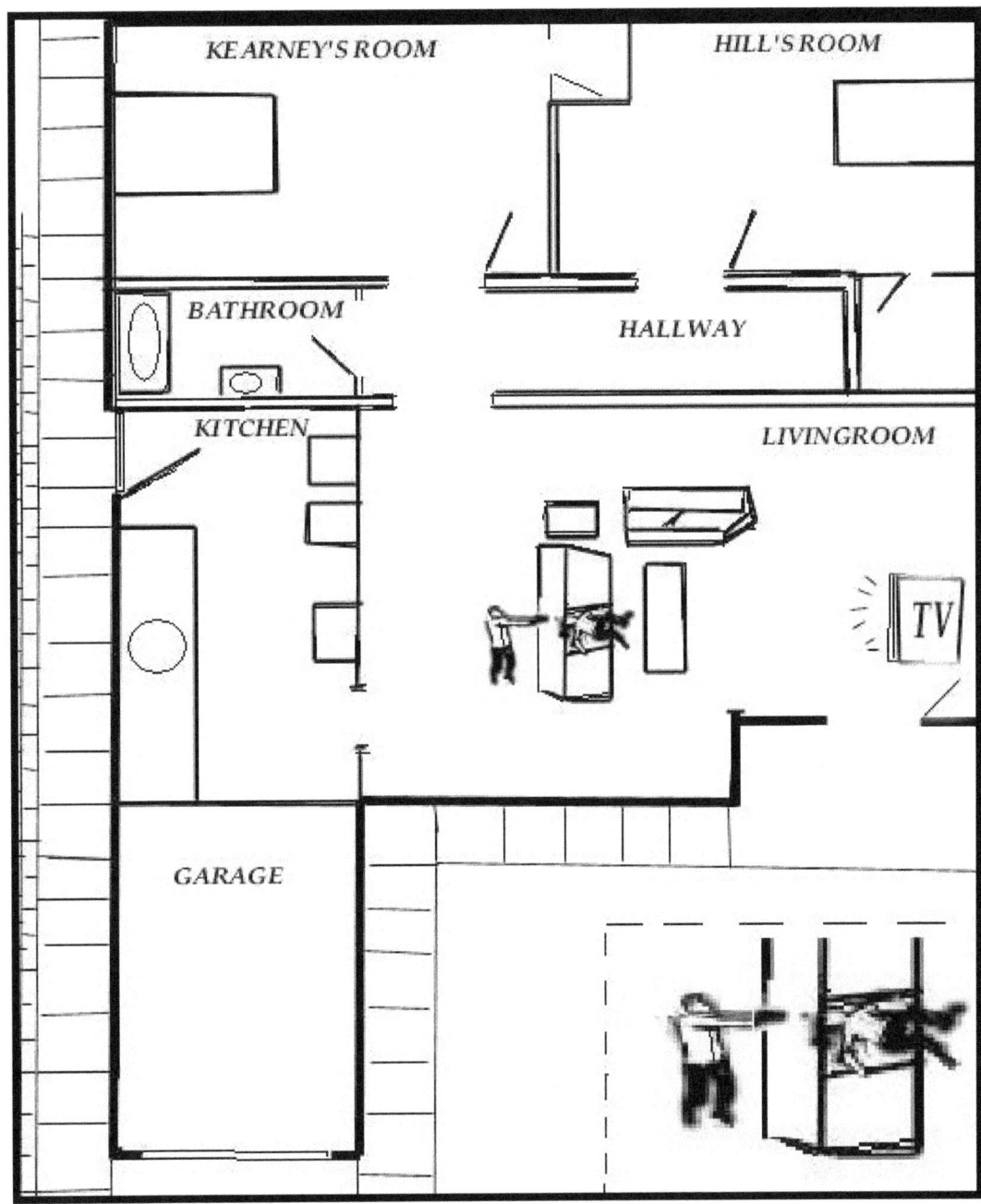

Above: Killer Patrick Kearney walked up behind John LaMay, while he was seated on the living room couch at his Redondo Beach residence, and he shot him behind the left ear. LaMay's murder would eventually give law enforcement the much-need break in the case that would bring the killer to justice. *Author's Collection*

SCRAPBOOK OF MURDER

"I don't know how to say it. When I was 8-years-old I felt like killing people and dismembering them. Have you ever seen that movie *Carrie*? You know you saw how they treated her and she was surprised at her prom, that's the way I was treated!"

Patrick Kearney (July 1, 1977)

John Otis LaMay was seventeen years old and was living in El Segundo, California, at the time of his death. It began when LaMay made a telephone call looking for David Hill. Patrick Kearney answered the call and told LaMay that David Hill wasn't home, but he would be returning shortly, which was not true. What was true was that Kearney was in the mood for another murder and was also extremely jealous of LaMay. Prior to the call, Hill had told Kearney that he would be gone for a few days. Supposedly without Hill's knowledge, Kearney agreed to pick up LaMay and he then bought him back to his residence on Robinson Street.

LaMay spend a few hours relaxing at the residence, while waiting on Hill to return, until he decided it was time to leave. Kearney claimed he had made a last-minute decision to kill LaMay, just before he was about to take him home. This remark would turn out to be another false statement he later told to officers. Next, Kearney walked up behind him, while he was sitting on the sofa and shot him in the back of the head. LaMay immediately collapsed and fell unto to the floor. Blood poured from LaMay's head as Kearney wrapped a towel around it, and then dragged him off the bathroom. Unhurried, Kearney began to sexually assault the teenager, before dissecting him in the bathtub. First, he cut off the hands at the wrists, carefully washing the blood off each hand.

Next, he hacked off both of LaMay's feet and carefully rinsed and wrapped each body part. Kearney continued this process while exploring each body part, until the entire body was packaged.

He dumped body in Temescal Canyon Road about 5:30 p.m. on Sunday, March 13, 1977. Upon investigation, police learned that the seventeen-year-old had told his next-door neighbor he was going to Redondo Beach to see a guy he'd met at a gym in downtown Los Angeles. The man went by the name Dave. When John LaMay didn't come home that night or the following day, his hysterical mother called the El Segundo police. She was certain that something had happened to him, claiming that her son didn't just go off for days at a time without calling.

On Friday, March 18, at approximately 9:30 a.m., the remains of John LaMay, a well-known homosexual, was discovered in a highway underpass, just south of Corona. The body had been placed in an old barrel carelessly covered by trash bags. It was noted that he had been carefully dismembered; with all the body parts washed and drained of blood. The pieces were neatly packed into five industrial trash bags, and carefully sealed with nylon filament tape. Three of the bags had been crammed into an empty 80-gallon oil drum, while the other two bags were left on the ground next to it. The boy's head was missing, but a birthmark would later be identified as belonging to John LaMay. The killer basically took the victim completely apart, like a science project that had gone bad. One of the witnesses, who had discovered the corpse named Mr. Guzman, had taken a pocketknife and cut open the top of a trash bag. Inside he found two pieces of what appeared to be portions of human leg or arm bones, but he thought it might be a calf. Apparently, people had dumped butchered calves had been dumped in the past. He cut open the larger bag and discovered human buttocks positioned upright, facing him. He immediately told his supervisor at the *Foothill Lemon Company*, and moments later the police were called. Prior to the identification of the victim, the body parts were taken to forensics for several tests, including an autopsy.

    The autopsy report noted that the victim was decapitated, and not only was the head missing, but also hands and feet were missing. To prevent immediate identification, the arms and legs were severed from torso at the shoulder and hip ball joints. Freshly cut, the bones were sawed at the neck, wrists, ankles and knees areas. Police determined that the death might have been due to strangulation, gunshot or some type of blow to head. There was a distinctive odor, which was similar to the smell of a fish market or a fishing dock clean up area. A pathologist examining the remains remarked that body had been washed thoroughly and drained completely free of all blood. During the autopsy, it was noted that the victim was estimated to have been dead from 24 to 48 hours, or may have even been closer to 36 hours, but more tests would be needed.

    The coroner anticipated the time of death by changes in the appearance and characteristics of the body, as well as the time the body was found. There are many different means by which the forensic pathologist can estimate the time of death. These methods included *livor mortis* (discoloration of the body due to settling of blood in the dependent portions of the body), rigor mortis (stiffening of the body after death), and *algor mortis* (change in body temperature after death). Other useful indicators included changes in the chemical composition of various body liquids after death, and other decomposition changes. Basically, tests showed that the longer the postmortem interval, the less accurate the time of death determination would be. Dr. Modglin and Deputy Coroner Carl Smith examined the corpse and opened the body cavity to take a urine sample. They noted that the bladder was full, which indicated the victim hadn't had time to relieve himself prior to his murder.

    Three hairs were removed from the fleshy part of the upper right thigh at the severed area. Two more hairs were found and removed from the left upper thigh, in addition to one hair being removed from the neck cavity and placed into evidence. Several photographs were taken of the victim's torso. It was noted that the victim's head had been severed at the C-7 cervical vertebra of the neck. A cut in the right forearm bone at the wrist was photographed along with a bruise on the right leg; also, the ends on the leg bone at the right ankle had been sawed. These items were filed as evidence.

    A thymus gland was removed and examined, and it was noted that the victim was probably less than 25 years old. There was an attempt to take blood samples, but the victims had been drained of blood. The heart showed signs of spotting, which meant the victim had suffered oxygen starvation or suffocation. This could have been caused by the shock prior to his death. Sections of the heart were taken, and the coronary arteries were dissected for analysis, which would indicate the victim was healthy and strong. The Dr. Modglin also specified that the victim had a horseshoe shaped kidney, which usually indicated some medical problems. Horseshoe shaped kidneys were very rare, with only one in a thousand used for identification purposes. The Liver, Kidney and muscle tissue samples were sent to toxicology, and the time of death was determined to be approximately

24 to 48 hours prior to the time when the body was found. The doctor's previous assumption on time of death would prove to be accurate. A more thorough examination placed the person's age approximately 17 to 21 years old. The measurement of the thigh was determined to be 50 millimeters long, which could help to determine the victim's height. The victim was labeled as John Doe victim 187 C.

Witnesses at the LaMay murder site were questioned, and evidence was gathered, which included photographs of vehicle tire tracks for compassion to eliminate witnesses as possible suspects. Photographs of the 55-gallon drum trash bag left next at the site were also taken. One of the witnesses who cut open one the trash bags said he thought it was a slaughtered pig, and he pulled out a leg. When he realized he was holding a human leg, he became frightened, and tossed it about 20 feet away from the other remains. John LaMay was killed about nine or ten o'clock in the evening. Prior to his death, the victim had told a neighbor that he was going to visit someone named Dave in Redondo Beach. This became a starting point for the police investigation, listed as case number B177062008.

The Riverside police associated the name "Dave" as the same person that regularly appeared on the sign-in sheets at gay bathhouses. Soon detectives located an address and were knocking on the door of Patrick Kearney's modest home in Redondo Beach to question David Hill about the whereabouts of John LaMay. Kearney answered the door and politely invited officers into his home. When acquired about LaMay's disappearance, both Hill and Kearney seemed genuinely concerned. The officer's told the two suspects about a neighbor who stated that LaMay was going to visit someone named "Dave" in Redondo Beach.

Officers questioned a nervous David Hill about his connection with the victim. Hill responded by saying he hadn't seen LaMay in a few days. When asked about their relationship with LaMay, both Hill and Kearney admitted having a homosexual correlation with LaMay. Officers asked for some hair and carpet samples, both men agreed to cooperate. Hair samples were taken from a hairbrush and a comb in the bathroom. Carpet samples were taken from the living room area and officers also took pubic hairs from both men, which were labeled and placed in sealed evidence baggies. The officers took all the samples and told Kearney and Hill they would be in touch.

Even though Kearney did not appear nervous or suspicious while officers were present, he was quite irritated and doubtful about the motive of the visit. The moment officers departed, Kearney began deposing all of his newspaper and magazine articles on his idol, Texas serial murderer Dean Corll. He also grabbed one of his recent .22 caliber murder weapons and tossed everything in a trash bag. He told Hill that he needed to drive to the store and would be back shortly. Kearney tossed these items in a trashcan behind Lucky market, before walking into the market to purchase a few groceries.
Whether or not Hill was aware of this particular murder is uncertain. If Hill was aware of this murder, the two probably discussed the unexpected visit from police and what they needed to do to cover their tracks. The pair in all probability, made a quick search of the house and vehicles to remove any possible incriminating evidence. Hill most likely watched the house while Kearney dumped the guns and other items. After they felt comfortable Kearney and Hill prepared some lunch and turned on the television to relax. The topic of LaMay was avoided for the time being, but both were no doubt still thinking about the murder and the recent visit by officers.

It was far from over though, and Riverside police would soon return to the Kearney residence a second time with more questions. This time the officer's lives would in grave danger. Patrick Kearney was planning to exterminate Riverside police officers like he had his many other victims. Hill wasn't home during this visit by officers and the questions were much more demanding and persistent. Officers pressed on about issues including Kearney's whereabouts on specific dates and times in question, and whether he could provide proof to establish these locations. Kearney was becoming annoyed with all the questions and felt strongly that officers were building a case against him for the murder of John LaMay. Kearney was convincing, but officers doubted his innocence. Kearney was sure that officers knew something, but they did not have enough evidence to make an arrest, so he kept his guard up.

During an interview with the author Tony Stewart, Homicide Detective Roger Wilson relayed new information that he received from Kearney during an interview at the Chino State Prison involving a plot to kill several Riverside police officers.

Stewart: Roger, during our several talks, you had mentioned that Patrick Kearney planned to kill four Riverside officers from the Sheriff's Department who were investigating him at his residence in March of 1977. You described how the officers sunk down into Kearney's couch and it would have been difficult for the officers to reach their guns quick enough. You also said Kearney had a weapon close by ready to fire, is this correct?
Wilson: Yeah, he sat in the chair that had the .357 Magnum in it.
Stewart: Where was the gun located?
Wilson: In the cushion, on the side. He had slid his hand beside the cushion and had his hand on the gun.
Stewart: Did he really think about killing these officers?
Wilson: Yes, that's what he told us.
Stewart: What about David Hill? Was he present?
Wilson: No, not at this time.

On March 17, a warrant was issued and signed by Riverside Superior Judge John H. Hughes to search the residence. Two days later, on March 19, the police went back to Robinson residence and arrived at 6:50 a.m. Riverside officers were not aware of it, but they were in grave danger. During questioning, Kearney sat on the arm of his love seat and slid his hand down the side of the cushion. He wrapped his hands around a .357 Magnum and placed his finger on the trigger. Kearney's heart began to pound, as he was about to pull out the gun and kill all four policemen. Suddenly, one of the officers stood up, and Kearney released his hand from the weapon. He decided against killing the officers, because he knew he would have been killed too. Instead, he decided he and his partner David Hill would escape by leaving the country. The officers had no idea how lucky they were at this moment. Even if one or two of the officers had managed to return fire and hit Kearney, he would have severely wounded or even killed two to three of the officers by the time they figured out what was going on. The result would have been fatal for all involved, and Kearney would have been killed in the process.

      According to Kearney, on the evening of his murder, John LaMay called him at the residence looking for David Hill, who wasn't home at the time. Kearney answered the phone and in a kind persuasive tone, he lied, and said that Hill would be returning home soon. Then, he offered to pick LaMay up, and the teen agreed on the ride. Kearney arrived at LaMay's El Segundo residence and waited patiently outside for his victim. LaMay came walking up a few moments later and climbed into the automobile. The cheerful teenager drove off down the highway with his killer, not knowing the fate that awaited him. They arrived that Kearney's Robinson residence about fifteen minutes later. Kearney told his guest to relax and offered him a drink.

      A short time later, LaMay asked how much longer it would be before Hill returned. Kearney told him "he should be back soon." LaMay mentioned that he had bought some good marijuana from David Hill and asked if he could smoke some. Kearney gave him the "Okay," and LaMay proceeded in getting high. After several hours had passed, Kearney claimed that LaMay asked to borrow some money, and this upset him. Then, LaMay asked for a ride home. Kearney said he agreed to give LaMay a ride, but then stalled, stating that he would be ready in a few minutes. He asked LaMay to sit down and relax while he gets ready. Next, Kearney quickly walked up behind LaMay and shot him in the head, while he was relaxing on the sofa in the Living room. LaMay collapsed and fell over on his side. Kearney quickly dragged his body to the bathroom for sex and dismemberment. Kearney would later dispose of the .22 cal. murder weapon into a dumpster behind Winchell's donut shop near Culver City, after dropping off the body. Kearney would later tell police that the motive for the killing of LaMay was because the teen wanted to borrow money, and this annoyed him. He added that the murder was a last-minute decision, but the truth is that Kearney planned to kill the teenager the minute he answered the telephone earlier in the evening.

      Kearney didn't want the police to believe that any of his murders were premeditated, because this act could have led to the death penalty. Accustomed to murder, he would later admit it didn't take much to get him mad enough to kill LaMay. The senseless killing involved Kearney's jealousy and his sexual urge with the dead.

      According to Michael Trainor, a friend of John LaMay's older brothers, Tom, and Jim LaMay, the victim had come to his residence about 10:00 p.m. on March 13, 1977 and stayed for about five minutes. Trainor had told the brothers that LaMay was going to Bob Edgecomb's house to call Dave Hill and added that they were going to find some girl's that they had picked up the night before. Michael Trainor said LaMay had a baggy full of marijuana on him that he believed he acquired from Hill. Trainor said he met Hill only one time, and that was when he went to pick up LaMay. He was told the man's name was David Hill, but he had not been formally introduced.

      Next, Riverside officer Daniel Wilson and Deputy DA Bacalski went to El Segundo Police Department to interview Bob Edgecomb. Edgecomb told officers that he knew LaMay for about three and half years. Edgecomb said the two hung out at his house quite often, until LaMay began working the Swing shift hours so he could attend school during the day. He said the last time he saw John LaMay was on March 12, 1977 and Michael Trainor was present. During another interview with Michael Trainor, he was asked about

LaMay ever having any weapons. He replied, he did not know of any guns LaMay had, but the teen did tell him that Dave Hill had been shooting cats in his back yard with a .22. LaMay told a friend that he had known David Hill for eleven months and they had become close friends. Patrick Kearney was aware of this friendship and was jealous of LaMay, which may have sparked his murder. Kearney knew he was going to kill LaMay the moment he picked him up at his house. Even though later he would lie to officers and say he decided to kill LaMay at the urge of the moment.

On April 28, 1977, the carpet samples the Riverside Sheriff's Department had previously obtained from Kearney's residence were sent to the Department of Justice laboratory for comparison along with the carpet fibers found in the residue from the tape on the trash bags in which LaMay was found. Detective Fay Springer also compared the fibers found in the Banning and Elsinore cases, and the fibers did not match the predominant type found in these cases.

On May 17, 1977, Riverside Sheriff's Department contacted Deputy District Attorney (D.A.) Dan Bacalsky to discuss most recent developments on the trash bags murders as well as suspects Patrick Kearney and David Hill. After reviewing the case, Bacalsky contacted Riverside Superior Court Judge John H. Hews, and convinced him that they had enough circumstantial evidence to issue a warrant allowing officers to search the residence at 1906 Robinson Street in Redondo Beach.
Then on May 19, at 7:30 a.m., armed with a warrant, officers proceeded to knock on the door of the Kearney residence and but there no answer. District Attorney Bacalsky and several officers arrived the at the residence at 6:50 a.m. accompanied by Department of Justice Criminologist Fay Springer, and investigators - R. McIver of Elsinore Police, Larry Miller from Banning Police Department, Investigator Roger Kahl of El Segundo Police and Sergeant Don Stephan of the Redondo Police Department. Officers noticed that vehicles belonging to Kearney and Hill were gone. Hughes Aircraft was contacted, and officers learned that Kearney had called in sick a week prior and was not expected back to work.

Officer's resorted to jimmying a front window and forced entry into the residence.

At 8:19 a.m., during a routine search a hacksaw was discovered in Kearney's top right dresser drawer and tagged as evidence. Fay Springer located a small amount of blood approximately 17 inches from the bathtub and 4 ½ inches from the baseboard on south wall, and blood on the north wall, about fourteen to twenty inches above the tub in a crack between the wall and shower door molding on the tub enclosure. Springer scraped the blood as evidence into a container to be sent it off the department of Justice laboratory for testing. Other items taken for evidence was a Winchester .22 caliber single shot rifle model 67A with missing bolt, found in Kearney's bedroom closet, a yellow jacket liner with blood on shoulder and phone bills found in closet. More bills were found in suitcase next to the dresser.

Also taken for evidence from the residence was shell oil company receipt for service on Kearney's pick-up truck, Master charge credit card receipts, Lucky's Food Store grocery receipts, and a business card from Tortilla Pete's Restaurant in Inglewood. Springer also gathered dirt samples, fiber samples from the toilet seat cover, and debris from a Sears *Kenmore Powermate* vacuum cleaner. Thirteen photo slides of young nude males were found on the top of refrigerator and taken along with an empty Smith and Wesson gun and an empty CDM brand gun box found in the attic. Carpet fibers were taken from Kearney's room, also from an Afghan rug in Hill's bedroom, and a golden doily was in the living room. The thorough search of the premises was completed at 3:05 p.m., seven hours after it had begun. Receipts were left at the residence for all the items taken, along with a copy of the search warrant. The hacksaw taken from Kearney's residence was sent to Los Angeles Coroner Dr. R.L. Taylor for microscopic testing in an attempt to match a cut on the bone of victim John LaMay.

On Thursday, May 26, 1977, while the D.A. and his detectives waited for results from the lab, they received a call from Mr. Frank MacDuffee of Hughes Aircraft in Culver City. MacDuffee told detectives that he had received a "Letter of Resignation" from Patrick Kearney that was delivered by his grandmother, Mrs. Mabel Phalen. The resignation was addressed to his Hughes Aircraft Supervisor Gert P. Arnstein. Arnstein told detectives that Kearney hadn't been to work since Friday, May 6, 1977. He added that he received another letter from Kearney that contained key to his desk and had an attached note that read, "Copy of letter attached." Meanwhile, Fay Springer had received test results from the hacksaw from the (D.O.J.) Department of Justice lab. The blood results on the hacksaw tested type O, which were the same type of blood as slain victim John LaMay. The evidence was quickly mounting against Kearney and Hill.

The following day, detectives drove to Hughes Aircraft and requested copies of Kearney's vacation and sick leave documents from 1964 to the present. According to records, Kearney had called into work on *Wednesday,* May 11, 1977, stating that he was sick. He called again on Wednesday, May 18, 1977 stating that he would be arriving in a few days to resolve any work-related problems and requested extended vacation time. Each time he called Hughes Aircraft, he spoke with Secretary Irene Hilburn.

Detectives also learned that on May 20, Kearney had picked up his paycheck at Hughes and didn't talk to anyone. Patrick Kearney's grandmother, Mrs. Phalen, had made phone calls to Hughes Aircraft, and warrant was issued on 5-31-77 to search her residence in Barstow, CA. About 8 p.m. the same evening, Riverside detectives arrived at the residence and knocked on her door.

Phalen was questioned and was very cooperative with officers. Mrs. Phalen stated that she received a phone call from her grandson on 5-19-77 and was told that a friend of theirs had been killed, and police were harassing them. She told officers that Patrick Kearney and David Hill had paid her a visit, but she wasn't sure if it was May 7 and 8, or the 14 and 15. She did remember that Mr. Hill had been so nervous and jittery that he could not eat or do anything. Mrs. Phalen knew something serious was going on, especially with David Hill. One reason for Hill's nervousness may have been the fact that Kearney opened up and explained everything to him. He told Hill the reason he quit his job, and why they had to sell the vehicles, the house, and personal items, and then flee to Canada. Hill was nervous because he knew about the murders and may have been involved. Hill was scared but he didn't want to go to Canada, he wanted to go home, back to Texas. Another reason Hill may have been so nervous is perhaps he was directly involved in the murders and he knew the gig was up. He had to know that they were about to face prison and this is why both he and Kearney were contemplating a life in prison or perhaps suicide.

These feelings of guilt were catching up to him and he was trying to escape it with his lover Patrick Kearney. Kearney told Mrs. Phalen that he was extremely worried that Hill would commit suicide if he were arrested. He said that David Hill's father had committed suicide while in jail, after being arrested on public intoxication.

Hill had also developed suicidal tendencies at age sixteen, after the death of his father. Hill's suicidal tendencies may have even been hereditary, along with his personality disorders passed down through his family.

Mrs. Phalen stated that on May 21, she had received a "Special delivery letter" post marked from Los Angeles. Inside was a letter, which she believed to have been written by David Hill, and directed by Patrick Kearney, there was carefully thought out instructions. Also enclosed within the letter were keys to Kearney's truck, house keys and a letter addressed to Hughes Aircraft that contained Kearney's work badge, I.D. card, and letter of resignation. The letter addressed to Mrs. Phalen contained precise instructions from Kearney and Hill to sell their residence and personal property, including their vehicles, and all money from proceeds was to be used to pay off depts. Mrs. Phalen voluntarily released these items along with her "Power of Attorney" records to officers.

Detective Larry Miller gave Mrs. Phalen a property receipt for the items that he retrieved as evidence. Since Mrs. Phalen was completely cooperative with detectives, as a result the search warrant was not served. Next, the two suspected killers went to the post office and put in a change of address, so that Mrs. Phalen could take care of their bills. After receiving the letter, Mrs. Phalen became very upset and contacted Pat Kearney's father, George in Kemp, Texas. She requested that he come to Los Angeles immediately, because she did not know what was happening. Pat's father and mother quickly flew out to Los Angeles and checked into the Holiday Inn near the airport at Century and La Cienega Boulevard.

According to police reports, on Tuesday evening of May 24, 1977, Patrick Kearney's parents George, and Eunice Kearney, arrived at their son's residence on 1906 Robinson Street in Redondo Beach, his Grandmother Mrs. Mabel Phalen, and David Hill's ex-wife Linda Gayle, accompanied them. Upon arrival, Mrs. Phalen unlocked the front door with the keys Kearney sent her and the group noticed the house was extremely messy. They immediately realized the residence had been thoroughly searched by police. They didn't disturb or touch anything. George Kearney took a copy of the search warrant that was left on May 19. Being a former Los Angeles police officer, George Kearney knew the seriousness of the document left by Riverside detectives. That same evening, Patrick Kearney's parents flew back to Texas, where the press could not reach them. The family was completely shocked at the disturbing information inscribed on the warrant, which indicated that the premises were being searched for evidence of foul play and suspension of murder. The warrant was convincing enough to traumatize the family, which caused them to disappear almost immediately, to escape any devastating implications that may occur. It wouldn't be long before the parents would learn the truth about their son.

While in pursuit of the suspected serial killers, police contacted newspapers and arranged a nationwide search to help locate the missing suspects Patrick Wayne Kearney and David Douglas Hill. The newspapers reported that the suspected killers were noted for cruising up and down the California coast looking for homosexuals. Although not all of Kearney's victims were homosexuals, police tried to label the victims as such. Actually, in all probability several of the victims were straight males that were killed mainly because they resisted Kearney's gay sexual encounter. Many of Kearney's victims were just children hadn't even reached puberty yet. They were still virgins and were too young to even have a sexual preference. On May 27, detectives contacted a friend of David Hill's named George (not to be confused with the George that was murdered by Kearney) who had worked part-time with him at a liquor store. George was questioned about his association with the suspected killers, and he told detectives that he usually contacted Hill in the evenings by phone or in person. The man said he hadn't been able to reach David Hill in two and a half weeks. After calling several times he even went to the residence, but no one was home. George added that this was quite unusual because he and Dave were very close and had no idea what had happened or where they would be.

Based on evidence collected by detectives and new developments, another search warrant was obtained on Friday, June 2, by Judge Howard M. Dabney. This warrant was to be served on the following day. On Friday, June 3, 1977, Riverside Sheriff's Department returned to the Kearney residence armed with another more in-depth search warrant. The suspects were now wanted for questioning in three murders.

Below is a list on property taken in conjunction with a search warrant that was served to search Patrick Kearney and David Hill's address at 1906 Robinson Street in Redondo Beach. Item numbers attached and labeled on each piece of evidence and dated June 3, 1977, in reference to file: A 187PC, E177077025.
Some of these items would reveal several dark secrets about both Kearney and Hill. Items found included:

Item # 1 - 1 each small and brown suitcase containing miscellaneous papers and bills.
Item # 2 - Miscellaneous papers from desk drawer in Patrick Kearney's bedroom.
Item # 3 - One box of manila coin envelopes from Patrick Kearney's bedroom.
Item # 4 - Miscellaneous mail from living room floor.
Item # 5 - 23 each books from Pat Kearney's bedroom bookcase.
Item # 6 - 2 pieces from plumbing from box in Kearney's bedroom.
Item # 7 - One pair of rubber gloves from Kearney's bedroom.
Item # 8 - Four each holsters from drawer in Kearney's bedroom.
Item # 9 - One box of .22 caliber long rifle Hollow-point ammunition from drawer in Kearney's bedroom.
Item # 10 - One partial box of .22 caliber short ammunition from drawer in Kearney's bedroom.

Item # 11 - 12 each .357 caliber rounds from drawer in Kearney's bedroom.
Item # 12 - 3 each Speed Loaders from drawer in Kearney's bedroom.
Item # 13 - 1 each Speed Loader case from drawer in Kearney's bedroom.
Item # 14- 1 each tear gas pen and five cartridges for same from drawer in Kearney's bedroom.
Item # 15 - Handcuff key from drawer in Kearney's bedroom.
Item # 16 - 3 knives from drawer in Kearney's bedroom.
Item # 17 - 1 each partial box of 3 .38 caliber special ammunition from drawer in Kearney's bedroom.
Item # 18 - 1 partial box of 357-magnum ammunition from drawer in Kearney's bedroom. Item # 19 - 1 full box of .38 caliber special ammunition from drawer in Kearney's bedroom. Item # 20 - 1 each Lee hand loader for .38 caliber ammunition from drawer in Kearney's bedroom.
Item # 21 - 1 each dog chain from drawer in Kearney's bedroom.
Item # 22 - 1 each blank gun from drawer in Kearney's bedroom.
Item # 23 - 5 packages of hack saw blades from drawer in Kearney's bedroom.
Item # 24 - 1 each rifle bolt from drawer in Kearney's bedroom.
Item # 25 - 9 credit membership cards from drawer in Kearney's bedroom.
Item # 26 - 1 temperature gauge from Kearney's bedroom.
Item # 27 - 4 each 35-millimeter photo slides from Kearney's bedroom.
Item # 28 - 1 business card from Kearney's bedroom.
Item # 29 - 3 each ham operator's cards from Kearney's bedroom.
Item # 30 - 2 boxes of checks from Kearney's bedroom.
Item # 31 - Business papers from gray tool chest in Kearney's bedroom.
Item # 32 - 1 package of 13 cent stamps from drawer in Kearney's bedroom.
Item # 33 - 18 .357 magnum caliber bullets from drawer in Kearney's bedroom.
Item # 34 - 1 gray box containing ham operator papers from Kearney's bedroom.
Item # 35 - 1 Ross loss medical card from Kearney's bedroom.
Item # 36 - Personal papers in manila coin envelope from Kearney's bedroom. Item # 37 - 1 each photograph with (BLACKED OUT) on reverse side from Kearney's bedroom.
Item # 38 - 1 each check book in the name of B.W.Kearney from Kearney's bedroom.
Item # 39 - 1 each special agent badge from drawer in Kearney's bedroom.
Item # 40 - 1 each diploma for B.W.Kearney from El Camino College found in Kearney's bedroom.

Item # 41 - 1 each .22 caliber cartridge belt from closet in Kearney's bedroom.
Item # 42 - 1 each green rifle scabbard from closet in Kearney's bedroom.
Item # 43 - 1 each package of papers from closet in Kearney's bedroom.
Item # 44 - 1 each certificate of navigation from shelf above closet in Kearney's bedroom.
Item # 45 - Miscellaneous personal papers from top of speaker in Kearney's bedroom.
Item # 46   2 each boxes of 35 millimeter slides from top of shelf in Kearney's bedroom.
Item # 47   1 each notebook with Spanish writing from Kearney's bedroom.
Item # 48 - Miscellaneous magazines from dresser in Kearney's bedroom.
Item # 49 - 1 each photo album from top of dresser from Kearney's bedroom.
Item # 50 - 2 each books from Kearney's bedroom.
Item # 51 - 1 each International Private Investigators badge from Kearney's bedroom.
Item # 52 - 2 each pair of gloves from dresser in Kearney's bedroom.
Item # 53 - 1 each pair of shorts for Mc Arthur Part YMCA, found in from dresser in Kearney's bedroom.
Item # 54 - Miscellaneous personal papers from in Kearney's bedroom.
Item # 55 - 1 each bar fly book from dresser in Kearney's bedroom.
Item # 56 - 2 each cassette tapes from over bedroom door in Kearney's bedroom.
Item # 57 - 1 each maroon robe from hall closet
Item # 58 - One each notebook from top shelf in Dave's room containing notes pertaining to alibi.
Item # 59 -   One each book of pictures from Dave's closet.
Item # 60 -   One each Selective Service card in the name of Dave Hill from dresser in Hill's Bedroom
Item # 61 -   One black book and Decker jig saw from shelf in Hill's bedroom.
Item # 62 -   One book on sex and witches from shelf in Hill's bedroom.
Item # 63 -   Eight books from shelf in Hill's bedroom.
Item # 64 -   One packet of BLANK cards in Hill's bedroom.
Item # 65 -   One each pocket knife from top dresser drawer in Hill's bedroom.
Item # 66 -   One each Derringer holster from dresser drawer in Hill's bedroom.
Item # 67 -   One each book entitled "Show of Violence" from shelf in Hill's bedroom.
Item # 68 -   One each book entitled "Helter Shelter" from shelf in Hill's bedroom.
Item # 69 -   One each book entitled "Sue the Bastards" from shelf in Hill's bedroom.
Item # 70 -   One each book entitled "Route 66" from shelf in Hill's bedroom.
Item # 71 -   One each book entitled "Infamous Irratics from shelf in Hill's bedroom.

Item # 72 -   One each book entitled "Heitman's Inferno" from shelf in Hill's bedroom.
Item # 73 -   One each book entitled "Kill Three" from shelf in Hill's bedroom.
Item # 74 -   One each book entitled "Distility" from shelf in Hill's bedroom.
Item # 75 -   One each book entitled "Adult Lad Lovers" from shelf in Hill's bedroom.
Item # 76 - Miscellaneous bits of clothing and black billfold from trash can in Hill's bedroom.
Item # 77 - Miscellaneous notes and a pair of sunglasses from trash can in Hill's bedroom.
Item # 78 - One each loaded .22-caliber revolver from under mattress in Hill's bedroom.
Item # 79 - One each torn photograph from trash basket in Hill's bedroom.
Item # 80 - One each file box with porno films from hall closet.
Item # 81 - One each file box with letters and papers in attic.
Item # 82 -   Five boxes 35-millimeter slides from shelf in front room.
Item # 83 -   Three each stacks of papers from attic.
Item # 84 -   Three each sheath knives from attic.
Item # 85 -   One each hack saw from toolbox in Pat Kearney's room.
Item # 86 -   One each checkbook in name of David Hill.
Item # 87 -   One each address book from drawer in living room.
Item # 88 -   One each discharge and DD214 form in the name of David Hill   from desk drawer in living room.
Item # 89 -   One each card from Regency Club with name David Marshall from desk drawer in living room.
Item # 90 -   One each receipt from Lucky Stores from desk in living room.
Item # 91 -   Two each rolls of scotch tape from living room desk.
Item # 92 -   Five each white envelope's with blue interior from desk drawer in living room.
Item # 93 -   One each page of notes from desk drawer in living room.
Item # 94 -   Miscellaneous film negatives from desk in living room.
Item # 95 -   One each empty notebook from living room desk.

Item # 96   Miscellaneous bank statements from living room desk.
Item # 97   One box of 35-millimeter slides from kitchen cupboard near utility room.
Item # 98 -   Five pair of rubber gloves from utility room.
Item # 99 -   One box of slides from box in attic.
Item # 100 - One envelope of personal papers from attic.
Item # 101 - Miscellaneous letters from box in attic.
Item # 102 - Two each tissue or paper towel holders from hall closet.
Item # 103 - Two each empty barrel's in attic.

Based on facts collected on May 19th, along with new evidence that was establish during a recent search of the Robinson residence, warrants were officially issued June 3, 1977, for the arrest of Patrick Wayne Kearney and David Douglas Hill. During a nationwide hunt, Kearney and Hill had fled to El Paso, Texas, New Mexico and to Tucson, Arizona looking to evade justice. While in Arizona, Kearney was avoiding his parents, but did purchase a birthday card for his mother, and then mailed it to her. He was frightened to face his father after the serious crimes he had committed. Kearney was afraid to return to his residence, in fear that the police may show up. After viewing their own names and faces in the newspaper with a report that the two were wanted for questioning involving several murders, Kearney contacted his grandmother and other relatives, and they advised him to surrender, before it was too late. Kearney and Hill knew they needed surrender before authorizes came after them. They came to the realization that they may be shot if they resisted or avoided arrest in any way. The suspects knew that the Riverside Sheriff's Department was closing in on him, and it would be just a matter of time before they would be apprehended. The two talked it over and decided to surrender, but they took their sweet time returning to California. It was during this time that Kearney and Hill took a good look at their options and contemplated suicide.

As Kearney later put it when speaking with detectives, <Sic> "We always wanted to move. Had to get out of town within these areas, looking around. We were in El Paso, Texas almost exactly a month. I like being close to the border. We left Mexico about Thursday, last week; we traveled by bus. We took our time; we didn't want to get here on the weekend. We read in the newspaper in Tucson that you guys were out after us, we decided to come and turn ourselves in. We were sure you were looking for us until we read the newspaper, Saturday L.A. Times. We spend two weeks in kind of indecision and Hill is very nervous. He wanted to commit suicide for some minor misdemeanor a year or two ago. It wasn't like we were running away, it's like we were gonna. I can't remember, we never really got pinned down, just that we did it and there may have been psychological undercurrents we were both really thinking, you know, other than on the surface. We spend two weeks just taking it easy, two weeks on vacation around the area, and it was, I guess, towards the middle of the second week that I dreaded to leave. We went to El Paso, just took our time getting there. We looked around Arizona, Tucson. We were in El Paso most of the time." <End Sic>

In California the evidence was rapidly escalating against Patrick Kearney and David Hill. They were moved up detectives' ladder into the slot of prime suspects. On June 20th, Riverside detectives picked up an invoice from Sergeant Al Sett and his partner Roger Wilson of the Los Angeles Sheriff's Department Homicide Division. These invoices were previously obtained from Gale Supply Company in Los Angeles, who supplied Hughes Aircraft with Micro brand vinyl trash bag liners, similar to those used on several dead bodies found in five counties, including LA. The invoiced showed that over 7500 of the Micro trash bag liners had been supplied to Hughes Aircraft in various sizes in over a four month period from June of 1973 to October 1973.

On this same date, June 20, Riverside Investigator Larry Miller received a call from Mr. MacDuffee of Hughes Aircraft that a check for $500 had just been sent to Kearney's grandmother in Barstow. The check was reported as vacation pay that Kearney had coming to him. The net was beginning to close on Patrick Kearney and his lover David Hill. On June 21, detectives returned to Kearney's grandmother's house and she turned over Kearney's Master Charge card, along with several purchases made by Kearney. The receipts indicated that Kearney traveled to San Bernardino, San Diego, Mission Viejo, and Calexico areas, between May 9 and May 20. The latter day, he stayed at the Villa Sur Motel in Calexico. Kearney grandmother advised detectives that she had returned the $500 check to Hughes Aircraft, as she was unable to open an account to pay Kearney's bills as requested by him previously.

On Wednesday, *June 22, 1977,* Riverside detectives contacted the FBI and requested that agents in the Calexico area check out the Villa Sur Motel for any information they could obtain on Kearney on March 20, when he was registered there. The Federal Bureau of Investigation sent agents in the field to the Villa Sur Motel, and confirmed that two men in question stayed at the evening and checked out the following day. Credit records indicated that Kearney's credit card information was on file, but the attendant was certain that two men had stayed the night. This was about the time John E. Demchik disappeared and the credit receipts proves Kearney and Hill were in the vicinity. On Thursday, June 23, a joint homicide meeting was held in Riverside at the Academy of Justice building with all the law enforcement officers that had previously been involved in eleven unsolved murders in the Los Angeles area. The meeting was held in order to disburse evidence obtained during the investigation into the deaths of LaMay and Marquez so that officers may review their own evidence, and witnesses' statements. This congregation of minds established a connection between the previous unsolved homicides and the apparently related homicides under investigation. There were killers on the loose and it was time to bring them to justice.

The question remained, who would be in charge of the case? Who had jurisdiction? Bodies were discovered all over southern California, but most of the victims were killed in Los Angeles.

When asked why Kearney and Hill turned themselves in to Riverside Detectives when the fugitives lived in Redondo Beach, *Homicide Detective Roger Wilson* of the *Los Angeles County Sheriff's Department* responded, "Because when we put it out in the newspaper that Riverside had a search warrant on his (Kearney's) house on evidence, and had brought it back to a judge, that probably never even read it, and then issued a warrant on him (Kearney). Kearney found out about it in a Texas newspaper and then surrendered to Riverside officials." *Homicide Detective Roger Wilson*

Lead Homicide Detective Al Sett revisits the location where the mutilated body of John LaMay was located. John LaMay Inset. *Author's Collection*

Detective Wilson believed that Riverside Sheriff's Department presented their evidence to the judge and the public official who in turn issued a warrant for the arrest of Kearney and Hill without reading the evidence. From a civilian's point of view, one must question if this is how the justice system really works? There appears to have been a lack of communication and perhaps some favoritism between judges and law enforcement officers. Also, this contributed to a lot of jealousy between police departments involved in the Kearney case. Everyone wanted the credit for catching a killer. Even though it was a team effort and all departments were involved, there were a few departments that went beyond the call of duty to assure their credit in the case. We will get more into this in our final conclusion.

MISCARRIAGE OF JUSTICE

"They did tear the bathroom apart. They found blood in the bathroom drain. They found blood behind the pressboard and tiles and they found blood in some of the carpeting. In several areas, they found a lot of blood."

Lead Homicide Detective Roger Wilson

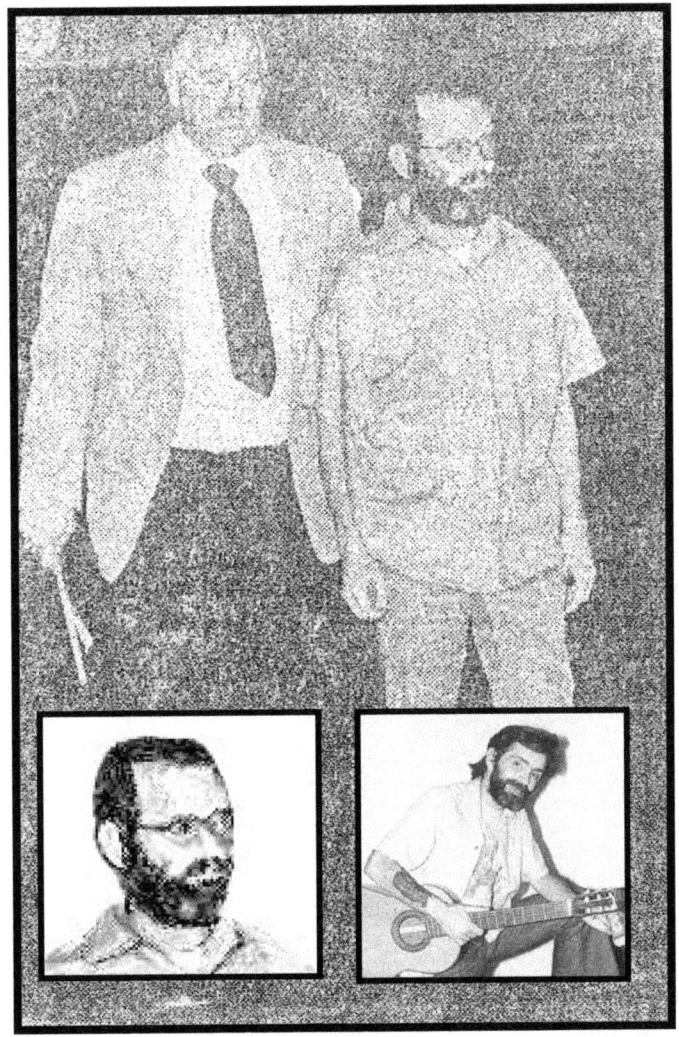

Looking an awful lot like Charley Manson (inset on right), Patrick Kearney seen here in custody on his way to the county jail to face more murder charges. Manson was Kearney's neighbor at Corcoran State Prison in California during the mid-nineteen nineties.

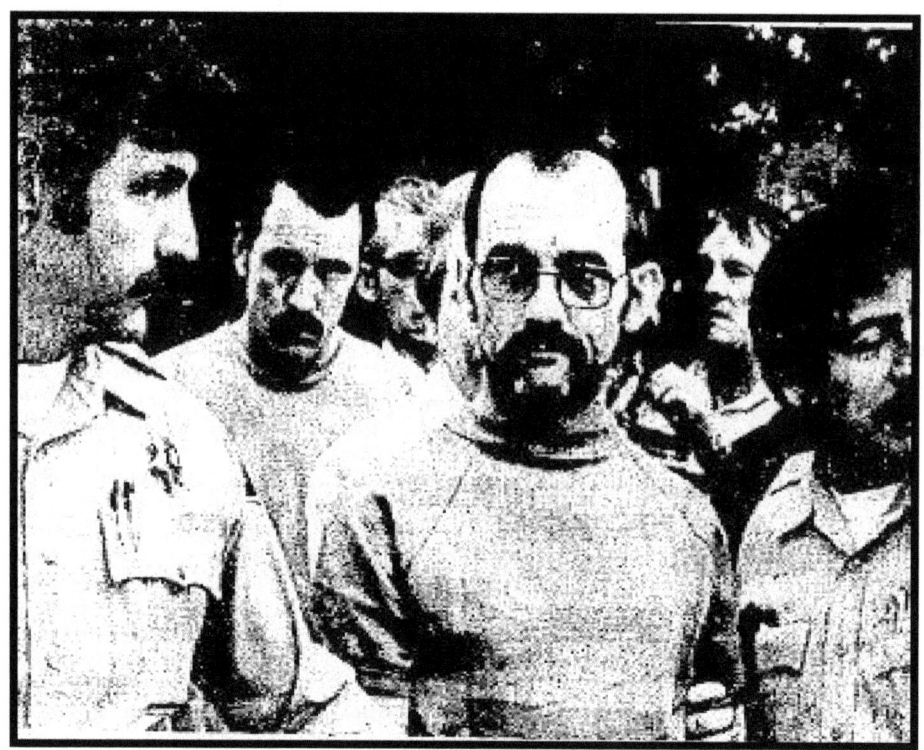

Kearney eyes Riverside County police officer while on the way to his pre-arraignment hearing on several murder charges. **Photos Author's Collection**

The killer looks up at a reporter, while David Hill (back row) looks down in shame.

Another photograph of Kearney in custody where he belongs, while Hill looks on in the background.   *Author's Collection*

Back in the early 1960's, Patrick Kearney and David Hill became so obsessed with murder stories and began reading anything they could find. Several books they collected would become legal evidence years later, during a search of their residence in Redondo Beach, California. Detectives found several books of interest in suspect David Hill's room. For a man who Kearney claimed was not involved in any of the murders, Hill seemed to acquire a taste for reading about hurting and murdering adults and young children. Some of the murder books taken as evidence included, *The Show of Violence - A World-Famous Psychiatrist Tell Why People Kill* by Fredric Wertham. The book describes the murders and reasons that 14 people slaughtered in Texas, 13 women strangled in Boston and 8 nurses killed in Chicago. Another murder book found in Hill's room was *Helter Skelter* by Vincent Bugliosi, which involved Charley Manson, the drug addict cult leader who ordered the deaths of Sharon Tate and LaBianca's in 1969. These killers even cut the baby from actress Sharon Tate's stomach with a knife during the gruesome attack, as she desperately begged them to spare her life. Another book from Hill's collection was "Kill Three" which described by *The Daily Telegraph as,* <Sic>Devilish simple…diabolically ingenious…a nut with a grievance and a Chelsea-type dolly kidnap three infants and inform a firm of solicitors that they will be killed unless the solicitors produce €100,000. <End Sic>

Nova described the book as "Not for those with queasy stomachs…appears to borrow something in the way inspiration (for children cruelty) from the Moors murders…slick and readable." The Moors murders occurred between July of 1963 and October of 1965, when Ian Brady and Myra Hindley sexually assaulted and brutally murdered five children from ages 10 to 17 in Greater Manchester, England. The killers were declared sexually sadistic psychopaths. There was also a book from the dark side on *Sex and Witches* with several chapters that discusses "*The fear of women power, Manhood through Violence, Man's fear of Women and sex,* and *Handmaids of the devil.* The book describes, "Sex *and The* Witches' *Sabbath* and the *Witches' Gathering*, which became known as the Sabbath, which drew more attention from the investigation than any other aspect of *Witchcraft.*"

Normally, these books and others found at the residence would not have been a big deal, but in this case, scores of people were murdered at the residence. The books became legal evidence along with several other items, which included the loaded .22-caliber revolver found under David Hill's mattress in his bedroom. Why would David Hill keep a loaded weapon under his mattress? Was he aware of Kearney's murdering addiction or was he actually involved? Or perhaps Hill knew about the murders and was keeping his guard up. We do know that Mr. Hill and Kearney both chased my brother in a pickup truck on at least two occasions, which proves that Hill had some knowledge of Kearney abducting children, but we are not completely sure how in-depth was his involvement? David Hill was never thoroughly investigated like he should have been. Also, he refused to take a lie detector or polygraph that may have shined some doubt on his innocence.

Serial killer Dean Corll's army photo August 10, 1964

He admitted that he could not take the polygraph, because he would fail, but still no charges were ever filed. By 1973, Kearney began reading about Dean Corll, a homosexual serial killer and pedophile who murdered seventeen adolescent boys in Houston, Texas. Kearney was so infatuated that he began keeping a "Scrapbook of Murder," collecting newspaper articles and following every detail of Corll murders. But Patrick Kearney wasn't just another avid reader; he was becoming drawn in the stories with a strong fascination with these murders. He couldn't wait to try these methods on his own victims. Dean Corll was born in Fort Wayne, Indiana on December 24, 1939. It is interesting to note that David Hill was also on December 24, 1942, although he was three years younger than Corll. This probably made Kearney feel closer to both Hill and Corll.

After Corll's parents divorced, he moved to Pasadena, Texas, with his mother, Mary Robinson, and a younger brother. The family moved to an area just south of Houston. The mother opened a Candy store and made Corll the Vise-President by the time he was nineteen years old. He received the nickname, "The Candy Man" because he would often hand out candy to neighborhood kids. On August 10, 1964, he was drafted into the army, but was honorable discharge on June 11, 1965, after his aging mother wrote a letter requesting, she needed her son's help running the store. Corll began hanging around young children and teenage boys, and although it seemed particular for a grown man to be hanging around such a young group, no one connected him with the missing children in the community. In 1968, Corll's mother moved to Colorado and the two kept in touch by phone. Corll did not have the business skills as his mother did, so the candy business soon failed, and closed. Corll teamed up with a crime associate named Wayne Henley and together they tortured and murdered dozens of young boys. Many of them were listed, as runaways despite protests from parents who insisted their child would not have run away from home. In the early seventies, Corll and Henley got into an argument that ended with the death of Corll. Police were called and several bodies were located along with all the bloody details of the murders.

Oddly, in 1972, Henley told police the exact location where other bodies had previously been buried, but the officers felt they had enough victims, and the search was called off. Police did report seeing two men digging holes in Galveston County, during this year, but would not search for more bodies, since the case was officially closed. Why would police give up on victims with parents and relatives worrying and wondering what happened to their loved ones? This is very strange, but the same situation had also happened in the Kearney case. Several of his victims have still not been recovered, and police gave up questioning Kearney on this matter.

Kearney used Corll's methods of killing, to later become a copycat killer, while adding mutilations to the death mix. Houston newspapers described how employees at his Corll's work said they seen him with several clear rolls of thick plastic, similar to the plastic trash bags that victim's bodies were found in. Kearney read how victims were raped, tortured, shot and strangled. Some their public hairs were plucked out one by one, some had objects forced into their rectums, genitals were removed, and all victims were sodomized. In 2008, a Houston forensic anthropologist named Sharon Derrick, who was working with the medical examiner's office, was still trying to identify several victims thirty-five years later. One of these teenagers was Randall Lee Harvey who had been missing since March 9, 1971. Kearney's murders seemed to have slowed down in California, from 1969 to 1972.

Since Kearney and Hill had family in Texas, it is very possible that the two men were in Houston in March of 1971 and committed this murder as well as other unsolved murders in the area. Without credit card receipts or information from officers who are unwilling to reopen this case to the public, we will never know the entire truth, and criminals like Kearney may have got away with many other murders. When Los Angeles Homicide Detective Roger Wilson was asked if he believed Kearney killed in Texas, Arizona and Mexico areas, he responded, "He may have, I wouldn't know, this wasn't our jurisdiction." It sounds like police departments were only interested in crimes that occurred in their areas, even if the killer may have been involved in other crimes elsewhere. Perhaps it has to do with jurisdiction. This failure of communication and cooperation has led to many unsolved crimes and "Cold cases," as they are called. These cases remain unsolved.

Kearney had collected several newspaper articles on the killer over the years, and was infatuated with Corll, who murdered an estimated 27 teenagers in Houston in the early 1970's. Kearney used some of Corll's techniques of wrapping victims in plastic, sticking items into the rectums and plucking public hairs from victims, but he also added many of his own procedures too, such as beating and sexually assaulting his victims even after he killed them. Along the way, Kearney would make mistakes that would nearly get him caught. On one occasion, during a drive to the desert to drop off a trash bag of body parts, he suddenly blew a tire. After realizing that his spare tire was also flat, he was forced to call a tow truck. The attendant repaired the tire and never questioned the trash bags in the back of the truck that were beginning to smell.

Kearney was nervous and even considered killing the man. Another time he locked his keys in the car and it took hours to jimmy it open with a coat hanger, while body parts were in the back seat. Nervously, he looked up every time a car approached, waiting for one of them to be the police. It was this carelessness that would later lead to his surrender. Since Kearney left semen in most all of the bodies of victims, if DNA would have been available in the nineteen sixties and seventies, he would not have lasted as long as he did.

Also, there were some fingerprints taken off trash bags, and the police department in Long Beach, California had Kearney prints on files from his arrest for trying to solicit sex around a public restroom where homosexuals were known to frequently hang out.

If detectives involved in the case would have communicated better with other *departments*, Kearney's identify would have been discovered early on. This lack of communication would allow the killer to thrive for over ten years undetected. At one point, Kearney believed he would never be caught.

"Kearney and Hill welcomed them in, they are calm, and seemed concerned about the missing boy. While there, though, investigators helped themselves to a few carpet fibers, because for the first time in a trash bag murder, carpet fibers had been caught up in the nylon filament tape used to seal the bags. The fibers matched."
Detectives confront Patrick Kearney about the death of John LaMay

The man behind the mask, confessed murderer Patrick Kearney during their surrender to the Riverside County Sheriff's Department in July of 1977. *Photographer unknown*

We know about all murders that Kearney did confess to detectives, but what about all the murders that he did not confess too? He told officers that he couldn't remember all the victims he killed, but there were several others that Kearney did not want officers to know about. These victims remain lost forever. So, do these cases just remain unsolved and the killer is never charged for them? Is this how the justice system works? Every murder victim should be accounted for and Kearney needs to provide all the answers. Why do detectives close a case that includes many more unsolved murders? It just doesn't make much sense, because all victims should matter. And every single person should be accounted for. Kearney should not even be able to sleep until he confesses to the whereabouts of every victim. The families deserve closure.

We know that on July 1, 1977, Patrick Kearney and David Hill walked into the Riverside Sheriff's Department and stood patiently at the receptionist counter. A moment later, the woman behind the counter asked, "May I help you?" Kearney spoke; "Yes," and then he pointed at a "Wanted poster" hanging on the wall and announced that they were the suspects at large. She looked up at the two faces in front of her, and then glanced at the poster they were referring too. The wanted poster described two men wanted for questioning in a series of murders in five counties. The names read Patrick Kearney and David Hill of Redondo Beach, California. She asked the men "Are you Patrick Kearney and David Hill? They both replied in a polite calm tone, "Yes." Nervously, she quickly called for backup. She had every reason to be nervous, because it is not every day that serial killers walk into a police station and surrender. The men were both immediately handcuffed and placed under arrest, their rights were read, and both were held on $500,000 bond. While Kearney and Hill were detained behind bars at the Riverside Police Department, the Los Angeles Police Department prematurely announced that they had acquired enough evidence to link the suspects to as many as forty-three similar murders in the southern California area from the mid-nineteen sixties through the nineteen seventies. The L.A.P.D were out to claim all the credit even though they actually had little to do with working on the case at the time.

Although often confused by the public, the Los Angeles Police Department is a different entity and is not affiliated with the Los Angeles County Sheriff's Department. Los Angeles Police Department (L.A.P.D.) is a City Police Department, whereas the Los Angeles Sheriff's Department is County that works with all the community areas, including 58 contract cities that pay for police protection. The Los Angeles County Sheriff's Department covers all these jurisdictions. Riverside Police Department was outraged to hear that the Los Angeles Police Department was releasing premature facts to the press. According to Homicide Detective Roger Wilson of the L.A. Sheriff's Department, and the L.A.P.D. did things differently. The L.A.P.D. attempted to make a big deal out of the case by using the press, long before even having all the facts. Other counties such as Orange County, San Bernardino County, Imperial County and San Diego didn't appreciate the grand standing by the Los Angeles Police Department, especially during an official investigation.

These selfish acts of trying to hog all the credit would cause problems for the Los Angeles Sheriff's Department. The moment the L.A.P.D. tried to claim all the credit, red flags were raised that made it difficult for the L.A. Sheriff's Department to convince Riverside detectives to cooperate with them. It took a frustrating three weeks of requests with Riverside detectives, before the L.A. Sheriff's Department was finally allowed to interview Kearney on murder charges that occurred in their jurisdiction. Detectives became frustrated with the whole situation. However, it became obvious that Riverside police, the L.A P.D. and the Los Angeles Sheriff's Department were at odds with each other, which would cause conflicts between all those working on this case. Even though, this should have been a team effort out to stop a serial killer and save the lives of the innocent.

When L.A. Sheriff's Department *Homicide Investigators* Al Sett and Roger Wilson were finally allowed to meet with Kearney, he agreed to accompany deputies on a five-hour search of an area near the U.S. – Mexico border. The officers befriended Kearney as a ploy to get him talking by merely pretending to be his friend. It was Riverside police who succeeded in getting Kearney to talk, but it was Detectives Al Sett and Roger Wilson that talked Kearney into giving up the bodies. This was a major breakthrough in the case.

During the initial search, no bodies were located, but the killer was definitely talking. County Coroner Lou Hettinger mentioned to detectives that Kearney pointed out two areas where unidentified bodies have been dumped in the past. The areas were searched, and bodies were found around February 1973 and April of 1976. This was just the beginning of a serial killer's initial confession, and the body count would soon grow at a steady pace.

One newspaper local read: *"Trash Bag Murderers David Hill and Patrick Kearney surrendered on July 5, 1977, which ended a ten-year nightmare for dozens of victims and their families. Kearney and Hill calmly walked into the Riverside Sheriff's Information Center, looked up at a wanted poster on the wall displaying their photographs and Hill said, "We're them." Later the charges were dropped against Hill, when Kearney refused to associate him to any of the murders. Hill was released for lack of evidence, after Kearney said he had nothing to do with the murders. Did Kearney cover for him? Kearney was worried about Hill killing himself, because his father had hung himself in jail year's prior. Hill walked free and fled back to his homeland in Texas."*

Kearney attempted to express remorse when he told officers that he wish he hadn't killed Arturo and Nicholas Hernandez, because they were more or less friends. He said, he actually said he felt bad that he done it, but was he telling the truth, or was this just part of the charade that he created in his sick ingenious mind?

"I think it just became a habit. I probably had some nutty reason for killing them. I was going to say something about my beliefs and religion, and when I try to talk about religion, I here recently wanna cry" Kearney said.

Was Kearney out to win the best "Killer Actor" award with this comment? Most serial killers are good at acting, and this is how they stay active so long.

Kearney tears of emotions were certainly not for the victims, but because he could no longer play God and the devil in his senile mind. It was over. After his arrest Kearney became Prisoner# B-88913, and nothing more. During initial interrogations, Riverside police climbed deep into Kearney's mind, and pulled out the distorted reality of this psychopathic killer.

Riverside Sheriff's Department: What was the reason you dismembered your Victims?

Kearney: Ah, well, partially but I dismembered quite a few others as you probably noticed you know, ah, there is a certain skill in doing it there (Kearney's residence). I've got medicinal practice. (Meaning, he believed he had the power to heal, tending to or used to cure a disease or relieve pain). "He wasn't in a bag. I just buried him" Kearney is talking about victim Mark Andrew Orach.

Riverside: Did you dump them by anything specific at all?

Kearney: Yeah that you mentioned it, uh, later I came back by where when in was light and I think there might have been some kind of power station or something on the other side of the road nearby. It didn't seem like there was anything specific there. And there might have been some kind of road to pull off here, I pulled off in nothing and got the car struck in the sand and locked myself out (Kearney laughs). I found a piece of wire or something to get the car open and managed to back, you know you can sometimes, back out of being struck, hoping the Highway Patrol or somebody wouldn't come along, but they didn't.

Riverside: What made you start dumping along highways rather than trash cans?

Kearney: I, (pause)…started dumping along the roadway first, I used to live in Arizona, and I noticed that things disappeared very rapidly out in the desert. You could put a small animal on an anthill, and it disappears right in front of your eyes.

Riverside: We had often made the comment when the good Lord says, 'Stand up' that desert gonna be awful crowed out there." (Laughter) Pat, going back over the last ten years, I know you might not be able to, but just an estimate as the number of uh guys you have killed would it be over 50?

Kearney: It might me over 30 or 40 and uh I uh didn't keep count or records purposely tried not to remember anything, in case I had a lie detector test or something. I couldn't have remembered most of these names if I hadn't seen them in the paper. I may uh have inadvertently, I lived in Long Beach, I did a lot of corresponding with people with different kinds of adds in the free presses and everything. It's a good chance that I come across a guy or some of the people, or some of the victims, but I don't know anything about them or anything that would help. I did a lot of corresponding you know, try to find people who were interested in going to Mexico with me. You guys know by now I go to Mexico almost every weekend, find people who share in driving and stuff.

Riverside: What do you do down there?

Kearney: I maybe just wander around back alleys and back streets, steam baths, and stuff. I like Mexicans, I like being there and you know I often didn't do anything to anybody. I might enjoy sex other than steam bath

Riverside: Did you kill anyone down there?

Kearney: Negative (Note: Mexico was not an area that Kearney wanted to admit committing a murder.)

Riverside: Did you travel mostly at night with these people after you killed them

Kearney: Um, some of the, um yeah, I, you know picked them up late at night an what have you, and some of them uh like I say Dave was gone for several days at a time and I would kill them and dismember them and the next day I would go out in the daylight and drop parts in garbage can to garbage can.

Riverside: You always take all their clothes. Except you overlooked Woody. How come you left him clothed?
Kearney: Well, he uh had dirtied himself. I didn't want to get it all over the car.
Riverside: Do you know the whereabouts you left him?
Kearney: It was San Diego somewhere near the border.
Riverside: Do you remember where you picked him up?
Kearney: Yeah, I picked him up by my house.

Kearney admitted killing over 40 victims, yet he was only charged with 21 murders. So, what about the remainder of victims that have not been recovered? Also, Kearney mentions that he corresponded with people that he invited on trips to Mexico. How many of these people went on this road trip with Kearney to Mexico and never returned? These are questions that the author sent to the killer via U.S. mail, but he would not reply.

Below: Tony Stewart asking Homicide Detective Roger Wilson questions about David Hill's part in the murders and fleeing the counter with Kearney.

Stewart: Mr. Wilson, from a detective's standpoint, do you feel that Kearney protected David Hill?
Wilson: Yeah, I think so.
Stewart: You also mentioned something about an airplane incident, in which Kearney and Hill were trying to dump a dead body out of an aircraft, but failed. What happened?
Wilson: Hm…the guys (Kearney and Hill) were in an airplane, and they were gonna throw the one guy out, but they couldn't get the door open.
Stewart: Do you have any idea who the guy was?
Wilson: No, Kearney would not repeat the story, when asked again.
Stewart: Now, who told you this story? Kearney or Hill?
Wilson: Kearney
Stewart: It sounds like Kearney backed out of that one, because Hill's name was involved, and wanted to protect him. The kind of thing two lovers would do to protect each other.
Wilson: Yeah.
Stewart: In May of 1977, Kearney contacted his grandmother, Mrs. Phalen and asked her to sell his house, truck, and personal property. He told her a friend of theirs had been killed and police were harassing them, and he and Dave Hill were going to Canada. It sounds like they were leaving the country. What are your thoughts on this? Were they about to escape the country? It appears an innocent Hill was fleeing with him. Mrs. Phalen also said Mr. Hill had been so nervous and jittery that he could not eat or do anything Wilson: It sounds like Hill knew something at this point.

Also, Kearney and Hill waved their Constitutional Rights. Hill stated because of his nervous condition, he felt he was unable to conduct a good polygraph examination and would not be able to state his opinion as to the subject of truthfulness about the night of March 13, 1977, which was the same night John LaMay was murdered. After the examination was terminated and the police could not find enough evidence to indict Hill, he transported back to his residence in Redondo. It doesn't sound like the actions of an innocent man.

There is another alternative to this story. What if David Hill was the actual killer and Kearney was his whippy assistant that helped to lure in the victims? Hill was about 6'3', he was a big guy, while Kearney was barely 5"7'. Kearney worked while Hill did whatever he pleased. Looking at the relationship, it appeared that Hill was the "Man of the house, "whereas Kearney seemed more the woman that complained a lot, but he did what he was told. The last night that I was at the Kearney residence, the latter seemed very nervous as soon as Hill walked in the front door.

Did Kearney take the rap for Hill, or were they both involved? One thing is for certain, whatever the real story was, Kearney and Hill took a long vacation to get their stories straight just before they surrendered to police. The stories were well rehearsed. Many have begun to question David Hill's innocence, and even today this suspicion remains. Before Kearney told officers that Hill was completely innocent of murder changes, he began asking questions about, "What if Hill was guilty or an accomplice or an accessory to the crimes, would he go to jail?" The officers told him that would depend on the actual time when Hill became knowledgeable of the murders, whether he would be guilty or not. "David will probably get a year or two for all this, and it will probably do him some good; it'll allow him to grow up," said Kearney. Kearney also said he was worried about Hill, because his friend was a nervous man who may try to commit suicide like his father had done year's prior, while in jail. Kearney said David Hill didn't have any idea about the murders until police had come to the house and began their investigation. He added that Hill was neither involved in nor aware of the murders. Then Kearney admitted to committing all the murders, while Hill was away, which his lover and companion in crime, a free man. There was more to this story that Kearney was hiding.

Did Kearney take all the blame to save his nervous lover from jail, or was Hill innocent of murder changes? Either way, Kearney succeeded to clean the blood off Hill's hands. According to Kearney, it was Hill that caused him to go out and kill; yet Hill was not physically involved. When Hill was gone, Kearney's jealous impotent frustrations had reached a boiling point.

There was only one thing that he knew that would satisfy those feelings of repressed rage, and that was "First Degree" murder. Kearney said that when Hill left the house after a fight or disagreement, he would go prowling for victims. He'd jump in his Volkswagen and go out to pick up hitchhikers or young men from gay bars. Being of slight build, he had a surefire system of subduing his victims; first, he used kindness to lure them in and then without warning, he shot them in the head with a .22-caliber pistol. Sometimes he would be driving down the highway, paying strict attention to the speed limit with his left hand on the steering wheel, he would shoot his victim in the passenger seat with his right hand. Other times Kearney turned the heater in his car on high, and eventually his passenger would get tired and begin to fall asleep. Kearney would watch them closely, and the minute they began to falter he was shoot him in the head. After looking at all the evidence, the Riverside County Grand Jury refused to indict David Hill.

Riverside District Attorney Byron Morton told that the press the evidence against Mr. Hill was weak. Morton added that much of the information unearthed by Riverside investigators exonerated Hill of any crimes. McMillan said he was not surprised the grand jury refused to indict Hill, stating that he did not think there was enough evidence to hold him in Superior Court. Both Riverside District Attorney Byron Morton and Public Defender Malcolm MacMillan said there was insufficient evidence to hold David Hill on any charges? No Charges? What about the fact that both Hill and Kearney admitted having a sexual homosexual relationship with LaMay and others? LaMay was 17-yearsold, which made him a minor, and I believe Hill could have been charged with statutory rape of a minor at the very least. Also, there were several other minors that both Hill and Kearney admitted have sexual relations with.

According to California Penal Code Section 288a, Partial clip of the law (b) "Any person who participates in an act of oral copulation with another person who is under 18 years of age shall be punished by imprisonment in the state prison, or in a county jail for a period of not more than one year. 2) ... any person over the age of 21 years who participates in an act of oral copulation with another person who is under 16 years of age is guilty of a felony. (c) (1) Any person who participates in an act of oral copulation with another person who is under 14 years of age and more than 10 years younger than he or she shall be

punished by imprisonment in the state prison for three, six, or eight years."

So why wasn't Hill ever charged with having sex with minors? Was it because they were all murdered? Did Hill's attorney walk his client, who may have been murderer or rapist out the police department to freedom? Did he free a guilty person?

Another important fact that was brought up by Detective Roger Wilson of the L.A. Sheriff's Department that points to Hill's possible involvement in a murder was in a confession from Kearney. During the years when Kearney worked at Hughes Aircraft, he decided to take up flying like his brother Michael. Michael Kearney was President and chief executive of Spacehab in Texas, a large company that worked directly with NASA. Patrick Kearney was always jealous of his younger brothers and their achievements. In the next several years, Kearney would earn over three hundred flying miles.

It is interesting to note that Kearney verbally confessed to Homicide Detective Roger Wilson that he and David Hill tried to dump a body by throwing it out of the small airplane, but failed, because they couldn't open the pressurized hatch door. When Wilson questioned him for more details, Kearney's changed his story, and denied Hill's involvement. Wilson heard the confession with his own ears that Hill was involved, but Kearney refused to repeat the story twice, because this would have put Hill behind bars for life. Kearney felt responsible for Hill. He fought and lied to keep his friend and lover out of jail. In fact, this is one murder that neither Kearney nor Hill wanted to talk about. Let's look closer at the facts. Men and young boys were being slaughtered and dumped along highways between Southern California and Mexico borders in the mi seventies. After gathering vital forensic information, the investigation focused on Patrick Kearney, the electronics engineer from Los Angeles and his unemployed roommate David Hill, and neither one looked nothing like the stereotype Serial Killers of the day. Nevertheless, Kearney would eventually confess to several cold-blooded killings. Initially, he only pleaded guilty to killing only three men. Authorities knew there were many more murders and offered Kearney a life sentence deal, to come clean. Kearney would not receive a death sentence in exchange for his full cooperation and a complete list of victims. Quietly standing before Los Angeles Municipal Court Judge Dickran Tevrizian Jr. asked how he pleaded, and Kearney replied, "Guilty, Your honor." The killer ultimately confessed and pleaded guilty to eighteen additional homicides. As agreed, he directed officers to the bodies of victims that were previously not discovered. Kearney would admit to another eleven murders that he was never prosecuted for, bringing his grand total to 32 killings, but there were several more that would never be recovered.

Kearney was smart. He knew he was guilty of a lot more murders, so he kept the eyes of detectives focused only on certain cases. He held on to the names of some bodies to use as a dealing tool to spare his life or to buy his freedom.

On Thursday, *July 7, 1977,* Kearney wanted to talk to detectives in regard to a knife that would become evidence and added that maybe he shouldn't say anything. Then, he changed his tune and agreed to cooperate. He was playing with the police, pretending to be the good guy. Kearney said it was the knife he used on a victim called Woody. He punctured Woody's throat and then cut him just above the groin area. Kearney advised detectives that the knife could be found on the bottom shelf of his left-side dresser drawer, in his office at Hughes Aircraft. He added that this was the same knife that he used on Arturo Marquez. Deputy Daniel Wilson of Riverside asked if the bayonet was used to cut LaMay and Kearney stated he did stick the bayonet in the rectum of an unidentified victim, but not LaMay. He stated the victim's name was possibly Larry, but the last name is unknown. Kearney mentioned that he used an Exacto-knife utility blade with a blade number 11 about 3/4" long to cut John LaMay.

On Thursday, *July 14, 1977,* Patrick Kearney was formally indicted on the first two counts of murder. Kearney rendered full responsibility for the murders, because…as he told police, "It excited me and gave me a feeling of dominance." By July 15, Kearney had signed confessions to 28 murders, 12 of which were confirmed. On December 21, he pleaded guilty on three counts of first-degree murder, and received three life sentences. The Judge filed a gag order in October 77, which was lifted in December and reporters could enter the courtroom after sentencing. After the gag order was removed,
Kearney declined to comment, saying, "I can't allow myself to think about it, it's much too painful." In documents released after his sentencing he told prosecutors how he killed

"coolly," but had some tense moments transporting the bodies.

In February of 1978, Kearney was charged with 18 murders, four of which were never recovered. He described without emotion to his psychiatrist, how he shot his victims in the head with a .22 caliber pistol in Redondo Beach and at his Culver City Duplex. This was the same day that both Kearney and Hill waved their Constitutional Rights.

No other counties had formally brought charges against Kearney or Hill. The Los Angeles County district attorney's office said they were considering prosecution of Kearney for as many as 21 other "Trash bag" murders, even though he had been sentenced to life for three homicides in Riverside County. "We have 11 counts we could file against Kearney and there are possibly 10 other murders we could connect him with," said, Deputy District Attorney John Breault. The decision apparently will rest on whether a multiple murder prosecution result, which decides whether Kearney receives the death penalty, if convicted in Los Angeles County.

"There is a U.S. Supreme Court opinion which says if he could receive the death penalty under both old and new and it is proper to seek the death penalty, but that question hasn't been taken up with the California Supreme Court, and what we have to decide is whether we'll take it up there in this case," said Breault. Breault added that the decision ultimately would be made by Chief Deputy District Attorney Stephen Trott, who said, "We'll make up our minds on this shortly. Orange County district attorney's office is also reviewing the evidence of other murders Kearney is believed to have committed in its jurisdiction." *February 22, 1978, Los Angeles Times.*

Even though Kearney was given amnesty from the death penalty for his cooperation in the case, capital punishment was still be considered due to the large amount of murders. The relatives of the victims screamed for justice, but they were only silenced by politics and changes laws that protects killers and forgets about the victims.

INSULT TO HUMANITY - No Trial

"He's in a protective housing unit like some of the others; otherwise, their safety would be jeopardized. This keeps him away from others who might want to do him harm. And it keeps him away from those he might want to hurt." Prison Sgt. Tony Diaz.
A bearded Patrick Kearney being transported to court in Los Angeles County

In July of 1977, "Killer Kearney" pleaded guilty eighteen more counts of homicide murder, and another life term for each count. When the judge asked about why he had killed his victims, Kearney politely declined to answer the question. It was after accepting Kearney's multiple pleas of guilty, to the murder of victims, ranging from 5 to 28 years, Municipal Judge Dickran Tevrizian said, "I feel I have some obligation to 18 people you silenced. The families of those victims want to know why. Can you tell us why? "I prefer not to," the bearded slightly built Kearney replied. This reply was an insult to families of victims who deserved answers. According to Deputy District Attorney John Breault "No Deal" was made with Kearney.   This was not entirely true.

The 39-year-old aerospace worker did agree to plead guilty, with a plea bargain that carried a condition that the prosecution could not seek the death penalty. District Attorney John Breault did make a deal with Kearney that spared his life for information rendered. Yet, Kearney played Breault and law enforcement officers like a fiddle, strumming all the tunes they wanted to hear. He gave them only the information that he wanted them to know. He outsmarted the judges, lawyers, and detectives with his lies of deception, as his story continued to change before their eyes. The justice system was blinded and bought every detail, as truth. According to Detective Roger Wilson, Kearney lied to the victims he killed, but was honest with investigators about the murders. This contradictory statement demonstrates how easily Kearney tricked officers into believing his deceiving details of so-called facts. He pulled the wool over their eyes, by telling detectives that he couldn't remember all his victims, because he purposely tried to forget them just in case, he ever had to take a lie detector assessment, even though later Kearney refused to take a polygraph exam. Detectives were convinced, he was telling the truth, but the only truth he was telling was that he did not want to die for his crimes. Wilson truly believed that Kearney was being completely honest about killing a total of twenty-one people, and no more, even though he had previously confessed to Riverside detectives that he killed "over 30 to 40 victims." During an interview with Detective Roger Wilson, he was asked about the three victims Kearney had admitted to killing in Long Beach, and Wilson responded, "I don't know, that wasn't our jurisdiction." Next, he was asked, "Do you think Kearney ever killed while living in Texas or Mexico?" Wilson answered, "I don't know, it's probably something that we wouldn't have got into, because we had so many of our own. We had to take care of our stuff first, and talk to him, but I don't know if anyone else was interested, other than the National Senate for missing and exploded children. When asked, "If Kearney had killed in Texas, would it have been difficult to pin on him, after all these years?" Wilson replied, "Oh yeah, that would be senseless, that would be a waste of money." Would the relatives of victims agree?

It appears that Kearney basically succeeded in getting away with several other murders that police didn't want to deal with, so they simply closed the book on these murders. These forgotten victims remain ancient history, except by relatives, who continue to suffer from these tragic memories of losing loved ones.

After entering his guilty pleas, in municipal court on the fifth floor of the downtown criminal courts building, Kearney was marched eight floors up to appear before Superior Court Judge Paul Breckenridge, who imposed concurrent life sentences. A concurrent sentence automatically guarantees Kearney the right to parole hearings every five to six years, and a chance to gain his freedom. The judge basically gave him a "Get out of jail free card," after serving one life sentence. Subsequent to handing out Kearney's sentence, Judge Paul Breckenridge said, "This defendant has certainly perpetrated a series of ghastly and grisly crimes…I can only hope the *Community Release Board* will never release Mr. Kearney. He appears to be an insult to humanity." Kearney was indeed an insult to the human race and to the children of America, killing and discarding kids like common garbage. He remains a nightmare to society and the parents who lost their children. Even though Kearney refused to talk about his crimes, Judge Tevrizian requested medical records that revealed some horrifying facts, from the files of his psychiatrist Dr. Seawright Anderson.

In Anderson's report, Kearney was reported as saying, "My first acts of homicide were motivated by curiosity and having sex with the victims after death." Riverside County Deputy Probation Officer Sue King quoted Kearney as saying, "It did not take much reason for him to kill anyone and that it became a habit." He also told her, "Hurting and killing someone sounded sexually exciting, but when it came down to do it, it wasn't." Jay Grossman, Kearney's attorney said he felt Kearney could have posed a strong psychiatric defense but insisted on pleading guilty despite his lawyer's advice. Kearney refused to admit that he might be insane or use this as his defense.

In the untidiness of the legal mumbo-jumbo, the *LA TIMES* newspaper reported that on Friday, *July 15, 1977*, David Hill was spirited out of jail about 11:20 a.m. The Grand jury that had deliberated only one hour after hearing three hours of evidence, refused to indict Hill in connection with the series of at least 15 and possibly 28 murders, that spanned ten years, in five counties. Hill was released even though there were still another 12 to 15 unsolved murders to investigate.

After his indictment, Kearney appeared before Judge E. Scott Dales where his arraignment on murder charges was set for July 28. One investigator told the LA Times newspaper that Kearney may have taken the blame for the slayings to absolve Hill, his roommate and lover of over fifteen years. Looking at the facts, it is not possible that Hill could have lived with Kearney well over a decade without knowing anything about the murders. Another attorney named MacMillian said he would continue to represent Hill and told his client to remain quiet because of potential murder charges in other counties. Deputy District Attorney Dino Fulgoni, the Prosecutor assigned to the case in Los Angeles County, told authorities that they have no immediate plans to take Hill into custody.

However, Fulgoni said he would "Completely review" all reports provided by Riverside County investigators before making a final decision. Chief Deputy District Attorney James Enright said Orange County authorities also plan to evaluate all the information and evidence before deciding whether to charge Hill aspect of the "Trash bag" murders. The investigation had reached it peak on Sunday, *April 13, 1975,* when the nude body of twenty-one-year-old Albert Rivera was discovered. The killing spree ended with the killing of John LaMay, Kearney's final victim.

Today, Patrick Kearney sits behind the bars of his jail cell and awaits his parole hearings every six years, hoping for the day when everyone will forget about his deadly deeds so he can be set free. According to the newspapers at the time, Kearney told Riverside detectives that he began killing in 1962, the same year he met David Douglas Hill in Texas. Kearney contradicted himself when stated in reports to Los Angeles Sheriff detectives that his first murder was committed in 1968 in Culver City. This was the murder of a man only known as "George."

In other statements, he claimed the murders began in the mid-sixties in the Tijuana and San Diego areas. In any case, Kearney's story kept changing. Oddly, these statements were not ever thoroughly investigated, because detectives were eager to solve the case. Kearney was pushing for a quick conviction to avoid the death penalty, and he got his wish. The killer later described how he would pick up young naïve guys in bars, bathhouses, at bus stops, and in places where gay men congregated, looking for a quickie in the bushes. "They were easy to find, easy to kill, and their bodies were easy to dispose of in the desert." This statement confirmed that there are more unidentified victims located in Arizona, Texas and Tijuana, Mexico. Kearney got away with quite a few other murders that he has not ever been charged with. The questions remain, Should Patrick Kearney be responsible and tried for murders that he most likely committed in Mexico? Did Kearney get away with murder in Mexico? There is a strong possibility that several more victims that Kearney never admitted having deteriorated into permanent incognito.

After all, if he is guilty of murdering innocent Mexican citizens, shouldn't he be tried in that country? Does the Mexican Government carry the death Penalty for first degree murder? Are Mexican officials even aware that Kearney may have murdered people in their country? Did the U.S. convey this information with the Mexican?
Government, or did they just not feel it was important enough? This would have helped the Mexican government clear up some unsolved murder cases. If these murders actually began in 1962, this would mean there could have been possibly even more victims in the state of Texas also. These were other murders that Kearney had never been charged with. He was only charged with about half of his California murders.

In fact, there are probably several cold cases of the 1960's to through the 1970's era in Texas and Mexico that could be cleared up by Kearney. The serial killer would never admit to murders of crimes committed in Texas or Mexico, knowing he might face the death penalty. Texas has lots of desert areas where bodies would never be found.

Crimes of murder never expire, so Kearney can still be tried for cold case crimes, and I'm sure he is aware of this fact. This is why he has managed to keep quiet all these years. Kearney is a smart man; he also knew what he was doing, and he knew how to beat the system. Kearney knew all he needed to do was, "Give them what they want to hear, but don't give them everything," and that is exactly what he did. The truth may only come out on his deathbed.

Kearney's characteristics were the combination of insane cannibal killer Ed Gein, a man with a psychotic disorder and Dr. Hannibal Lecter, a fictional character with genius uniqueness from the movie "Silence of the lambs," released on February 14, 1991. Kearney carried these similar traits; with the exception that Kearney didn't eat his victims. Ed Gein would butcher his victims and feast on them, like a hunter dining on fresh killed deer. Gein didn't waste any part of his victims; much like native Indians who would slaughter buffalo for food and clothing, except for that he was butchering human beings. This killer made soup bowls from the top of their skulls and clothes from their skin. Gein character influenced the October 1, 1974 movie," The Texas Chainsaw Massacre." Also, the 1960 movie *Psycho* from a story by author Robert Bloch, was based on the character Norman Bates, but was modeled after Ed Gein. Ed Gein was a real-life cannibal, whereas Dr. Hannibal Lecter was only a character in a movie. Lecter was portrayed more as a killer with the I. Q. of a genius, much like Kearney. One of Kearney's deceptions was that he falsely claimed to be a doctor just like Dr. Hannibal Lecter. Kearney even owned a little black bag containing some medical instruments so he could examine his victims prior to murdering them. This method was most likely used on several of his victims.

"Killing excited me and gave me a feeling of dominance."
Patrick Kearney told Homicide investigators

"Chance was strangled; Buchanan, Armendariz, McGhee, and Orach were all shot like pigs," said *homicide Detective Roger Wilson*. The rest of his victims were also killed, and after being sexually assaulted, they were gutted and mutilated. Records can only demonstrate the immeasurable suffering that Patrick Kearney has caused to the countless families of his victims. If these victims could speak out from the graves, what would they say? How would they feel about Patrick Kearney and David Hill? Patrick Kearney would surely know the answer to this question, but he would not care. Kearney quit caring about human lives, long ago. One thing is for certain, the victims would be extremely angry, because their lives were taken away so young, which caused great pain and suffering to their loved ones for generations to come.

Within the long trail of tears, Kearney has flooded many lives with endless worry, regret and sorrow. The victims would have chosen life rather than death, but this choice was taken away from them, the moment they met Kearney. All these victims did have one thing in common; they all trusted Kearney and were murdered without mercy. So many lives were taken for a killer's own bloody sexual pleasures and gratification. Below is twenty-five of the possibly 43 or more that Kearney bragged about killing. The other sixteen victims and perhaps many others have never been recovered and remain forgotten.

LET'S NOT FORGET THE VICTIMS

MURDERDED 1962 - Victims 1.2.3. Long Beach Victims (Body not recovered)
MURDERDED July 8, 1977 -Victim 4. George (Unidentified skeleton found under Kearney's house – Culver City) killed around Christmas 1968, (Body recovered)
MURDERDED Aug. 24, 1974 -Victim 5. Ronald Dean Smith (5 years old – Lennox) Body recovered in Riverside found 1974
MURDERDED Oct. 29, 1975 – Victim 6. Larry Gene Walters 21, missing (Body not recovered)
MURDERDED March 21, 1976 -Victim 7. Oliver Peter Molilor 13, (Body recovered)
MURDERDED April 6, 1976 -Victim 8. Kenneth Eugene Buchanan (17 years old – Lawndale) (Body recovered)
MURDERDED April 19, 1976 -Victim 9. Larry Armendariz 14, missing -(Body not recovered)
MURDERDED May 26, 1976 -Victim 10. Kevin Dewayne Portis (4 years old) (Body not recovered)
MURDERDED June 11, 1976 -Victim 11. Michael McGhee Jr. (11 years old) (Body not recovered)
MURDERDED June 21, 1976 -Victim 12. John Woods 23, Redondo Beach, found shot in head and dumped in San Diego (Body recovered)
MURDERDED Aug. 22, 1976 -Victim 13. John Doe (Body recovered)
MURDERDED Oct. 6, 1976 -Victim 14. Mark Andrew Orach 20, (Body recovered)
MURDERDED Oct. 10, 1976 -Victim 15. Randall Lawrence Moore 16,
MURDERDED Oct. 24, 1976 -Victim 16. Timothy B. Ingham 19, of Merced – (Body recovered)
MURDERDED Jan. 24, 1977-Victim 17. Nick Hernandez (28 years old – Los Angeles) found
MURDERDED Mar. 18, 1977-Victim 18. John Otis Lamay (17 years old – El Segundo) (Body recovered, but head remains missing)
MURDERDED Victim 19. Robert William Bennefiel (17 years old – Redondo Beach) Body never Recovered– dumped in South Bay Land Fill
MURDERDED -Victim 20. David Allen 27, (Body recovered) in Fall Brook Area
MURDERDED- Victim 21. Wilfred L. Faherty (20 years old – Redondo Beach)
MURDERDED -Victim 22. Albert Rivera (24 years old – Los Angeles)
MURDERDED -Victim 23. Arturo Marquez (24 years old – Oxnard)
MURDERDED -Victim 24. Merle Chance (7 years old – Venice Beach) (Body recovered)

Eighteen other victims have never been recovered.

RELATIVES OF VICTIMS SPEAK

What do the relatives think about their losses that were caused by this killer? Torrance resident Marcia Born has been assured by the Los Angeles County Sheriff's Department that her brother's killer has no chance of ever being released, yet Killer Kearney goes up for parole every six years. If there is no guarantee that this killer would ever be released, then why is this killer even available for parole? Is there a chance for freedom, even after committing an estimated 43 murders? The very same court that set David Hill free, also gave Kearney the parole hearing option, which may allow him to one day be liberated.

Justice in this case screams out from the graves of victims, to bury this killer behind bars for an eternity. What Kearney did to the families is forever. While other serials killers have been executed and are lying dead in their graves for their murderous deeds, Kearney relaxes each day in his cell that includes free food and room service. Since so many have suffered because of this killer, why was he spared from the death penalty? Relatives of victims have the right to know. Kearney did his homework, and surrendered, while the death penalty was still inactive? This was a big part of why he surrendered, when he did. Capital punishment would have most likely been the penalty, in this case, if Kearney had waited one more month before surrendering. Did Kearney's punishment fit his crimes? Was justice served?

California serial killers such as the Night Stalker, the Hillside Strangler's, Tex Watson, Charley Manson and other killer, who received death penalty never died because of California's unlimited appeals process. Why are these killers allowed to continue these relentless appeals to avoid paying the penalty in which they were charged? California's legal authorizes response to this is that they want to make sure there is no room for errors. The scales of justice seem to be unbalanced whereas some murderers are put to death, while others who have killed either celebrities or large numbers of people are usually spared the death penalty. We need to ask, "Is this a fair justice?"

If you kill somebody like John Lennon, John F. Kennedy or Sharon Tate, your life as a killer is spared. Why are plea bargains legal? "I'll give you something...you give me something." There should be no deals for murderers. Bundy tried to make a deal and tell where bodies of victims were located, and the state said, "No deal"...he was electrocuted 3 days later.

Patrick Wayne Kearney's mandated parole hearing comes up like clockwork every six years. When the clocks ticks and the hands of time bring forth his next hearing, Marcia Born starts making telephone calls and writing letters, *"Just in case," she said.* Born has remained dedicated in keeping this killer locked up. She said, "Out of respect for my brother, I feel I must go." Born also lost her best friend, teenager Jacqueline Lamp, who was killed by Lawrence Bittaker and accomplice Roy Norris. The two were convicted of kidnapping, torturing, and murdering five girls. After losing her brother and her best friend, Born commented, "I thought I was jinxed. When I was younger, I thought I was protecting other people by not being their friend."

Born said it was in 1975, when Patrick Kearney picked up her 17-year-old brother Robert "Billy" Benniefiel, and he never returned home. It was on Valentine's Day of 1981 when Kearney confessed to her brother's murder. She would visit the South Bay Landfill where her brother's remains were dumped, and she would bring flowers and bow in prayer to his memory, but today she has moved on. "Not anymore. Not after 21 years. We moved on, but it's always in your head. It doesn't go away. There's always going to be anger and bitterness. I mean, my God, he killed my brother."

Born explains how a year and a half after his disappearance, her family and local police believed that Benniefiel had simply run away, but it would turn out to be not that simple. She recalls that it wasn't until a neighbor showed the family a newspaper article that ran a story on Kearney's confession and a description of a victim. The victim's description sounded like Robert Benniefiel and the family made a connection. The family took a photograph of Benniefiel to police headquarters to determine whether or not he was a victim of Patrick Kearney.

Born said, police took a picture of Robert to Kearney, and asked him, "Is this one of your victims?" Kearney identified him immediately. To this day it eats my other brother up that the picture he took out of his wallet was the one that slime looked at." Kearney confessed to Benniefiel's murder in 1981, but the body was never discovered. Kearney told officials that he dumped a few other bodies in the South Bay landfill. He added, "You'll never find him." He was right; Benniefiel's body has never been recovered. Born said, "She'll never forget. She can't."

"It's almost like killing my brother wasn't the worst of it," she said. "It's what he did to the family. Every time the (parole) hearing comes up, it just dredges it all up."

Born told reporters that she and her family have always felt guilty for her brother's death, because they persuaded him to move out to California from Louisiana. She wonders if her brother would still be alive if he had stayed in the South. Born said that her other brother still speculates about the day Billy was picked up by Kearney, and relives this day, remembering when he and his brother had parted ways. He believes that if they had stayed together, maybe he'd still be alive. This is common among relatives who lose someone close. Today, Marcia Born isn't sure what her brother would be doing if he were still alive. "He'd be in his late 40s, probably living a simple life, sometimes Born finds herself wondering if he isn't doing just that." Perhaps he is doing what he loved best in heaven.

"I don't know if it's doubt or hope," she said. "We don't have a body, and Kearney didn't know my brother's name. There's always that little bit in your mind. For so many years, you see someone who looks like him, you take a double take, even to this day." Marcia Born will always remember her older brother and they is no amount of time that can ever change this. Maybe her brother is looking down and smiling upon the family that was a part of him.

Benniefiel dedication – Tony Stewart talking with Roger Wilson

Stewart - You mentioned that one the mother of victim Robert Benniefiel started some programs. Can you tell me what they were?

Wilson - Well, the first one was after we told her (Benniefiel's mother) the pieces were up at the landfill in Palos Verdes, and she got the county to dedicate a piece of land, and they all planted trees, the five families, actual four, one of them didn't give a shit about anybody. They have a row of trees up there dedicated with their names, and that was Benniefiel, Ortar, McGee, and Walters.

Stewart - Marcia Born says she goes up there quite often and says it's very beautiful.

Wilson - If that's any consolation. She got involved in M.A.D.D. Mothers Against Drunk Driving and it's something like P.O.M.C. Parents Of Murdered Children. I forget the exact wording.

After reading about Kearney's upcoming 1996 hearing; the families of victims told The Daily Breeze Newspaper, they wanted to make sure he never gets out of prison. They wanted to clear their minds and vent their rage. The article spoke about having someone you love to disappear and pray relentlessly that they would reappear, only to receive a call from the police stating, "A body has been found." Then you are asked to stop by to examine the clothes, and bring a picture, medical and dental records to confirm the victim's identification. He was charged with 21 murders, multiply that times the family members who were affected, and he has bought tragedy to a few hundred lives.

Steven Demchik, father of 13-year-old victim John Demchik, reacted by saying, "That son of bitch!" After the disappearance of his son in 1975, Steven Demchik told his wife and four children that he was off to Northern California to find a better paying job, in truth, he left to search for his son.

"I figured he might be up in San Francisco. I used to spend my weekends just driving around the city and, on the highways, just to see if I could spot him. I dreamed of him up there. The last dream I had, he was in a dungeon. He was calling me. I asked him, 'Where are you.' He never answered. I went through a lot of hell. "

"Six years after John Demchik disappearance, Kearney confessed to the murder and told where he'd buried the boy." Six long years of suffering and agony, the family had to endure. "Police asked Norma Demchik (mother) to identify her son's clothes. His killing 'haunted' his mother, one daughter recalled: I think she just didn't want to go on. Already stricken with cancer, Norma Demchik died soon after learning about her son.

"He's not coming back," Steven Demchik said. "There's nothing that can bring him back. I knew that after the police called and his mother identified his clothes," I said, 'That's him.' There's no use grieving over it anymore. There are times when I remember him on his birthday or Christmas. That's hard, but I must reach back and say, 'He's not coming back,' said Steven Demchik."

Another article in the Daily Breeze reported on the family of victim 5-year-old Ronald smith. After his murder, his mother, grandparents, and his aunt, all fled far away from the South Bay area to try to live again.

"Ronnie was the baby of the family, and there's not a holiday or day that goes by that we don't imagine what he'd be doing, what he'd look like now," said his aunt, Ronnie Jewette, in a telephone interview from her home in Washington state. "His death was so terrible, and it made me afraid to let my own children go out anymore. When Ronnie died, we all learned you couldn't be too trusting. His death changed everything, everyone. Especially his mother, JoAnn O'Conner, age 45. She married, and then divorced. Quit her job as a bookkeeper and moved to the Seattle area. She'll never forget, she can't forget. Ronald was her only child," said Ronnie Jewette.

"I can still smell what his skin smelled like and how his hair felt, and when I close my eyes, I can hear his voice, JoAnn O'Connor said during a telephone interview with reporters." She continued, "Your life will never be the same after something like that. My life went through radical changes …I quit work and moved and changed everything in my life. You choose to change your whole environment. If I were going to survive it, I had to make some changes." On his birthday, October 18, O'Connor said, "All the family has pictures out and we talk about Ronnie freely. It's nice to be able to put those pictures out and share those happy memories. I won't attend the hearing; I've already gone through the mourning and healing from the anger. I don't think it'd be good for me to attend. It's like dead flesh, you don't bring it up because it stinks."

Bertha Chance lives alone with memories of her 8-year-old son, Hondo, who disappeared while riding his bicycle. Kearney later confessed to killing the child and dumping his body in the Angeles National Forest.

"I had four other kids, but he was my baby. I can't describe what it made me feel like. It wasn't easy. It was not easy. I stayed by myself every day. I went out to his grave every day. I would take flowers and sit and talk to him. If people saw me, they thought I was crazy because I was sitting there talking to a headstone."

Chance held on to her grief for a long time. She worked for years at an assembly plant supporting herself and stays busy at home where she enjoyed raising her grandchildren. Although, she doesn't feel strong enough to attend Kearney's hearings, over the years she has sent hundreds of letters demanding that he stay behind bars.

Kearney also killed 13-year-olf Michael McGhee of Redondo Beach, California. The family contacted the parole board after Kearney was sentenced to let them know they would be attending his hearing. "I want to let them know the slime he is. I want to tell them how he affected people's lives. He needs to account for what he has done," said Elizabeth McGhee, Michael's sister. She added that she knows he will never likely be released, but she needs to tell the parole board about the lives he took, and about the lives he ruined. "He took my naivety away. Before this happened, I used to go down to the beach at night and walk along the ocean, but he took that away. I realized I couldn't do that anymore. There were a lot of things I wouldn't do anymore. It wasn't safe. I realized how sick the world is."

Deputy Attorney Diane Vezzani said she wishes the diminutive Kearney would attend his hearing to have to face the friends and families of his victims. She said she would also like to confront him. "I'd like to tell him, 'Big man, what a big man you are! Had to use a gun to have your way with little boys. What a big, brave man."

Guy Sorensen and his father Robert C. Sorensen also knew Patrick Kearney. Robert was a close friend of Kearney's and was also his co-worker at Hughes Aircraft. Guy's comments give us another insight of who this killer really was.

"I knew Patrick W. Kearney since I was 6 years old. He worked with my father at Hughes Aircraft in El Segundo. He had been a friend of the family for 11 years, until he was arrested.

I thought I knew Patrick very well, but obviously not. We lived in Costa Mesa when I first met Pat. I liked him immediately. He helped us move from Costa Mesa to Cerritos in the early seventies. He was my father's best and only friend. I sat in the truck with him many times alone and he was always friendly. We had gone to several company picnics and Pat would always greet us. He was also very fond of going to Tijuana. My father, Robert C. Sorensen and a friend of mine would go with Pat down to Baja and they would go their way and we would go ours. My dad said that Pat would bring him to bathhouses in TJ. I knew Pat very well from the mid to late sixties up until his arrest in '77.' Pat had murdered my girlfriend's brother. I say the body count is a little shy of how many young boys and young men fell prey to Pat's insatiable appetite to dominate and destroy every male he could get his hands on, but his preference was young surfer types.

"He spoke the language fluently and he couldn't take his eyes off my friend, and I thought that strange and actually began to get a little jealous why he was giving my friend so much attention. My friend was muscular, with blonde haired and blue eyes. Pat's preferred prey item. I couldn't get a word in edge wise he was trying so hard to engage my friend in conversation it made me feel uncomfortable and a bit awkward. My friend just thought he was cool. David Hill knew everything Pat was very conscientious when it came to the people he trusted. He was very protective. That's one of the reasons he didn't run. He was protecting the people he was close to from having to answer some embarrassing questions by the police. My father went with him to buy the gun used in some of the later murders. He wanted to get caught, He was tired of killing but he had lost control and could no longer stop himself. If you know Pat at all you know he's a multiple personality. Thank God my father was his best friend and my father was also 6'3" and a heavy weight golden glove boxer who was the preverbal gentle giant his fists are the size of bricks. Pat was a real paradox when it came to the people he sincerely liked and the people he pretended to like. I truly am thankful you and your brother got free of his grasp, he was a true genius, but like most highly intellectual persons, he fell short on sincere emotion and was severely stunted."

ANOTHER TWIST: ZODIAC KILLER?

Faces of Patrick Kearney

Police stretch of the Zodiac Killer

Were Patrick Kearney and the Zodiac, one and the same? The Zodiac experts will argue that the killer had a completely different schema and a diverse persona than Patrick Kearney had, and they are correct. However, they can't argue the fact that Kearney had a striking resemblance to the inexplicable Zodiac killer. Without stating that the *Zodiac killer* and the *Trash bag murderer* are indeed the same person, we first need to consider weighing the possibilities and compare the evidence. Not only were the facial descriptions of the two are similar, but both murderers, Kearney and the Zodiac, were both active around the same time period. The San Francisco police have questioned 2,500 Zodiac suspects, but no one has ever been convicted. Could serial killer Patrick Wayne Kearney actually be the mysterious Zodiac killer of the late nineteen sixties and seventies? The same set of circumstances applies in this scenario involving many senseless murders. Kearney unquestionably had the aptitude and characteristics to kill innocent people without ethics or mercy, as the Zodiac killer did. Also, both traveled up and down California's coastlines during these murderous quests. There is a noticeable difference in these killers; whereas Kearney maintained a low profile, the Zodiac craved attention. Both Killers had more than one personality, perhaps even multiple personalities. The Zodiac killer developed a relationship with the San Francisco Chronicle and used his press to taunt the police, publishing newspaper messages that contained secret astrological number and codes that would supposedly revealed his identity?

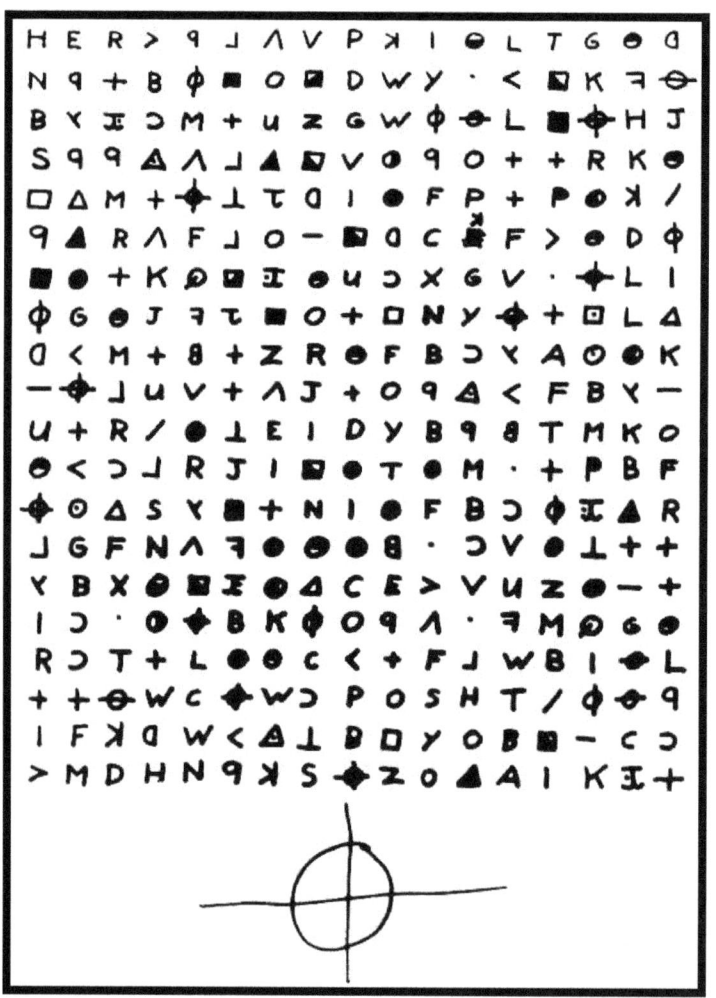

The Zodiac's cryptograms messages sent to the San Francisco Police Department consisting of astrological numbers

The Zodiac criticized the Chronicle with deadly threats that his killings are to be front-page news. Also, we know that Kearney killed people in several California counties, but there is still no strong evidence that he killed in the San Francisco Bay area.

One Zodiac related victim that he supposedly confessed to, but has not been confirmed, was eighteen-year-old Cheri Jo Bates. She was stabbed to death was killed in Riverside county on October 30, 1968, in the same location where Kearney had dumped several bodies. This was also the same year that Kearney admitted killing his first victim known only as George. We have evidence that Kearney made a statement to Homicide Detective's Al Sett and Roger Wilson that he wanted to kill a couple, while parked at "Lovers lane," just like serial killer Caryl Chessman (The Red Light Bandit) did years earlier. The motivation to kill a couple at lover's lane also fit the Zodiac killer's M.O. in the sixties. The Zodiac had seven confirmed victims from 1968 to 1969, two of whom survived to give the police a description of the killer, which displayed a strong resemblance to Patrick Kearney.

With an I.Q. of 180, Kearney was unquestionably a genius that thought outside the box, and undoubtedly might have taken on a whole set of other personalities. If fact, he may have had multiple personalities during his murderous career, which is common in serial killers. Once in captivity Kearney also bragged about his murders, much like the Zodiac did to newspapers. By not volunteering all his murders to detectives, possibly including the unsolved Zodiac killings, a part of Kearney was allowed to remain free within his psychopathic mind. When asked if Kearney could have killed more people than he previously admitted, detectives responded by saying, "Patrick Kearney was completely honest and very cooperative with us, we believe he confessed to all the murders and we really doubt that there were any other victims."

Detectives in several counties were dealing with a psychopathic genius that was much more intelligent than anyone who questioned him. This gave Kearney a full opportunity to pull the shade over their eyes of homicide investigators, as he did. By pretending to be completely cooperative and honest, and giving detectives exactly what they wanted to hear, he was able to convince them of anything. He took advantage of this. Detective Al Sett questioned Kearney, and said, "He wanted to talk. For some reason or another, he wanted to talk. I was known as a pretty good interrogator, but Kearney really wanted to talk. He wanted to get this stuff off his cheat."

Kearney was overly eager to converse with detectives, but he suspiciously refused to take a lie detector or polygraph examination. Why? Because he was worried that officers would find out he wasn't telling the entire truth. There was much more to the story. He was guilty of a lot more murders, which would have proved he was the deadliest killer in U.S. history. Kearney was smart; he completely gained the investigators trust, and then withheld several key facts to prevent receiving capital punishment.

Patrick Kearney said he would kill after arguing with his roommate David Hill, which is interesting when we view their Zodiac signs. Kearney's Zodiac sign was Libra while Hill's sign was Capricorn, and according to the Zodiac scale, Libra has a difficult relationship with Capricorn. This fact shines true in Kearney's character. According to the Zodiac scale, "The origin of the word Libra is derived from the Latin meaning balances or scales." Often, seen as a statue entitled "Goddess of Justice" that is seen holding the scales or balances erected over the domes of modern courthouses.

If Kearney was indeed the inexplicable Zodiac killer, perhaps he felt he needed to judge and condemn people that he felt were guilty. This way he could attempt to archive balance as written in the Zodiac scales. By doing so, as the Zodiac, he would murder single women and couples that contaminated this balance the world of impurities, or those against homosexuals. After achieving this goal, he could then sodomise and kill young males as a reward for his own sexual pleasures. This theory may or may not sound farfetched, but the behavior of many serial killers is quite delusional with illogical thoughts contained inside their demented minds. Within a serial killer's world, anything was possible, especially with Patrick Kearney, who definitely thought outside the circle of reality.

"Perhaps the greatest fault of the Libra Sign is indecision. Libra individuals find it difficult to make up their minds and strongly dislike taking sides. Although they have an aversion to those who are rude, they themselves can frequently be disconcertingly brash and blunt."

This Libra description describes most of Kearney's personality, but leaves out the word "Murderous." With a genius level I.Q., Kearney may have used his intelligence to disguise his own handwriting. We must examine his writing to see if it can be a perfect match to the Zodiac's own handwriting? It was time to find out the truth.

To determine whether or not Kearney allegedly wrote the Zodiac letters, handwriting samples of several letters and drawings from both killers were collected and sent to an expert for forensic examination and comparison. To authenticate or disprove this theory, these sample pages were sent via email transmission to Marion Briggs, an expert in Forensic Document Examination Handwriting Identification.

On February 12, 2008, documents sent to Marion Briggs were examined for critical comparison of writer habits and handwriting characteristics to determine the truth and prove whether Kearney and the zodiac were one in the same. Below these are the results of this forensic analysis.

REPORT: Forensic Examination and Comparison

A total of fifteen (15) questioned documents allegedly written by "The Zodiac (Q-#1-15) and five (5) Known documents, written by Patrick w. Kearney, (K#1-#5) were received February 12, via email transmission.

All documents were examined, and critical comparison of writer habits and handwriting characteristics was conducted to determine, if possible, whether any or all the Questioned writings were or were not written by the same person who wrote the Patrick W. Kearney Standards.

Findings and conclusions:
It should be noted that the writings of both the Patrick W. Kearney and the Questioned Zodiac documents were written by someone who is precision and technology-oriented, which each of their hand-drawn graphic chart represents.

Therefore, the erratic line quality, penmanship skill and numerous misspellings throughout the Zodiac writings are contradictory and can reasonably be attributed to an attempt by the writer to distort the natural, spontaneous writer habits and handwriting characteristics and, therefore, to protect personal identity.

Some similarities in writer habits and handwriting characteristics have been located within the Questioned writings, compared with the Kearney Standards. They are:

- Formation: c, i, l
- Punctuation: period
- Underscore of misc. words for emphasis

A preponderance of differences in writer habits and handwriting characteristics has also been located. They are:

Individual letter formation:
 A,B,D,E,e,F,G,H,I,J,K,M,m,n,O,p,R,S,T,t,u,V,W,w,y
Numerals: 1,2,3
Letter combinations: AT,AND,BY,could,make,RE,THE,the,HE,ER,ICE,mo,WA,ing,Dear
Symbols: ± (plus sign) & (ampersand), arrowhead, and , (comma)

SIMILARITIES

KNOWN: Patrick W. Kearney	QUESTIONED: "The Zodiac"
1. profit. (K-1)	1. nights. (Q-4)
2. UNDER (K-2)	2. not (Q-...)

DIFFERENCES

KNOWN: Patrick W. Kearney	QUESTIONED: "The Zodiac"
1. VOLATILITY (K-3)	1. A+ (Q-3)
2. BY (K-1)	2. BY (Q-7)
3. could (K-1)	3. could (Q-10)
4. make (K-1)	4. make (Q-10)
5. REVENGE! (K-1)	5. "THERE (Q-1)
6. THE (K-2) HEDGE (K-2) the (K-2)	6. The (Q-2) This (Q-2) the (Q-6)
7a. OVERPRICED (K-2)	7. rather (Q-11) nice (Q-11) police (Q-14)
7b. UNDER-PRICED (K-2)	
8. MONEY (K-2) more (K-3)	8. most (Q-10)
9. Wall (K-1)	9. Washington (Q-9)
10. pricing (K-4) CRUNCHING (K-3)	10. speaking (Q-2) speak (Q-9)
11. Dear (K-4)	11. Dear (Q-3) Dear (Q-10) Dear (Q-12) Dear (Q-14)
12. A+B (K-5)	12. A+B (Q-11)
13. $ (K-1)	13. + SF Exam (Q-4) + Twisted (Q-6)
14. TOP (K-3)	14. empty (Q-2) list (Q-6)
15. 1 (K-1) 2 (K-2) 3 (K-3) 3 (K-3)	15. -12 (Q-2) -38 (Q-2) 13 (Q-5) 13 (Q-6) (Q-14)

DIFFERENCES

KNOWN: Patrick W. Kearney	QUESTIONED: "The Zodiac"
1. A. (K-2) analysis (K-4)	1. Area (Q-2) Jug (Q-15) ~~Clean~~ (Q-12)
2. BUY (K-2) TALIBAN (K-4)	2. Bay (Q-2) Became (Q-9)
3. AND (K-2) PRICED (K-3)	3. and (Q-3) complied (Q-2)
4. DEFINITIONS (K-4)	4. SFPD (Q-5) Editor (Q-10) Exam (Q-14)
5. the (K-4)	5. Page (Q-15)
6. FALLING (K-1) For (K-4)	6. Fry. (Q-15)
7. GLOSSARY (K-4) "HEDGE (K-2)	7. T O (Q-2)
8. Here (K-2)	8. Here (Q-4)
9. IF (K-2)	9. If (Q-4) I (Q-5)
10. Jets (K-1)	10. Judas (Q-10) Judas (Q-13)
11. Stocks (K-1) STOCK (K-2)	11. think (Q-7) killed (Q-7)
12. MARKET (K-1) MISPRICED (K-1)	12. Map (Q-2) Meannies (Q-9)
13. "FORMULA" (K-3) htm (K-4)	13. much (Q-7) money (Q-7)
14. OPTIONS (K-1) enterprise (K-4)	14. thing (Q-3) now (Q-11)
15. OSAMA's (K-1) One (K-3)	15. Others (Q-5)
16. OPTION (K-3) STRIP (K-3)	16. Maple (Q-9) prove (Q-9)

(Chart #2)

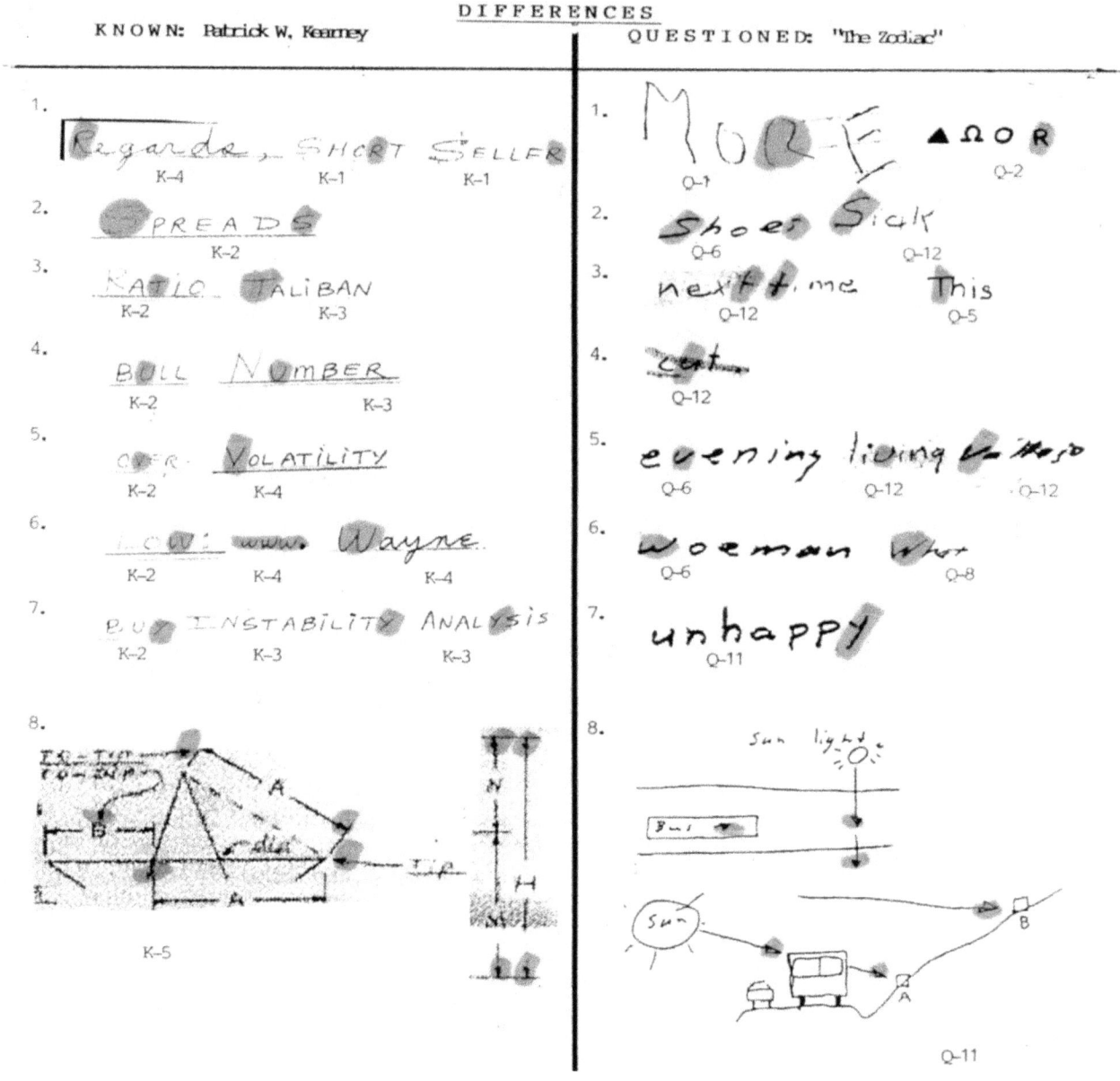

Final determination of Marion E. Briggs analysis derived from above writings and drawings is now conclusive.

Based on the available evidence, the questioned Zodiac writings were probably not written by the same person who wrote the Patrick Kearney Standards.

Verification of opinion is contingent upon examination of original documents.

Submitted by:
Marion E. Briggs, BCFDE, CFE

Even though there were some similarities found in the handwriting analysis by expert Marion Briggs' the samples were determined as not written by the same person. Thus, confirming that Patrick Kearney was not the Zodiac killer. So, if Kearney was not the Zodiac killer, "Who was the Zodiac killer?" There were thousands of suspects, but many experts believe that Arthur Leigh Allen was most likely the real zodiac killer. This theory began when expert Donald Harden unraveled the Zodiac's cryptograms messages and mysterious ciphers to reveal the hidden name Arthur Leigh Allen. In July of 1992, a surviving Zodiac victim named Mike Mageau picked Arthur Allen out of a police photo lineup, "That's him! He's the man who shot me!" replied Mageau.

On August 26, 1992, Allen died of natural causes at age 58, after a history of diabetes and heart problems.

Two days later, on August 28, 1992, police armed with a search warrant searched Allen's residence and found many interesting items including videotape that was strangely labeled with a "Z." Police never revealed the contents of the video, but in of October 2002, Allen's DNA was compared to samples found on a confirmed Zodiac letter and the results were determined to be negative. If Allen was indeed the Zodiac killer, in the end, he has succeeded fooling the world. One day the truth will surface, but either way, the killer is most likely dead or in a nursing home by now.

FINAL ANALYSIS

Serial Killer Patrick Kearney is seen here shackled, while being transported to Los Angeles County Criminal Court to face sentencing for twenty-one accounts of "First Degree," *Cold-blooded* murder, less than half the murders he committed.

**Kearney's present home at Mule Creek State Prison 2010
California Department of Corrections and Rehabilitations – Google Images**

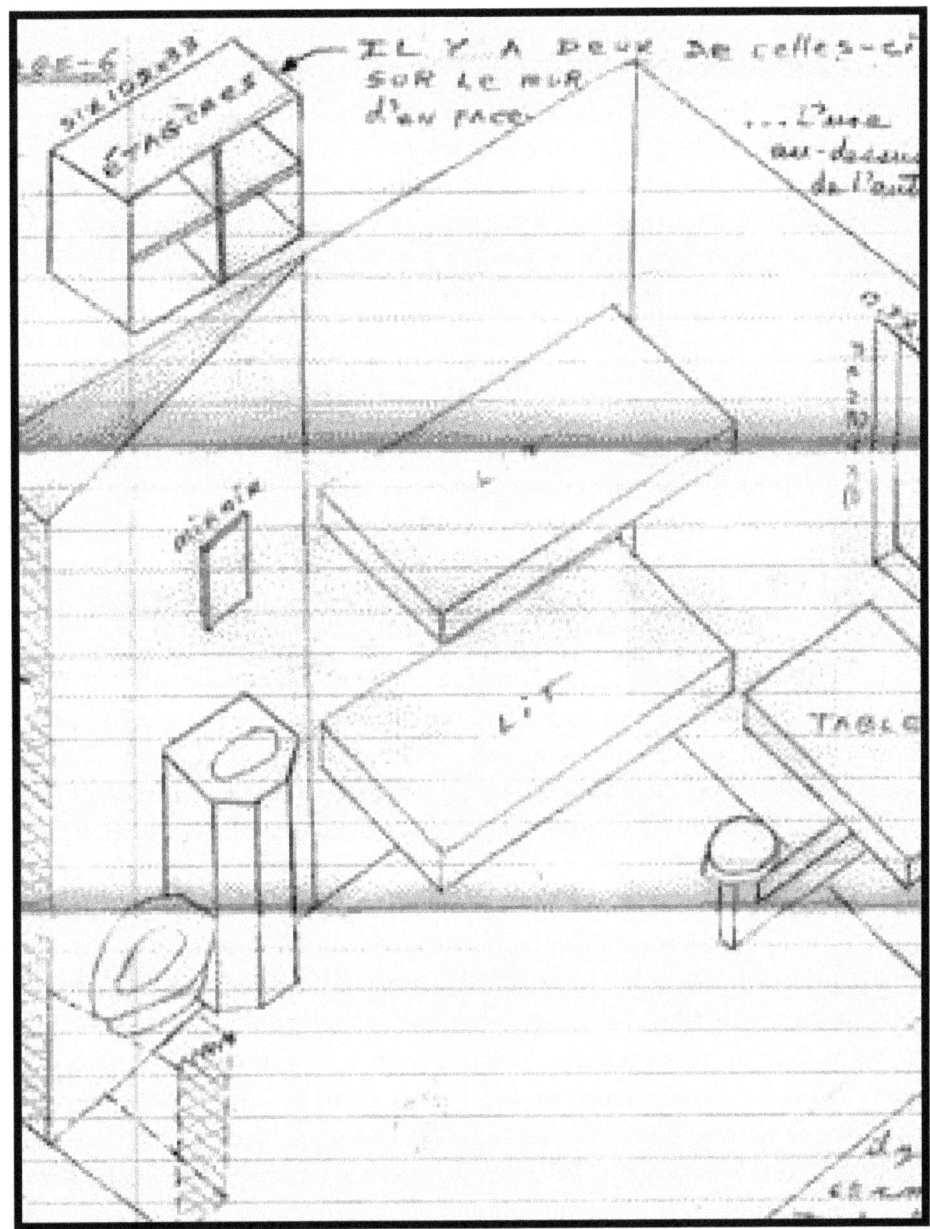

Kearney's prison cell, drawn by the killer with words inscribed as,
IL Y A Deux De Celles-ci sor Le Mur d'en face. Translated to English reveals: "There Two of These To The Sea on face." Could this be a code or formula for a future escape, or a hidden message for his lover David Hill? Kearney twisted mind should not be taken lightly; others have made the same fatal mistake and paid with their lives. It was Kearney's modus operandi that earned him the nickname *The Trash Bag Murderer*.

It was Riverside Sheriff's Department that deserves the credit for bring Kearney to justice, but because most of the victims were from Los Angeles. So, the ball was passed on to the Los Angeles Sheriff's Department that did the final legwork on the case, which placed the killer behind bars. Today, Patrick Kearney resides at Mule Creek State Prison in Northern California, about an hour from Sacramento. The parole board reviewed Patrick Kearney's case listed as Booking # B88913. He was up for parole on Feb. 2010, but was denied, and his next hearing will be in 2016. Mule Creek State Prison located at: Physical Address: 4001 Highway 104, PO Box 409099, Ione Ca 95640.

The actual mailing Address is P.O. Box 409099, Ione, CA 95640 and phone number (209) 274-4911. Anyone can contact the facility and try to attend these hearings to keep this killer behind bars.

According to authorities, Kearney doesn't have any contact with the outside world, and is only aloud out of his cell for twenty minutes a day. He is not allowed to correspond with anyone. Mule Creek State Prison's annual operating budget is $135 million to house over 3,500 other prisoners. Taxpayers pay $38,571 dollars to feed, clothe and house Kearney each year, not counting medical expenses. This is more money than most American even earn in a year.

He has served time in Chino State Prison in San Bernardino County, California, and was later transferred to Corcoran State Prison located in Kings County where he served time with convicted killers Charley Manson, Sirhan Sirhan, and Juan Corona. In the early 1990's, he was transferred to Calipatria State Prison located in Imperial County and is presently serving time with murderers Tex Watson and Lyle Menendez at Mule Creek State Prison in Sacramento, California.

In his perplexed mind, Kearney found justified reasoning for the killing of every one of his victims. He described his victims as worthless transients, homosexuals, runaways, thieves, male prostitutes, drug users or old friends that turned against him. Only a handful of the victims fit these profiles. In most cases, he was completely wrong in his descriptions of his victims. Many were not transients, homosexuals or runaways as he predicted; instead they were just ordinary people from loving families out to enjoy life, when Kearney disrupted it. Even if he had taken the time to get to know these people better, would this have saved their lives? The answer is "No," because Kearney even killed his own friends. There were a few victims that were into drugs or minor crimes, but they were not bad enough to be killed outright and turned into a science experiment. Some of these people needed assistance, and Kearney would be right there to offer his help. Kearney always appeared as the innocent party that was just trying to help those he killed. He thought it was acceptable to kill and sexually assault the courses, because the dead felt no pain. "They were easy to find, easy to kill, bodies easy to dispose of in the desert," boastfully, Kearney bragged.

Kearney proved to be a demon monster behind the invisible mask he wore. I find it chilling to realize that I had personally talked to this serial killer alone at his home, where he killed so many, and I survived. Now, I would like to share my experience. There are important measures that we should take as parents, citizens, children, and survivors of violent crimes. We need to take precautions that can save lives against these serial predators. This is serious business, there are over 400 serial killers out there right now searching for easy victims. Look at the bulletin boards at stores like Wal-Mart, and several other places that list missing children. Our children are disappearing, and it needs to stop.

In Arlington, Texas on January 13, 1996, little Amber Hagerman was thrown into a pickup truck. Neighbors heard the little girl scream and witnessed the abduction. The incident was reported to police, along with a description of the man, but he was never apprehended. Four days later, Amber's body was found in a drainage ditch, four miles from her home. Her throat had been cut, and the autopsy showed she had died two days after her abduction. Nine months after Amber's death, her parents, and Marc Klaas, the father 12-year-old Polly, who murdered in 1993, joined together with other supporters of child protection laws and succeeded in having the Amber Hagerman Child Protection Act passed into law by President Clinton.

America's Most Wanted host John Walsh also lost his son Adam on July 27, 1981. Adam was abducted from a *Sears Department Store* at the Hollywood Mall, which was located directly across from the Hollywood Police station. Adam's mother had dropped Adam off in the Sears toy department briefly, while she looked for a lamp. When she returned, Adam was missing. Sixteen days after the abduction, Adam's severed head was discovered in a drainage canal, 120 miles away from the Walsh residence. John Walsh later founded the *Adam Walsh Child Resource Center* on November 9, 1988, located at: SUITE 306, FT. Lauderdale, 33322.

There are several organizations that can help such as *The Amber alert at* http://www.amberalert.gov/, *National Center for Missing and Exploited Children at* http://www.missingkids.com. You can even contact John Walsh's *America's Most Wanted at* http://www.amw.com/.

WHAT CAN WE DO TO HELP STOP VIOLENT CRIMES?

By being aware and understanding the characteristics of these serial killers we can keep our children safe. This works for us adults too. This is a very serious matter. It can be really scary knowing that there are hundreds of lunatics out running lose just like Kearney that haven't been caught yet. These killers are searching for victims at this very moment as we speak. With good police work and the watchful eye of citizens, one-by-one, we can put a stop to these senseless murderers. Meanwhile, more innocent people are being brutalized and killed by someone they thought they could trust. I've looked a serial killer directly in the face, and couldn't see anything past the compassionate person, that they wanted me to see. So how could I tell this man was a killer? I couldn't. Serial killers are the most difficult creatures to catch, because they appear to be so ordinary and they're extremely careful not to get caught.

The smartest things we can all do to protect ourselves are, "Do not ever hitch hike, or go anywhere with strangers, no matter how nice they seem to be." Look out for your friends and family, don't ever let them leave with strangers either. Most serial killers search for people that are out late at night, or those in desperate need of assistance. These are the most common victims, but these killers also go out to clubs to find people. Be aware of strangers who are eager to offer you a ride home or invite you to be their guest for dinner. Several of Kearney's victims never made it home after he treated them to dinner. It would be their last meal. You don't have to live your life in fear, just be aware and stay alert. It is important that we provide information to educate the public to help them to be more alert. The more people can learn about the way these vicious killers operate, the better they may be able to defend and protect themselves and their families. Once you've lived of this kind of horror, you never forget. I was very fortunate to have survived to share my experience. My good friend Marion Briggs told me she truly believes that life is a classroom and that everything that happens to us is part of the education we need for something. I couldn't have said this better. We can lay a wager that Kearney regrets knowing that my brother and I survived to tell his shocking story. My goal has been to remind the victim's families and educate millions of people of what he has done. This will furthermore help to keep Kearney behind bars where he forever belongs, until the day he dies.

Instead of using his time behind bars to show remorse for the victims he murdered or their families, Kearney wastes his time ridiculing and fanaticizing about his world within his cell, comparing prisons to large ships on the ocean. Before we conclude and close the cover of this book, there are several unanswered questions to address. Patrick Kearney and David Hill are perhaps the only ones, who answer many of these questions, but since they have continued to remain quiescent on the subject, we will attempt to answer these questions based of the evidence provided.

Without trying to sound overly presumptuous, let's begin with Kearney's admitted homosexual lover, and murder suspect David Hill. We do now have evidence that strongly suggests Hill may have also been guilty of first-degree murder by association, or perhaps even directly involved. Please keep in mind that Hill was never actually convicted of murder, but was a suspect on these charges, until freed. Regardless, Hill was not completely innocent upon his release. He was guilty of having sexual relationships with minor boys. Also, he did flee California with Kearney with plans of escaping to Canada. The first question of great importance is why did David Hill go free when he had guilt written all over his face? If Hill wasn't guilty, then why didn't he contact the police the moment he learned about Kearney's deadly activities? This is a logical question. Was he possibly protecting Kearney or was it the other way around? Was Kearney preparing Hill for questioning by police, so they could get their stories straight? Under legal law, fleeing with a criminal is called referred to as *harboring a felon*, which is punishable by imprisonment. Kearney later told police that when he fled California with Hill, they were not yet considered as suspects. This statement was actually not true, the two were suspects and this is precisely why Riverside detectives were taking several samples from their residence.

    Upon release of Hill, both Riverside and the Los Angeles Police Departments stated, "We don't have enough evidence for an indictment." Not enough evidence for an indictment? What about an indictment on charges of "Harboring a felon" or "Accessory to murder?" There were several reasons to hold Hill on suspicion. Hill even refused to take a polygraph examination to prove he was not guilty. Hill was diagnosed with an undetermined personality disorder. A condition that was severe enough to get him discharged from the army. The military didn't easily grant discharges to everyone that claims they had a problem, especially in the nineteen sixties. Was Hill's personality disorder severe enough to meet the criteria as a murderer? Most serial killers do have some type of psychiatric personality disorder. Hill fits this description and was around murders daily for fifteen years.

    A normal person usually doesn't kill another human being, but Kearney and Hill were far from normal. Finally, we do have new evidence that includes testimonies from eyewitness that proves both Kearney and Hill were involved. Both men were present and chased Ron Stewart, on at least two occasions in a pickup truck. There had to be a motive behind this type of action, and it proves that Hill was most definitely involved. Stewart collected coke bottles from Hill and Kearney, and he knew exactly what they looked like, there was no mistake. They were both involved. So why did Hill walk away a free man without being charged? Over the years, I tried to forget about Kearney and Hill, but after deciding to write my autobiography, their names came up again. I decided to take it a step further. Since, I knew that murder never expired, I thought the police would like to know about Hill's involvement. I would later find out that I was not the only one who believed Hill was involved in the murders, but I soon learned this was a door, that no one wanted to open.

    In 2009, I personally contacted the main detectives directly involved in the case to let them know about Hill's involvement, and was only told to leave a message with homicide. So I called and was connected to voice mail. I left essential messages of vital importance, stating that I had new evidence to offer that may implicate Hill in the trash bag murder case. No one returned my calls. Without any luck by telephone I googled the Riverside County Sheriff's Department web pages and contacted Lieutenant John Ruffcorn via email. I told Ruffcorn that it was important I contact lead Detective Al Sett of the Patrick Kearney case and asked if he knew how I might reach him? Ruffcorn was kind enough to reply to my email, but he wasn't much help.

    He replied, "Good Morning. This is Lieutenant John Ruffcorn of Riverside County Sheriff's Department, Technical Services Bureau. I checked with several people within the department and I could not locate anyone who knows how to contact Detective Al Sett.

Thank you for using our website." I sent him another email requesting any information available on the trash bag murderer case, which had been closed for over 30 years.

He referred me to the *Information Services Bureau and* said they will be able to tell you more about what information we can or cannot provide you. Next, I emailed Ruffcorn again and said, "I also need to reach Detective's Louis Danoff, Roger Wilson, and John St. John, because they were also involved in the Kearney case. It is very important that I reach them. My brother and I, were nearly victims of Kearney and Hill, and I have some new information of interest."

After I mentioned I had new evidence regarding the case, Lieutenant John Ruffcorn never sent me another reply. I was not giving up that easily. I followed up by contacting *Information Services Bureau* that Ruffcorn had referred me too, but they were not too eager help either. I wondered why the Riverside Police Department and the Los Angeles Police Department were being so secretive. I asked myself, what did they have to hide? It would surely be bad public relations, if proven that the case was handled inappropriately and unprofessionally. This would be a great embarrassment to the force. The department could even be held liable, if Hill would have killed anyone after his release. As far as they were concerned, the case was closed and that is how they wanted it to remain. Perhaps the answer was because it could come out that these police departments might have released a guilty man involved in dozens of murders. Without the help of police, I realized I was on my own. The fact is that murder cases never expire, and you can be charged many years after the murder took place. With today's technology, bodies can be exhumed and with forensic DNA testing can prove whether Hill was guilty or not. The families and the public have the right to find out, if there was any foul play going on here. I was not out to tarnish the reputation of the police, but to find the truth. I praise these departments for solving this case that stopped the murders from continuing, which saved scores of lives.

The police were honored for such an incredible heroic feat, but I feel we still need to open the case and investigate Mr. Hill to get answers to vital questions. Why did he and Kearney chase my brother? Why did he flee to Mexico with Kearney, if he were innocent? And on what grounds did police release Hill? Was it really due to lack of evidence? If so, what "Lack of evidence" are they referring too? Was it the fact that Kearney, "a confessed killer, said Hill wasn't guilty of murder? That is not a fact; this is hearsay of a killer who was trying to protect his homosexual lover. This is not justified, nor does it validate or substantiate the fact that Hill was innocent. They had plenty to hold him on while the investigation continued. There is something surreptitious about this case, and the fact that Kearney was hushed off to jail without a trial, under a shroud of confidentiality.

Today, he is basically a forgotten serial killer and that's how he wants it to remain. I can't stress the fact enough that he wants people to forget, so he can be paroled someday. Other questions of crucial importance are the matter of opinion that Patrick Kearney's victims didn't suffer during their untimely deaths? Kearney stated under oath that he shot his victims in the head and it was a painless death, quick and instantaneously. Let us pray that he was telling the truth. It is not my intention to insert further pain to the victim's families that continue to suffer, but it is significant to show the heartless cowardly monster that Kearney was. The truth is that most victims rarely die immediately after being shot in the head by a .22 cal. For example, let's look at Senator Robert F. Kennedy, who was shot in the head by Sirhan Sirhan with an Iver Johnson .22-caliber pistol. He survived for twenty-six hours, before dying.

In 1980, an intoxicated and depressed male nicknamed Crazy Joe decided to kill himself over an argument with his girlfriend. Without hesitation, he placed a five shot .22 caliber handgun between his eyes "Point blank" and pulled the trigger. The bullet entered his brain and surprisingly didn't even knock him out; he remained conscience, while he was rushed to the hospital. He later said that he had bled a lot during the incident, and it hurt like hell, but he survived.

Today, the bullet is still lodged in his brain but the seizures he has had for years afterwards, have finally stopped. He is alive and doing well. Another woman was shot between the eyes by a .22 caliber handgun, while leaning down to change a target practice board for her husband. She recalled hearing her husband call out, "Oh dear" and as she looked up the bullet went down between her eyes and she spit it out her mouth. She blacked out, but survived, and her husband was hauled off to jail to face attempted murder charges.

So, it is very possible to survive such an incident. If you recall, Kearney shot his first victim George between the eyes. And I'm willing to bet that George didn't die instantaneously either. I'm sure Kearney remembers this painful death, but he had no remorse for George or anyone else for that matter. Kearney stated that some of his victims were shot several times, because they were suffering and would not die. We pray they blacked out and died quickly before Kearney experimented on them, but this is probably not the case. He was a cold-hearted ruthless killer that was fascinated by murder.

From the evidence presented, Kearney had stated he usually shot his victims in the head from behind and dragged the bodies off to the bathtub to drain the blood, where the victims suffered and died helplessly. Most of the victims were sexually assaulted and beaten, while they were dying. Then, Kearney began sawing off limbs, while victims may have even still been alive. It is a horrible thought, but almost undoubtedly true.

Kearney was sentenced on twenty-one accounts of murder, even though he admitted to killing thirty-two people. Plus, there were another thirteen murders that also carried his signature (M.O.), which would have bought the number to quivering forty-three victims. This number seems to be closer to Kearney's confession, not included other victims from Mexico, Arizona and Texas. Kearney is one of the deadliest serial killers alive today that beat the death penalty. He liked leaving his victims where animals could quickly devour the evidence. Where did he get this idea? It just so happens that his prior residence was Texas and Mexico, and both include a lot of desert landscapes where you could easily ditch bodies. If we search the unsolved murders of the late early 1960's when Kearney was present in the area, there may have been several more victims that remain on the missing persons list. We need to check the similarities in Texas to Kearney's victims and perhaps clear up some more unsolved murders.

Kearney knew that Texas and Mexico carried the death penalty, so he cleverly played the nice guy, admitting to deaths in California to avoid these other states. Then he plea-bargained and agreed to help detectives for a guarantee that he would receive life instead of death for his crimes. We need to educate people so multi-murderers like Patrick Wayne Kearney never gets out of jail or sees the light of day again. In November of 1981, in a handwritten petition Kearney wrote, "I didn't kill anybody. That's all I'll say at the moment."

Following this statement, he asked to be released from prison, claiming he did not commit the gruesome murders he was convicted of, and that his attorney that poorly advised him. Kearney added, "The person in custody pleaded guilty to felonies, which he did not commit. The pleas were given due to threats and other forms of duress." According to lead Detective Roger Wilson, he said this was a personal message directed at him and his partner Al Sett to let them know he is still alive and well. Wilson and Sett had befriended Kearney just to get information out of him. They made Kearney feel like he was part of the team during the investigation, and the killer played along.

This book has been a long road, reviewing a trail of documents and interviews with several people, including the relatives of victims, FBI, several police departments, and homicide detectives involved in the case. These long hours of reviewing hundreds of files have revealed quite a few unknown and startling unpublished facts.

Evidence presented in this book has been thoroughly researched, but many of the aged files were saved on the old Xerox copiers. This was the only method used to copy and duplicate important documents in the 1960's and 70's. The only problem was that over the years the ink tends to saturate, and files are barely allegeable to read. Today police agencies utilize high tech equipment and computer technology to copy and store files on microfilm. The old Xerox copies were similar to duplicate checks, and receipts books that are still employed today. Even though Kearney was only charged and sentenced for 21 murders, Imperial County Sheriff Detectives said Kearney and David Hill were accused of several other crimes that were never thoroughly investigated.

Oddly, when you search the *Riverside Sheriff's Information Center* for information on Kearney, it comes up showing no results found. It's like the killer never existed. Even though Kearney went to jail, it doesn't change the fact that he got away with murder. Victims are dead and the relatives are still suffering, while the killer sits in his jail cell every day, relaxing with no remorse ever documented on record. David Hill has never come forth to offer sympathy to the families of victims either.

In front of homicide detectives reviewing the case, Kearney refused to talk about his family religion, saying it make him too emotional, but no sympathy ever comes to those who destroys the lives of others for their own satisfaction. It doesn't matter what rational motivation Kearney believes he has given for his murderous deeds; there is no justification or argument that makes murder acceptable. Kearney began to lose his mind at age eight and continued until he committed several senseless murders and needed to be locked up forever. He is now living in a cage just like the animal he had become. It often angers me when I read articles about Kearney, and his victims are rarely even mentioned.

These victims lost their lives due to the violent acts of this perverted necrophilia killer, also known as thanatophilla and necrolagnia for their attraction to corpses. These people seek comfort or overflowing feelings of isolation and self-esteem by expressing power over homicide victims. So often, killers are the ones who are long remembered, while the victims are forever forgotten. Sadly, unless the victims happened to be a celebrity or someone famous, they became ancient history, to everyone except family and friends. The friends and relatives of the victims have all suffered tremendously in this case. Regardless, Kearney genuinely enjoyed blasting bullets into the brains of his victims, as much as the anal sex, experiments and mutilations he performed on them. He was one sickly insane individual. It takes a certain kind of person to kill like Kearney did. Just because he knew the difference between right and wrong, this alone doesn't make him sane. He knew it was immoral, but he still killed. Murderers always believe they have good motives for what they did, which gives them reason to continue.

The law says that if a criminal knows the difference in right or wrong, they are legally sane. Even though Kearney confessed to a string of cold-blooded murders, even his own psychiatrist, and the courts declared him sane. The law states that if a criminal knows the difference between right and wrong, he is declared sane. What kind of insane law is this? There were over twenty-one confirmed murdered victims, and as many as forty-three. Does this sound like a sane person? A sane person does not go around killing and butchering people. Perhaps, it is the Justice Department that is insane. After all, it was the Justice Department that sentenced Patrick Kearney to life with the possibility of parole.

Parole? ...really? Where's the logic here? Parole should have never even been an option. He was a cold-blooded mass murderer who killed, raped, beat and butchered his victims. The only thing he deserved was the death penalty. This is an insult to relatives of victims. When Kearney turned himself in, the death penalty wasn't active, but one-month later executions became legal in California. Bodies were still being discovered well into August, and with capital punishment reinstated, Kearney was not only a prime candidate for the death penalty, but he also deserved to be executed. So why do criminals like Kearney slip through the net? Many California serial killers who receive death penalty like the Night Stalker, the Hillside Strangler and many others have never been executed, because of the state's unlimited appeals process. Kearney always felt responsible that the Hillside Stranglers killed, only after reading about his murders. Why are convicted killers allowed to continue these relentless appeals to avoid paying the penalty in which they were charged? California's legal authorizes response to these appeals process is that they want to make sure there is no room for errors, so they allow appeals to continue. Most of us don't believe in taking a life, but these killers were sentenced to death for a good reason. They were killing children and would do it again if they could have a second chance.

The scales of justice seem to be unbalanced. Many murderers who have been sentenced to death are executed, while others who have killed either celebrities or large numbers of people are spared the death penalty. We need to ask if this is fair justice? If you kill John Lennon, John F. Kennedy or Sharon Tate, your life is spared. Why are plea bargains legal? I give you something -- you give me something. There should be no deals for murderers. Serial killer Ted Bundy was sentenced to death. He tried to make a deal with authorities and tell where bodies of victims were located, but Florida state said, "No deal"...he was electrocuted three days later.

Today, while the confessed Trash Bag murderer ages in his jail cell, he most certainly enjoys his fond memories of the victims he tortured and killed. Thirty years later, cowardly, he still refuses to look the families in the eye. At the time of his arrest, Kearney talked about his murders as easy as cool water flowing through a mountain spring of Colorado. This is the only time he has ever talked about the murders. Kearney said he never planned his murders, stating that these killings were last minute decisions. This was one of many lies that Kearney hand fed to detectives and the courts, which not only swallowed it, but also digested it as the truth. The truth is that Kearney went on the prowl and searched for victims to deliberately kill. Kearney picked up hitchhikers that he genuinely intended to bring to his home, sexually molest their corpses and then carve up like a Thanksgiving turkey. These are crimes called kidnapping and pre-meditated coldblooded murder in any law book in the state of California.

When the death penalty was reinstated, pre-meditated cold-blooded murder was listed as a capital offence with death as the punishment. Kearney played cards with the prosecutor and had the winning hand that helped him escape the death penalty. The Justice Department and the prosecutor should have made a special exception in this case. Patrick Kearney most certainly qualified after boldly stating he killed over 40 victims, many of which have never been recovered. Kearney answered, "Morbid curiosity and sexual gratification" "Why did he carelessly kill these innocent people?" There were several reasons that he claimed was the reason he did it, such as anger, rage, fright, curiosity, sex and perverted fantasies. Kearney left behind many unhealed scars on thousands of people. He did not get the death penalty, but he did get life in prison, which can often be worse than death. Over the years Kearney has sworn off his parole hearings, because he doesn't want to face relatives of victims. Another reason is because he is afraid that people in prison will find out that he sodomized and dismembered corpses, and then dumped their remains in trash bags on the side of highways like common garbage. Many serial killers like John Wayne Gacy, Ted Bundy, and several others that were executed for their murderous crimes, yet Kearney victims were just play things to him, they were not even human beings. On May 27, 1921, in California, USA. Chessman was executed on May 2, 1960, in the gas chamber. He was another criminal idolized by Patrick Kearney. Staff writer from the Daily Breeze newspaper reported, "The last thing any killer wants is for the yard to hear, he was a child molester," which would an automatic death sentence in prison among inmates. This statement stands true even today.

While housed in Corcoran State Prison, Kearney's neighbors included Charles Manson, Sirhan Sirhan, and serial killer Juan Corona. Patrick Wayne Kearney became just inmate number B-88913. It is in prison where he continues his studies on Japanese/Chinese philosophy and reflects his personal views on the interior architectural and design of prison cells, including the distinct atmosphere of his environment. In an attempt to add elegance to the structures of his habitat, he wrote his own variation of the dark side, criticizing prison furniture as *"Classical dungeon;"* adding comparisons with elements from the early *torture chambers* and *plumbing fixtures* that are painstakingly copied from provincial morgue decorative motifs. This guy remains trapped in his own devilish world. Although, he is not allowed contact with the outside world, some of his writing and drawing have managed to slip onto the Internet.

WRITINGS OF A SERIAL KILLER

Interior Decorator

<Sic>Before we examine the finer points of the inner ambience, I first need to remind you that, in the aesthetic content, these buildings must respond to their own inner, formal determinants, both cultural and functional, and can effectively ignore the regional setting; although, the choice is optional.

While stylistic features of interior decoration may vary considerably, and the programmatic organization logically contains reinterprets, and accommodates features of the traditional with that of the site, four basic themes prevail:

The walls are cleverly colored with decorative motifs, which attempt to imitate the best features of contemporary freeway underpass.

The furniture is provided in matching sets, which can best be described as Classical Dungeon, borrowing select elements from the early torture chambers of the Inquisition.

The plumbing fixtures are painstakingly copied from provincial morgue decorative motifs and are located conveniently close to the head of the beds.
And, the doors are rough replicas of the best traditions of Early Roman Zoo<End Sic>.

Prison Design

<sic>"Purpose-built structures like prisons generally lack the qualities of refined aesthetics and creative use of materials of traditional architecture and may confront an alien environment that has its own deeply imbedded historical and visual vocabulary resulting from both cultural & functional paradigms. Revivalist, Historicist, or any design based solely on traditional principles, will retard creativity. The romanticism of prison architecture is imbued at San Quentin where the earliest and architecturally most significant building clearly reflects the need for historical belonging. Other traditional designs, borrowing select elements from traditional and Post-Modern architecture are often architecturally nondescript with no architectural elements added to the generally crude aesthetics or the barn-type form as either decorative motifs, as direct visual iconic references to their intended purpose, or as unambiguous statements of their correctional character. Some have attempted reinterpretation of the traditional with mixed results;

however, it can be argued that the idea(s) of self-help construction and emphasis on appropriate technology may eventually work, and that the adoption of abstract geometry in the buildings can be seen as a search for individual architectural solutions.

Prison architecture should be expressive and understandable to all and should employ a form language, which invokes in prisoners a sense of belonging to the present and the hope of the future. Here, we have a design approach that is entirely innovative & functional while remaining environmental, morphological, and semiotic in a tripartite operational principle of modern conceptual design techniques, rather than a straight, literal transplantation of traditional character. Besides the obvious disregard for the existing built environment, and without capturing the essential symbols of the Valley architecture, it is a pseudotraditonal design with mixed products of uneven quality. The distorted expressions of prison buildings, the lack of garish colors & the use of prefabricated industrial materials only deny the heritage and the authenticity which old monuments like San Quentin embodied and which inspired to imitate medieval classics such as the Bastille, the Chateau d'if, or Reading Gaol...in which only the image of the monuments sought was important in reference to available visual sources. In his departure from this style, the architect here was seeking an affinity through the reinterpretation of certain arcane features borrowed from prisoner-of-war (P.O.W.) camps and through the expression of some esoteric and anachronistic features common to Gothic military fortifications. This is appropriate and historically contextual and is considered an improvement rather than a distraction. While the architect can be cited as disregarding the spirit--if not the letter--of Post-Modern American architectural vocabulary, he has reinterpreted that vocabulary into an everyday language which can be more easily fathomed...with literal readings of original thought. Clearly, this project shies away from addressing the conflicts and diversions of modern life and is a decisive departure from both the approaches of transplanted traditional architecture and its modern reinterpretation. The artist was not encumbered by conflicting perceptions of what a prison should look like nor by the difficult quest of expressing identity through form (without resorting to traditional imagery) -- which does not appeal to modern design sensibilities--and without recognizing the existence of past, local, building traditions. These simple, elegant buildings are functional and completely at home in their environment without being a landmark like their counterparts in scale." <End Sic>

While in prison Kearney has taken up Japanese/Chinese philosophy and interior design of prison cells, attempting to add elegance to the structures.

<Sic>"The distorted expressions of prison buildings, the lack of garish colors & the use of prefabricated industrial materials only deny the heritage and the authenticity which old monuments like San Quentin embodied and which inspired to imitate medieval classics such as the Bastille.

The effect goes deeper than subtle references through geometry or the obvious use of architectural icons and calligraphy. With all the grace and elegance of the Berlin Wall, the use of concrete construction further reinforces the expressive values of the design while providing climatically, thoroughly sound buildings without being encumbered with historical precedents. Of special interest to architects in pursuit of the silent eloquence of space and the quintessential presence of form, the innovative and unprecedented solid walls of the exterior give little clue as to what is inside, and narrow, vertically-slit, widely spaced windows--like gun ports of olden times--add to the buildings sense of impenetrability, reflects the designer's fascination with the mystical interpretation of prison architecture, highlights the relationship between architectural production and the cultural politics of identity, and illustrates the search for image with which most inmates, as well as the larger society, can be happy." <End Sic>

Ichi-Ban

<Sic>"Perhaps you have learned to count to ten in Japanese: Ichi (1), Nt (2), San(3), Shi(4), Go(5), Roku(6), ..., Ku (9), Ju(10), etc?
Actually, these numbers were borrowed from the Chinese. Japanese has its own, native numbers as well, but they are seldom used.
Along with the Chinese numbers, Japanese also borrowed a Chinese custom that seems strange to us, but is common to several oriental languages; that is, they seldom use numbers by themselves (as we do). Instead, they almost always add a suffix. There are about 250 of these endings. They are short, (just about 3 letters), and each one describes the class or general characteristic of the objects being counted, e.g., round, flat, thin, etc. If you say that you have 3 pencils, you'll add a suffix which means: "round, cylindrical object(s)." And, if you brag that you have 6 sons, you'll add 3 letters which mean:
"offspring."
They tend to use these number-and-suffix combinations as either a noun or a pronoun, but in places where we'd us a number as an adjective. For example, we'd say: " I have six sons." However, they'd likely say: "I have sons; there are six," except that they'd have to attach the suffix to the "six" that means: "offspring," and the result would tend to sound
(to us) like: "I have sons; six-offspring are they."
"Nisei" is in the English dictionary and is used to mean: "second-generation" Japanese (who were born over here). Obviously, "sei" is simply the suffix which means:
"generation." Thus, "sansei" would, of course, be the term for: "third" generation. "Ban" is the suffix to indicate the number of an object (in an order). For example, player number three (#3) on the team would be: "sanban," and item-number five (#5) on the menu would be: "goban." And, "ichi-ban" means: "number one."
"Number one," in English, can be used to mean: "first choice," figuratively as well as literally. That is, it can mean that something is the "best" (or the very best), "excellent," or even "super," i.e., it is "first class." The same is true in Japanese.
The term: "ichi-ban" was often picked-up by US servicemen stationed in Japan after WWII, and it is also starting to be seen increasingly more often (in print, etc.) in this country in recent times. It is a term that has become very useful to know.
The Japanese also have some interesting two-number combinations, which are often used to make coded (or circumspect) references to things. For example, "ichi-roku" (one-six) refers to a pawnshop, and "ku-ichi" (nine-one) is usually used to refer to a Jewish person, because: nine plus one is ten (9+1=10), and ten (10) is "ju" in Japanese.
Each language has its own ONOMATOPOEIA, i.e., words which are used to represent various types of sounds, such as: Buzz, Bang, Bark, Bow-wow, Meow, Click, Snap, Pop, Knock, Hiss, etc. For example, the onomatopoetic terms (in English) for the sounds that birds make are: Cheep, chirp, peep, tweet, etc. We might write: "cheep, cheep." However, in

Spanish they'd say:"pio, pio." And, where we'd say: "knock, knock," they'd write: "tun, tun."

For one of the sounds that a train makes, we learned to say: "clickety-clack, clicketyclack." However, in Japan they would say: "doe-des-ka-den, doe-des-ka-den, etc." i.e., "Where's it going? Where's it going? etc." <End Sic>

Ships At Sea

<Sic>"Some very famous writers from the past have tried to draw parallels between life in prison and life aboard ship, especially the old sailing ships of 80 to 200 years ago. They would often quote old seafaring stories like "Moby Dick." One comparison was, of course, that ships at sea, like prisons, were usually almost all-male environments. Nowadays, however, there may be more women aboard Navy ships and others too.

You could also say that both places (ships & prisons) are, effectively, separate and isolated worlds unto themselves. A big ship, especially an aircraft carrier, is like a city. There are thousands of men on board--as there are in many prisons--and each will have its own bakery, fire-department, barbershop, clothing-store, shopping-center (exchange), canteen, hospital, chapels, library, post-office, laundry, jail (brig), and so on. A prison does too. A carrier even has its own airport! Prisons and smaller ships often have heliports. There are also some similarities in the rules and the discipline. In fact, the job of a prison guard is effectively a para-military one. In both places, the rules must be enforced, and discipline maintained--even if it takes force to do so." <End Sic>

There is a lot of information on the Internet about serial killer Patrick Kearney, but many of the sites are poorly researched and unreliable sources. In lieu of Kearney's "Superior I.Q.," his intellect did not transmit the essential aptitude and ethical conduct needed to evade his senseless homicidal desires that eventually deposited him behind bars for life. Today, when I'm driving down the highways and I see trash bags on the side of the road, I can't help but to think about Serial Killer Patrick Kearney, and the faces of the innocent victims who died senselessly. Kearney has left behind intense eternal scars within me, as he did to all the families of victims. This type of loss never goes away. As previously mentioned, Kearney turned himself in one month before the death penalty was reinstated. He rushed to cooperate with detectives and show them where some of the victim's bodies were dumped. Kearney did not even receive a trial; he was quickly sentenced to 21 life sentences. Fearing for his life, he wanted everything out of the way before the death penalty was reinstated to escape capital punishment, and he succeeded.

Patrick Kearney did live in several other states, and even traveled out of the country into Mexico. In all probability, Kearney may have violated federal laws by committing several murders occurred in these areas. Kearney had dreamed of killing since he was eight years old, and he simply turned his dreams into a reality, that made him one of the worst killers of all time. The killer committed an "Integrity violation" by first gaining the faith of each victim with deceiving promises, and then luring them into shallow graves.

Most of Kearney's victims trusted him, but this trust only led to their demise. The killer came across as a concerned sympathetic person who was eager to help. Armed with a kindness and compassion, he befriended his young victims to the vicious drum roll of murder. The end result left behind over three-dozen nude mutilated bodies lying on the side of the major highways wrapped in heavy duty "Trash bags." Kearney stole the dignity, immortality and existence of each victim.

Kearney's violent instantaneous reaction to killing resulted from his strong desire for sexual gratitude. This desire was so great that his climax was worth more than a human life. In his twisted perverted mind, People became his personal experimental projects, and later his disposable sex toys. This demented romance with death would founder in the late nineteen seventies, eventually resulting in the killers surrender.

KILLER ESCAPES THE DEATH PENALTY

The death penalty was conveniently reinstated in August of 1977, exactly one month after Patrick Kearney surrendered. This saved his life.

Patrick Kearney had told officers that he was once married, but there are no public marriage records in California, Nevada or Texas.

George Kearney, (Patrick Kearney's father) the former L.A.P.D. officer died *on Saturday, December 31, 1994 in Texas.*

Kearney's mother, Eunice, might still be living, although she sold her home in Barstow, California in 1996. Her last known address was in Pennsylvania.
There is some controversy about David Douglas Hill being alive and well. Sources say that he lives under the radar of secrecy. Hill's last known residence was in Lubbock, Texas. Records indicate that he does not have a driver's license, nor he does not own a car.
Hill is not registered voter and has not served any time in Texas institutions in his town. He is not a registered sex offender either.

Since his days with Kearney, David Hill maintains a low profile. His wife and daughter still live in Lubbock, Texas where some sources say he maintains contact with them. There is also several online sites, including one site that mentions that David Hill played himself in an episode of "History's Mysteries: Infamous Murders" for the History Channel in 2001. However, according to Pat Pfremmer and the Texas Death Index, David Hill is listed as deceased on April 10, 1991, at age 49, which I believe to be correct. This footage of Hill on History Channel had been taken years prior.
According to his niece, after Kearney, Hill had returned to Lubbock, Texas where he went to school, and became a nurse. This was his occupation, until he passed away in 1991 from lung cancer. He is buried in Lubbock, Texas.

When asked what kind of punishment Homicide Detective Roger Wilson would recommend for killer Kearney, the detective replied:

"First, I'd remove his arm, sew it back on, and let it heal. Cut off a leg, sew it back on, and let it heal. Cut off another arm and let him heal. Then cut off another leg and let him heal, and then I'd let him soak in his own fluids."

Kearney was up for parole on Oct 30, 1996 but was denied. Five years later, his next hearing was set for 2001, also denied parole. He had another hearing February 2007, which was denied.

His next hearing was in 2012, which was also denied. Kearney has vowed not to show up at hearings, as long as any victims of relatives are present, because he is afraid to face them. Kearney's hearings are automatically denied if he refuses to appear. However, one day he could emerge from prison as free man, if relatives cease to materialize. As of 2012, Kearney still has no remorse for his actions. He has never publicly apologized for all the pain and suffering, he has caused the families of victims. Through God's eyes, we are taught to be forgiving, and not hateful, but when it comes to Patrick Kearney, I believe we can make an exception. He was as evil has a man can be, and personally, I will never exonerate this monster.

Today, every time I see trash bags on the side of the road, I think of the victims that Kearney tossed like common garbage. The killer left permanent scars, and tears have flooded the lives of hundreds, if not thousands, of innocent people who are also his victims.

In conclusion, we need to continue to send our prayers out to relatives of victims. Also, please continue to send your prayers out to my brother, Ron Stewart, who has won his battle with cancer and is now in remission. He was nearly a victim of this mad killer, but instead, he became one of the only two survivors of Patrick Kearney and David Hill. Our prayers are with you!

NOTE: 2011

I recently learned that serial killer Patrick Kearney is not happy with this book. This is excellent news. Perhaps, he has finally heard the victims speak from their own personal memoirs.
The killer has never appeared at any of his hearings, so that he would not have to face the relatives of victims and listen to their words of grief. This book is has given the relatives a chance to finally speak out and be heard by Kearney.

SUMMARY OF EVENTS

Note: Some of the dates may not appear in chronological order, due to dates victims disappeared and when they were found. Many of these reports vary in official police reports.

* 1952 - (L.A.P.D.) Los Angeles police officer and father George Kearney purchases a .22 caliber gun for his thirteen-year-old son Patrick Kearney and teaches him to kill pigs by shooting them behind the left ear; a method he explained that causes very little bleeding, and is very effective. 'Killer Kearney' later uses this method on human beings in one of the bloodiest slaughters in U.S. history.

* 1962 - Patrick Kearney brutally murders and sexually assaults the corpses of three Long Beach men, two brothers, listed as -- Mike and John Doe, and a cousin named -- Bobby. Kearney lured each victim separately to a shallow grave in the secluded wooded regions of San Diego, California and several surrounding vicinities. Each victim found shot, beat and rhythmically raped.

* 12-1967 - a frustrated Kearney kills his roommate – known only as "George." Kearney shoots George directly between the eyes at point blank range with his .22 caliber derringer, and watches as he collapses. He drags George off to the bathroom to undress, rape, thoroughly clean and mutilate the corpse. Worried that the bullet in George's brain may be traced back to his gun; Kearney decides to retrieve the bullet from the victim's bloody skull. Armed with a hacksaw and he cuts into his victim's brain, making a hole large enough to place his hand inside the head, and searched, until he retrieved the bullet. Afterwards, he dismembered and skinned the corpse -- removing the inner the organs. Next, he cut off the arms, and rinsed each part, sending all the blood down the bathtub drain. He buries George between two garage structures, at the rear of his triplex residence.

* 2- 9-1973, Kearney's appetite to kill and rape the dead grew as he spotted thirteen-year old -- John E. Demchik of Inglewood, hitchhiking during the early evening hours of the night. Kearney pulled over to the curb and offered Demchik a ride. As Kearney drove off with Demchik, the two engaged in some friendly conversation, until Kearney changed the tone and pulled out a .22 caliber handgun from his pocket, shooting Demchik in the head. Kearney quickly tossed a jacket around Demchik's head to catch the gushing streams of blood. Then Kearney drove down Highway 8 until he reached a quiet secluded area, located fifteen miles southeast of Calexico, California. The body was discovered five months later by a hiker who exploring the region. Forensics soon discovered that Demchik had a small hole behind his left ear, but this wasn't much left to work with. The victim had been inhumanly mutilated and left for the coyotes and buzzards could feast on. The body was so unrecognizable that police were unaware that they are dealing with a murder victim.

* 8-24-1974 - Ronald Dean Smith 5, of Lennox, California was last seen playing outside his house on Saturday. He was living with his mother, but on this day his kind grandmother that had given him permission to walk alone to Lennox Park, just a few blocks away. Kearney found Smith walking along the sidewalk and asked him if he wanted a ride. With a gigantic smile on his face, Smith tells the stranger, "I'm just going to the park." Kearney kills him and dumps the body. Saturday, October 12, 1974, forty-nine days after Kearney kidnapped the child, Smith's decomposed body was found in Riverside County, dumped like garbage on the side of the highway. It was just six day's short of Smith's sixth birthday, but he would never see it. Smith's decomposed face still had abrasions on the nose and chin, and confusions on his lips from Kearney's fingernails and pressure from the force applied from his palm.

* April 13, 1975 Albert Rivera age 21 of Los Angeles was hitch hiking to San Diego when Kearney picked him up in his Volkswagen (V.W. Bug). He turned on the heater and waited for Rivera to fall asleep, then shot him in the head. Kearney drove back to his Redondo residence to have his way with Rivera. The killer went inside his house to make sure David Hill wasn't home yet, leaving Rivera in the V.W. Next, he backed his car up to the front door, and dragged Rivera's body into the bathtub. Once in the bathroom, Kearney pulled public hairs from Rivera's genitals and then engaged in sexual recreation until the victim's rectum began bleeding. Kearney quickly stuffed the rectum with paper towels to prevent blood from getting on the floor. Next Kearney grabbed his hacksaw and Exacto type knife and began to mutilate the body.

* 11-10-75 - Larry Gene Walters 20, was hitchhiking on Manhattan Beach Blvd., when a stranger in a pickup truck pulls over and offers him a ride. Inside the truck is a stranger with a smile on his face. He asks, "Where are you going too?" Larry Walters replied, "I'm going to Redondo Beach to a friend's house." Walters forever disappeared, never to be heard from again. Kearney shot him in the head at his residence in Redondo Beach, and performed anal sex on his dead or dying body. At the conclusion of his climax, Kearney began dismembering Walters with a hacksaw and a razor knife. First, he cut off both feet, one at a time, rinsing each piece thoroughly of blood. Then he began cutting off the hands, and the head, placing each separate piece into a trash bag. In the next few days, he dumped head at Burger King. The hands and feet were dumped in the trashcans at Wenchell's donut shop, McDonald's, Burger King and several other fast food places. The corpse was dumped at the Palos Verde's landfill. None of Walters' body parts have ever been recovered.

* Fall 1976 - Robert "Billy" Benniefiel, 17, a student attending Aviation High School in Redondo Beach, he completely disappears after venturing off alone on a bike ride to the beach. He is last seen in Hermosa Beach near Pier Avenue, close to Aviation Boulevard, and Pacific Coast Highway, when he gets a flat tire. After chaining his bike to a street sign, he began walking, until offered a ride by Kearney. Shortly afterwards, he was executed and sodomised by Kearney. Billy's body was dumped in the Palos Verdes land field, never to be recovered.

* 3-1-1976 - Kenneth E. Buchanan, 17, of Redondo Beach is reported missing by his family. His nude body is found a month later on Wednesday, April 7, 1976. His badly decomposed body was found sixteen miles east of Hwy 98. Forensic experts determine that Buchanan was shot four times in head and viciously raped, while blood discharged from his body.

* 4-18-1976 - After a busy day at school, eight-year-old Merle Hondo Chance of Venice Beach is out riding his bicycle, when suddenly the chain brakes. Frustrated, he begins to cry out for help as he pushed the bicycle in the direction of his house. As he approaches a stop sign, Kearney drives up and notices Chance crying, and watches while he struggles to push the bike. A generous Kearney offers to drive the child to the bike shop to get it fixed, and Chance agrees. Kearney befriends the child and asks if he has ever been to Disneyland, and the boy replies, "no." Kearney promises that he will take him to the magic kingdom sometime, and the boy gets very excited. He tells Kearney that he can't wait to get home so he can tell his mother about the nice stranger that promised to take me to Disneyland. Unexpectedly, Kearney begins to panic at the thought of the boy telling his mother about the nice stranger and wraps a sweater around his head. He slides his hand up underneath the child's sweater and squeezes his nose real tight, with his hand covering the mouth, smothering him to death as the youngster fails to resist Kearney's deadly grip.

* 4-18-1976 - Larry Armendariz 15, is listed as missing by relatives. Armendariz was hitchhiking when he is picked up by Kearney. Soon afterwards, he is shot n the head, sexually assaulted, and dismembered according to a confession by killer Patrick Kearney, in his own words. His body is dumped at the Palos Verdes Landfill and never recovered. For years, his family prays he still alive, until Kearney admitted to murdering him.

* 4-1976 - Wilford Lawrence Faherty, 20, of Redondo Beach becomes another murder victim of Kearney. His mutilated Corpse is found on Aug. 28, 1976, on Otay Lake s Road in Southeast San Diego County. If is estimated that he was shot to death and sexually assaulted sometime between April and August of 1976. Maggots the size of grains of rice had eaten away much of the internal organs and the presence of sexual activity.

* March 21, 1976 -Victim 11. Oliver Peter Molilor 13,
(Body recovered)- Oliver Peter Molitor 13, is confirmed dead (body found) He was reported missing on March 21, 1976. Molitor remains were recovered, but Kearney later confesses from his jail cell that he dumped the body in Manhattan Beach. On December 23, 1977, the police received a letter from Kearney stating that he had killed a boy whom he thought was went by the name Ben. The lad had an uncle that was a manager of the Hermosa Beach Cove Theater located at Pier Avenue High School. The best he could recall, "it was in the summer of 1976" that Kearney killed him and packaged Molitor in several trash bags.

* June 11, 1976, the police received an urgent phone call regarding the disappearance of a Redondo Beach teenager named Michael Craig McGhee Jr. It was a summer day with temperatures reaching 89 degrees in Los Angeles County. According to his sister Elizabeth, Michael was a rebellious teenager who had dropped out of school at age 12. He was in and out of trouble, and well known by local police for numerous crimes including car thief, sexual offences and burglary. According to detectives, McGhee was a small-time

petty criminal who just couldn't seem to stay out of trouble. The teen had met Patrick Kearney one day while hitchhiking while walking along Inglewood Avenue near Lennox blvd Kearney picked up McGhee and gave him a ride to Torrance. During the ride, Kearney invited McGhee to go to Lake Elsinore (Kearney's favorite dead body dumping sites) on a camping trip some time. McGhee said he couldn't go at this time, but he told Kearney to call him in about a week. The following week, Kearney tried to call, but there was no answer. Kearney then drove over to McGhee house, and knocked on the door. McGhee sister answered and told the stranger that her brother was on restriction and couldn't go anywhere. As Kearney drove away, Michael McGhee raced after him on foot. He was never seen again.

* 6-20-1976 - John Woods 23, is found shot to death with his throat cut in San Diego, California according to L.A.P.D. The evening prior to his death, Woods was out on the town drinking with friends in search of what was understood to be the "Party of the summer" affair, but police broke up the memorable event around midnight. Woods was last seen at 12:30 p.m., when he requested that his convoy of friends drop him off at a local bar on Artesta Boulevard in Redondo Beach. His lifeless body was found less than five hours later.

* 8-22-1976 - Larry Espy was first identified as John Doe when found. He was a white male from age of about 13 to 17 years old. He was hitchhiking in the south bay area heading for the beach when Kearney picked up and gave him a ride to his Robinson residence. Espy and Kearney talked for a while, and then while watching television, his life ended. Kearney walked up behind him and shot "Point blank" into the back of his head, like the rest of his victims. Then he dragged Espy off to the bathroom to Sodomized his body, before cutting him up with a hack saw. After he was sexual satisfied, it was time to
dispose of the body like a used throwaway condom. Kearney used dead bodies to reach his climax. He was slaughtered and cleaned Espy like a fresh animal going to market, and then he placed into the trash bags to dispose like the others.

* 9-24-1976 - Timothy B. Ingham, 19, is discovered a few miles south of Borregos Hot Springs and east of Highway 74, along Ortega Highway, and a quarter of a mile west of Borrego Springs in San Diego County. He had been shot once in the head and was lying in a wash. His body appears to be in an advanced state of decomposition. Police noted that he was found nude, and shot just above the left ear. The flesh shows signs that animals had been gnawing on his mutilated body. There were no efforts to hide his body. Due to the extreme purification and maggot activity, there was no evidence of semen in the body found by the coroner.

* 10- 6-1976 - Mark Andrew Orach 20, first noted as an unidentified victim -- known only as "John Doe" was found in the same area of Orange County, California. Or ach was a resident of Ottawa, Canada. He was found alongside Ortega highway on the same day he was fatally shot. The unidentified man was found in the same location, with the exception that he was murdered on Aug. 22, 1976 along the Ortega Highway between San Juan Capistrano and Lake Elsinore. Both were sexually assaulted

* 10-10-1976 - Randall Lawrence Moore, 16, of Phoenix, was found on Highway 80, east of El Cajon on the same day he was murdered. Moore was hitchhiking from Arizona to San Diego, California. He was just outside San Diego on Hwy (8) when Patrick Kearney picked him up. Moore was a street-smart teenager. He didn't trust Kearney, but he needed the ride. Kearney made a pass at Moore, and he pulled a knife on Kearney as a warning not to try anything. Kearney shot him soon afterwards. He beat and mutilating the body.

* Fall 1976 - David Allen, 27, a Camp Pendleton Marine, whose body was found on a remote road in the Fallbrook area, about two miles west of Interstate 15. He disappeared the previous day.

* 1-24-1977- Nick "Nicky" Hernandez – Jimenez, was described as a popular male prostitute of Redondo Beach. Nicky had sexually serviced Kearney and Hill on occasions and was well liked in the homosexual community. Kearney eventually grew tired of Nicky hanging around the house, and murdered him in cold blood, with two bullets to the back of the head. The first shot tore through the back of his head, but it failed to kill him. Kearney noticed Nicky suffering and fired again sending a bullet through side of his head, killing him. He was found wrapped in a micro-type trash bag. He was found on Monday, January 24, 1977, when a manual worker practically stumbled over two heavy duty commercial type plastic trash bag liners. The bags were found in the Lennox Boulevard tunnel, underneath the (405) San Diego Freeway underpass. Inside the trash bags was the corpse of 28-year-old Nicolas Hernandez-Jimenez of Los Angeles. Like his other victims, Kearney had mutilated the body and drained all the blood from the victim.   * 3-3-1977 - Arturo Marquez (24 years old of Oxnard, California), "Kearney had known Marquez for just one day. He met them both at the Midtown Spa in Hollywood and took them out to dinner. Later that night he took Arturo near San Bernardino and killed him.
He later confessed that Marquez bled a whole lot, all over his clothes. "I wrapped a jacket around his head to try to keep it clean" said Kearney. He dragged Marquez's body face down, 500 feet east of Sunset Avenue. There were bloodstains found at the scene where Kearney eviscerate Mr. Marquez, cutting him open and removing his entrails, intestines. He had been dragged on his stomach to the bushes; Kearney performed this maneuver by placing the feet tucked within the waistband of his pant, beneath his belt.

* 3-18-1977 - John Otis LaMay 17, of El Segundo, California. LaMay had called looking for David Hill, but Patrick Kearney answered the phone. Kearney said David Hill wasn't home, but would return shortly, and agreed to pick up LaMay. He bought him back to his residence on Robinson Street. Kearney walked up behind him, while he was sitting on the couch and shot him in the back of the head. LaMay collapsed fell over on the couch and unto to the floor. Blood poured slowly from his head as Kearney dragged him off the bathroom. There, Kearney bent his body over the bathtub, and anally raped the corpse.

LaMay's head has never been recovered.

Surrendering on July 1, 1977, Kearney confessed to kidnapping, murdering, beating, and sexually assaulting from 32, to astounding 43 victims, disposing the mutilated corpses in trash bags, like common garbage.

ABOUT THE AUTHOR

Tony Stewart was born in Bloomington, Indiana in June of 1957. At age four, he moved to Los Angeles, California with his father, Estill, and younger brother, Ron. In 1967, he was introduced Stewart to serial killer Patrick Kearney by a Real Estate agent named Reid Wilson. Stewart was offered a job doing yard work for Kearney, in which he accepted. Later, both Tony Stewart and his brother Ron would nearly become victims of this mad Killer, but both would survive to tell the true story. It was this ordeal that inspired Stewart to extensively research and write this story, *The Trash Bag Murderer.*

As a survivor, and nearly a victim of this killer, I have long harbored thoughts regarding the damage that Kearney conveyed on others. He did not have any honor or compassion for human life. He especially targeted the younger male population, because they were much weaker than him. One thing is certain; Kearney was and remains a coward. Today, over 40 years after the murders, I still carry a mental picture in my head of Patrick Kearney that I can't seem to forget. In July of 1989, twelve years after Kearney surrendered to the Riverside Sheriff's Department, my brother called me on the telephone and said, "Hey, I heard on the news that Patrick Kearney got out of jail." The comment made me nervous, but in unconvinced tone, I replied, "Kearney wouldn't get out of jail after only serving 12 years in prison. There's no way!" He added, "Well that's what they said on TV." I told him, I was about to take my 15-month old son, Keith, to Alonda Park, and had to go, but if he heard any more on the matter to call me. My former wife, Linda, and I, packed up and few things, and left for the park around noon. It was a beautiful sunny day with not a cloud in the sky. My son laughed as we both slid down the slide together.

I took him on the merry-go-round, and then Linda and I, took turns pushing him on the swing while the other one filmed with the video camera. I had drunk several cups of coffee earlier that day, and suddenly, I began getting piercing cramps in my lower stomach. I had to find a restroom quickly to relieve myself, but didn't want to use the public restroom, because it was always filthy and disgusting, but now I had little choice. I told Linda to watch our son, while I run to the restroom. I located a small restroom close by and entered to find a toilet with no enclosure around it, a urinal, and a sink, all of which looked as though it hadn't been cleaned in months. I grabbed some paper towels out of the dispenser and wiped off the toilet seat the best I could, and placed toilet paper on the stool, and then quickly sitting down while my stomach rumbled. While I was doing my business, a shadowy figure appeared at the doorway and a silhouette of a man climbed the walls towards the entrance. As he walked towards the urinal, he glanced at his face and my blood ran cold. The man looked exactly like Patrick Kearney. I immediately thought about what my brother had said. I began to shake nervously, and my heart started pounding. Within seconds, I was up and out the door in a hurry. These disgusting bathrooms were known hangouts for homosexual creeps, and I did not want any part of it.

I wondered, "Was that Patrick Kearney?" As I raced towards Linda, and my son, I kept looking back over my shoulder. I yelled out to Linda and said, "Let's go now! Hurry!" She began to question me, but I grabbed all our things, our son, and headed towards the truck. I kept looking back to see if the man came out of the restroom. He did not appear, but I was sure it was Kearney. I had seen Kearney's face countless times and this man looked identical to him. The man wore thick glasses; he had dark hair, and even dressed like Kearney. He also needed a shave with about one week's growth with rough whiskers, sandpapering across his face. If this wasn't Kearney, it was his double. For a moment in the bathroom, I honestly felt like I was in danger. I raced home and called my brother. I told him everything that had happened, and he repeated his earlier statement. I determined that Kearney had not released and he remains confined behind bars.

Two years after nearly being killed by the *Trash bag murderer*, Stewart was accidentally shot in the stomach "Point blank" with a .22 caliber derringer. The bullet lodged into Stewart's small intestines, and it was surgically removed, but he survived. The doctor indicated that the wound could have been fatal if the projectile would have gone three inches in any other direction; Stewart would have been in grave danger. Instead, he has survived this and several other events on the streets of Los Angeles, to bring these countless facts of this case, to light with the assistance of several others.

BOOKS BY TONY STEWART INCLUDE:

MA BARKER IN OCKLAWAHA – *FBI's Longest Gun Battle* DILLINGER, THE HIDDEN TRUTH – *Gangsters and G-Men of the Great Depression era,*

TONY STEWART'S Poem's, Lyrics, and Short Stories,
JOHNNIE & BERYL DILLINGER – *A Page from the Past,* CRIME ERA - *Special Edition (1920's – 1930's)*
DILLINGER, THE HIDDEN TRUTH – *RELOADED.*
THE DILLINGER FAMILY SCRAPBOOK – *A Genealogy Record of Ancestors*
SCARS OF AFFLICTION – *Forgiven, But Not Forgotten*
THE TRASH BAG MURDERER
THE RUMOR MILL – *Whispers of Anguish* GANGSTER GALLERY – *A Pictorial of the Past*
THE SEARCH FOR LAUREN SPIERER
CRIME WAVE MAGAZINE

Accomplishments and interviews include:

*Appeared on American Badasses on the American Heroes Channel 2015
*Appeared on WTIU/WFIU Indiana News for program "History Through Headlines" on John Dillinger 3-2014.
*History Consultant for America: Facts Vs. Fiction on the Military Channel 2014 Interviewed by Workaholic Productions, Inc. Appeared in credits
*Contributed Dillinger photos to all-new series AMERICAN GUNS historic guns Oct. 2011. Listed in Credits.
*Appeared on National Geographic Channel on October 26, 2010 in an International 4part documentary film, entitled; "Making History - Rise of the Gangster." Interviewed by 360 Productions.
*Interview with Peter Boyles on 630 KHOW Denver's Talk Station 7-8-09 http://www.khow.com/pages/boyles.html
Interviewed on Crime Beat with Carl Brizzi Saturday June 20, 2009 (EST) on WIBC, 93.1 FM - WWW.WIBC.COM
*Interviewed by Don Babwin of AP Associated Press on June 18, 2009 about new Public Enemies movie. Also contributed to costume designs for actors, Johnny Depp, Christian Bale and others for film "Public Enemies."
*Appeared on location interview with Jupiter Entertainment on an updated documentary on criminals of the 1920's and 30's for the History channel to air in July/Aug. 2007 entitled Crime Wave.

*Unique on camera interview with Morningstar Entertainment of a new documentary for the Discovery channel, aired March 18, 19, 2006 entitled The Dillinger Conspiracy.

*Appeared in ARES World Defense Security Magazine September 2006 issue

*Appeared on Harry Boulade's Golden Rose Productions Radio AM 570 Journal, KCFJ AM 570, KCNO 94.5 FM in July 2006

History consultant in the making of several documentary films, including The Real Untouchables Series, by Atlantic Production, which aired April 2000 on The Learning Channel.

*Worked with Principle Films as a consultant in London on a program entitled IT Happened Here. The film aired on The Discovery Channel 2002.

*Interviewed in March 2005 issue of Yesterday's Memories magazine, continued in April 2005 addition.

*Produced a Blues Music Production with brother, talented recording artist Ron Stewart of Bloomington, Indiana on 91.3 with three hit songs in the top 10 MP3.com charts. Tony Stewart also Co-wrote a song entitled Seventeen with Ron Stewart.

Stewart is the Founder/CEO of True Crime Writers Association and is a book reviewer on Amazon.com and Barnesandnoble.com. He is the founder of The Dillinger Times Club and four "Award Winning" Historical Websites featuring a complete insight of his new book. These Sites have received well over 300,000 visitors with favorable results indicating a strong interest in his book. Stewart has been involved with student's worldwide, helping them to get a better understanding of crime and corruption during the Great Depression. In 1978, the author wrote a published article for Surfer Magazine called Unknown Surfers in Redondo Beach, California.

The author has studied Video Production courses in 1990 at Cal State University in Long Beach, California. Attended Vincennes University in Indiana where his studies included word comprehension and computer courses.

Presently, I am still searching for other family members of the victims. If you are out there I can be reached at email address: Dillinger72234@aol.com

http://www.lulu.com/spotlight/johnniedillinger

VITAL INTERVIEWS

KEARNEY QUESTIONED

July 1, 1977 – Riverside Sheriff's Department
Interview with Patrick Kearney

Miller: Okay, Having your rights read in mind and knowing your rights do you agree to speak with us now?

Kearney: Uh Huh.

Miller: Okay, How long were you in El Paso?

Kearney: Almost exactly a month. I liked being close to the border.

Miller: Did David Hill ever did catch you with anything in the bathtub or any blood in the bathtub or anything?

Kearney: No, he almost caught me with George. Ah David was supposed to be gone for a while, and he came back when I was about to put him in a bag and ah I ah managed to put him in my closet, he was already dead, and David came into the house ah, said his hello's and went to bed, then I went back in the bedroom and left him in the closet.

Miller: You seemed to have a good hand at foreign languages. They come easy to you. One of your books was on Arabic. Were you into that at all.

Kearney: I was looking into it ah, I considered maybe trying to get into something in that part of the world. For a while it looked like I might be able to go working with Hughes (Referring to Hughes Aircraft). Spanish goes back to my childhood.

Miller: Are you a religious person, your upraising, church or anything like that?

Kearney: I ah was going to say something about my beliefs and religion and when I try and talk about religion I here recently I wanna cry.

Bacalski: I understand you turned yourself in.

Kearney: Yes.

Bacalski: How did you find out that we were looking for you?

Kearney: We weren't sure until we read the newspapers.

Wilson: What did he (David Hill) think when you decided to leave.

Kearney: It wasn't like we were running away, just that we did it and there may have been psychological undercurrents we were both really thinking, you know, other than on the surface. When we left our decision was, well if you guys did get arrest warrants, you know, decided to come after us, than we would come back. Well, we spent two weeks, you know, we spent two weeks in kind of indecision and as you say, David is very nervous. He wanted to commit suicide.

Wilson: All the evidence we have connecting the crimes with you, tends to link both of you, and the residence. We don't know which one was actually involved to this point or how much.

Kearney: I guess that's what concerns me too, you know. That is, if one of us wasn't involved, what would happen to him. Especially, since we seemed to run away and tend to incriminate the other one as an accomplice or something. Not an accomplice, but you know, what about an accessory?

Bacalski: In other words, he didn't have any direct knowledge. He didn't see anything, is that what you are saying? He may surmise.

Kearney: He didn't have any idea before you guys began your investigation that anything was going on.

Bacalski: Did any of your victims know that they were going to die or that you were going to shoot them, before you did?

Kearney: No, it was a surprise.

Bacalski: Who was the next one you shot?

Kearney: Okay, I purposely tried not to remember things, and I have a memory problem. I really probably couldn't keep a straight list of or order. Bacalski: Pat, going back over the last ten years could you list victims? I know you might not be able to, but just an estimate to the number of guys you killed could it be over 50?

Kearney: It might be over 30 or 40, but I didn't keep count or records, purposely I tried not to remember anything in case I had a lie detector test or something. I couldn't have remembered most of those names if I hadn't seen them in the paper.

Miller: Did you kill Tim Ingram with the H & R Derringer?

Kearney: I'm sure I didn't because the derringer was kind of tricky. Every time I take them out of my pocket the barrel would start spinning and I had trouble getting it to work.

Bacalski: And other than cutting up the bodies, did you ever do anything else to the bodies after they were shot?

Kearney: Yes, I pulled out some of the pubic hair.

Bacalski: Okay, what was the reason for that?

Kearney: I wanted to see what it looked like. I pulled it all out, but this was after they were already dead.

Wilson: You just pulled their out. You didn't disturb their genitals at all.

Kearney: Not particular, I meant I don't think I left any marks or anything. I might have hit them or something, but they were already dead.

Wilson: Did you tie them up or bind any of them, prior to or after killing them?

Kearney: Well afterwards, I had to semi tie the package in order to be able to carry them by myself.

Wilson: But prior to their death, you didn't tie any of them up?

Kearney: I didn't torture anybody or anything. I thought of it, but I couldn't. I wouldn't have gone that far, where I could do that.

Wilson: How about any foreign objects on the bodies, like something in the rectum, after death and leave them like that.

Kearney: Oh well, paper towels and things that was mainly to keep the bleeding from getting all over the floor, while I was trying to get them in plastic bags. In the rectum, they had a tendency to bleed.

Wilson: Did you at any time have an association with someone else that you know that may have been killing people?

Kearney: I did a lot of correspondence, you know, trying to find people who were interested in going to Mexico with me. You guys probably know by now I go to Mexico most every weekend and find people to share in driving and stuff.

Bacalski: What do you do down there?

Kearney: I maybe just wonder around back streets and back alleys, steam baths and stuff. I meet people.

Bacalski: Did you ever kill people down there?

Kearney: Negative.

Bacalski: What was your main purpose for going down there?

Kearney: I like Mexicans. I like being there and often didn't do anything to anybody. I might enjoy sex and then steam bath and the atmosphere of seeing people. I've devoted most of my life to learning Spanish. I have a pen pal in Russia, and I learned to read and write her in Russian, and I've learned a lot of Japanese.

Bacalski: Can you tell us where you put his (John LaMay) hands, feet and head, we never found those.

Kearney: You probably won't, because they spend millions of dollars burning our trash near where we live, and the hands, and feet were mostly in a McDonalds, and Winchell's type places around where I lived. I believe we put the head in a very large supermarket trash can.

Bacalski: What made you dismember the bodies?

Kearney: It was partially to help me dispose of it and partially curiosity. I Don't know how to say it; when I was eight years old I felt like killing know people and dismembering them. Did you ever see the movie Carrie? You saw how they mistreated her, and she was surprised at her prom. That's the way I was when I was a kid. I don't what was going on. It seemed like the whole world wanted to mistreat me.

INTERVIEW WITH DETECTIVE ROGER WILSON

MURDER OF GEORGE 1st Victim (Kearney – Wilson, Interview 1978)

Wilson: Kearney gave us all the information on George, and we're still connected to the missing and exploded children. Were still trying to find out who he is. What did you do?

Kearney: Well, I laid his body on a shower curtain on my bed, and then I shaved all the body hair on him.

Wilson: What did you do next?

Kearney: Well, I skinned him. After I skinned him I took a hacksaw to his head went in and pulled out the bullet.

Wilson: The bullet had gone between the eyes all the way through his head and hit the back of the skull, and at the back of the skull, cause the back of the skull was fractured where the bullet had hit. I'm sure that a .22 loses velocity quickly and bounces around and that's how he kills them quick.

Wilson: You skinned him?

Kearney: Yeah,

Wilson: The whole body?

Kearney: Yes.

Wilson: What did you do next?

Kearney: Well, I opened up his chest cavity.

Wilson: What did you do?

Kearney: I pulled everything out and then, just curious Wilson and then?

Kearney: I cut the arms and legs off

Wilson: How did you do that?"

Kearney: I used an Exacto-knife, a number 11 blade, which is the little diagonal blade. Yeah, very, sharp as a scalpel.

Wilson: and ah, what did you do next?

Kearney: Well, I went out between the garages, and I dug a hole and I dug it underneath the cement foundation and then placed the torso, and then placed the legs because I couldn't carry everything at once. I placed the legs on top on the torso and the arms on top of that. Then I took all of George's possessions, I had even bought him clothes and stuff and I got rid of it and dumped the bloody shower curtain."

(STEWART – WILSON INTERVIEW)

Stewart: Roger, you had mentioned that Kearney had told you, there were four Riverside policemen at his house, and he thought of killing them as they sat on his couch, because it would had been hard for the officers to reach their guns quick enough. Did you say, "Kearney had a .357 Magnum, close by."

Wilson: Yeah, he sat in the chair that had the .357 Magnums in it.

Stewart: Where was the gun at? Was it on the side of the cushion?
Wilson: Yeah, in the cushion, on the side.
Stewart: and he really thought about killing these officers?
Wilson: That's what he told us."
Stewart: What about David Hill? Was he present?
Wilson: No.
Stewart: You mentioned you went out to Imperial County and met the Coroner there, he whispered to you while Kearney was saying, "The body was right here," that he did find a body about 50 feet away.
Wilson: Yeah.
Stewart: Well, you mentioned that Kearney walked about freely, and then came up and asked you, 'your partner isn't armed, but you are...how could you let me walk around freely?
Wilson: I told him that I was an expert shot, and we only needed one gun, and my partner carried a knife, and we've used Al Sett's knife more than we've used my gun, and I can pick your eyes out, so don't bother to run. He stayed real close to me from then on.
Stewart: What kind of knife did Al Sett have?
Wilson: Just a little pocketknife. (Laugh)
Stewart: He must have been pretty good with that knife.
Wilson: (laugh) you know, he did his fingernails and stuff. (laugh)
Stewart: I guess you guys only needed one gun anyway, because he seemed to be cooperative.
Wilson: Oh yeah, he knew he had it. He knew it was over.
   That was up on Angeles chest when we found the location of Merle Hondo.
Stewart: What type of gun did you carry on duty?
Wilson: I used a three-inch stainless-steel Smith and Wesson.
Stewart: and what caliber?
Wilson: It was a .357; it had .38 calibers in it, a factory model.
Stewart: Why do you think Kearney killed people? Was it sexual gratuity? Wilson Yeah, most of the bodies that we found, except for the deteriorated bodies, we found semen.
Stewart: Now, the ones that deteriorated the magnets ate away the semen?
Wilson: Yeah.
Stewart: Why did he drain the blood out of his victims?
Wilson: We'll when he washed them and cut them up in small pieces and put them in the bags, he didn't want the blood everywhere. And he knew about blood forensics and all that.
Stewart: He probably studied about all that kind of stuff.
Wilson: Well, you know his dad was a LAPD officer. I'm sure he learned a lot.
Stewart: Did he ever keep souvenirs of his victims?
Wilson: No
Stewart: In my research, I have learned that he tried to forget all the victims after he killed them.
Wilson: Yes, when your killing one a month.

Stewart: Can you tell me the longest period that he would keep a victim's body?
Wilson: Yes, he kept George. He had his way with him for a couple of days after he was dead, and I think one or two others overnight, and he cut them up the following day, after he had his way with them.
Stewart: Was the FBI involved in the case?
Wilson: No. There was no FBI. We were trying to profile the killer before the FBI, they were just getting started – and we were doing it. We were trying to pin down who killed Nicky Hernandez, who was a street running male whore, and found that the suspect was preying on homosexuals, and we went after that aspect of it. Nicky Hernandez had probably 250 to 300 scraps of paper with names and phone numbers in a drawer in his room. It was phone numbers of contacts of people he had had contact with, or he would call back. It was like, these are all my tricks and who should I contact tonight?' He would reach in that drawer and pull out a person with a name and phone number. We had to run all those numbers and attempt to contact them. Several of them were famous.
Stewart: Were they politicians?
Wilson: No, they were in the entertainment business, radio and television type stuff, and many of them – when you say who you are and why you were calling, they would just hang up.
Stewart: So that is one of the reasons why it was kept a low-profile case.
Wilson: Yeah, and so when we were turned off by many of them, some of them as soon as we'd say, 'who are you?' they'd hang up, they didn't want to talk to us because they found out who we were acquiring about.

Stewart: Didn't that make them look suspicious?
Wilson: Yeah, Riverside police came up and they were looking for the last people to see him alive. One of them was an attorney, and they were pushing him pretty hard, until he finally got mad. He told them not to contact him or any of his friends again; because they were, I guess innuendoes about where met in homosexual bathhouses and stuff like that.
It got a little hairy.
Stewart: Did Kearney ever say anything about his family?
Wilson: They were middle class and dysfunctional, as I understand.
Stewart: Was his father pretty strict?
Wilson: Yeah?
Stewart: Did Kearney ever say anything about his hating his family?

Wilson: He pretty much avoided us on talking about his family. That's generally how we start an interview. My partner and I would talk about their family, and get them talking, but he just wouldn't go that way. Stewart: I know you said that Kearney's father taught him to shoot pigs behind the left ear. I was wondering if Kearney resented his father? I read that Kearney avoided seeing his parents when he and Hill were on the run in Texas and New Mexico during a nationwide hunt for them.

Wilson: I don't know.

Stewart: Kearney lived in Redondo Beach. So why did he turn himself in at Riverside?

Wilson: Because when we put it out in the newspaper that Riverside had a search warrant on his house on evidence and had brought it back to a judge, that probably never even read it, and then issued a warrant on him. Kearney found out about it in a Texas newspaper and then surrendered to Riverside officials.

Stewart: Do you know how he felt about the Riverside police? I know you said you and your partner spoke more on his level.

Wilson: Yeah, and he responded to us quite well, and like I said, when Riverside cops stopped jerking us around, after he turned himself in, in Riverside. We requested time to go down there and interview him, and they said, 'But were not done yet.' It was a week and two days before we were called. They said, 'you can interview him this morning. He will be arraigned at 1:00 p.m. today, and after that. So, we boogied on down there and talked to him for about 3 hours. We got more out of him in the 3 hours, then Riverside out of him in a week. We came out of the interview an Investigator name Smuggley asked us, 'how much did we get out of him?' I told them, 'we got everything, he copped out to 21 murders, and they were shocked. They were shocked. We put together a team and when Riverside talked to Kearney, he would only talk about the ones that we put together so far.

Stewart: So, you guys got more information than Riverside did.

Wilson: Yeah, because we talked on his level. Riverside used words like 'so you fucked him" whereas we would speak more intelligent by saying, "So you sodomised him." Kearney appreciated that level of speaking.

Stewart: It also sounds like Riverside wanted all the credit, after making you wait a week before questioning him.

Wilson: Yeah, well the other police departments they'd do the same job we do, although we did it a little more thorough with the Sheriff's office, and knowing how the LAPD liked to 'grand stand." The L.A. Sheriff's office wanted to do the same thing, but we didn't. We would take our time and build a case, and we weren't that rushed to judgment, like inveracity, and then make the big splash. So, all the departments got together in Orange County to figure out who would lead the investigation and put it all together. Mainly because they figured everyone was murdered within LA County that we should handle it, and we said "Ok." We are the largest Sheriff's Department in the world and have more of a budget than anyone else and we could run with it, and we did. And we finally put it all together and had to get everything from all the other counties, and that's what we figured was the success of the case.

Stewart: So, you guys succeeded in getting guilty pleas in all 21 cases.

Wilson: Yeah, we were kind of disappointed that he wanted to cop out, because we had spent so much time putting everything together for the case, and the Judge had to read it in the morning, but he didn't read it, instead he went of the strength and the veracity of the L.A. County

Sheriff's department, and we submitted the books. He went by investigative report that Al Sett and I wrote, the synopsis from all the cases. There were 39 to 40 pages that were read to get an idea about Kearney.

Stewart: I have read articles on how you and your partner said Kearney wanted to talk to you. Sett said, "It wasn't much of a challenge, he wanted to talk."

Wilson: Yeah, we treated him like a friend. You know we'd joke with him and all that, and it worked out well.

Stewart: After the last three days you spent with Kearney, before turning him over to the prison officials, were there any final words?

Wilson: We took him out to dinner in china town.

Stewart: You took him out to dinner in handcuffs?

Wilson: No, he wasn't wearing cuffs. Kearney ordered the sweet pork with shrimp and all the extras. In fact, I think we all ordered the pork.' Stewart: So, was there any final words?

Wilson: Nope, I guess we were going to visit him in prison and talk more, one on one in state prison. We took him to dinner then bought him over to the jail compound. They opened up the gates for us. Al Sett drove around to where the buses make a circle and it's quite large, so we pulled as far away as we could from the booking center where all the press was, and he parked the car. So, we stopped and got out and all the lights began shinning on us and the cameras and everything. Kearney turned to me and he raised his arm, until I put my arm though and says, "Well, we might as well go." Arm in arm, we marched into the television cameras and into the booking cage. He was put in the county jail and then transferred up north to Soladad prison. So, we drove to Soladad prison and spent the whole day up there talking with Kearney.   Stewart: Did he say they were treating him ok?

Wilson: Yeah, because of his notoriety, nobody will touch him. I just told him to be cool and do your time. He said he had an idea that in prison he'd like to teach different languages including English to inmates. Kearney said he had never talked to his father about high profile killers; he said they have been separated during his entire life. Kearney has no contact with anyone, not even a guard. He is allowed to leave his compound one hour a day, if he wants too.

Stewart: You told me that Kearney's father taught him to kill pigs by shooting them behind the left ear; did he ever take part in the butchering of the pigs?   Wilson: Yeah, he did. I think his father did most of it. He was only 11 to 13 years of age.

Stewart: I wonder what his father thought of the killings, knowing that he taught his son how to kill animals, and his son later used his father's teaching methods to later kill human beings.

Wilson: Al Sett and "Jigsaw" St. John went down to talk to the family, while I was busy in trial with another case, but they wouldn't say much. They family requested to keep quiet after the whole affair.

Stewart: It looks like the grandmother, was a lot of help to Kearney. She became his "Power of attorney' and sold his house, vehicles and personal items to pay off his debts. At this point Kearney mentioned to his grandmother that they were going to Canada, because a friend of theirs had been killed and the police were harassing them. Roger, it looks as though they were planning a permanent escape to Canada and Hill was going with him. The grandmother said Hill was so jittery that he couldn't eat anything. It appears that Hill knew something about the murders back in May of 1977.

Wilson: Hill was that way all the time; that was normal for him, he was a weird guy.

Stewart: Do you see a big difference in forensic technology of the 1970's compared to today.

Wilson: Oh yeah, absolutely.

Stewart: Do you feel they could have found even more in Kearney's residence if the crimes occurred today?

Wilson: They could have, but they did tear the bathroom apart. They found blood in the bathroom drain. They found blood behind the pressboard and tiles and they found blood in some of the carpeting. In several areas, they found a lot of blood.

Stewart: Kearney had a bad side, but he also had a compassionate side.

Wilson: Well, one of the first things he said to us was that he realized he couldn't stop. He couldn't stop killing and was killing one a month, and he was getting a little scared.

Stewart: From a detective's standpoint, do you feel that Kearney protected David Hill?

Wilson: Yeah, I think so.

Stewart: You also mentioned something about an airplane incident, in which Kearney and Hill were going to dump a body out of the plane but couldn't get the hatch open.

Wilson: Hm. The guys were in the airplane and they were gonna throw the one guy out, but they couldn't get the door open.

Stewart: Do you have any idea who the guy was?

Wilson: No.

Stewart: Now who told you this story? Kearney or Hill?

Wilson: Kearney

Stewart: It sounds like Kearney backed out of that one because Hill's name was involved, and wanted to protect him. Kind of like two lovers would do.

Wilson: Yeah.

Stewart: I know about the same time Kearney was active...they also had the Zodiac killer in the San Francisco Bay area. I heard the first victim was killed was in Riverside. I was curious if you guys ever got involved in that case.

Wilson: No.

Stewart: I guess he was one they never caught. When I was in Junior High School, I remembered he had threatened to shoot the tires out of a school and kill the kids as they ran off the bus. A lot of kids were worried about this.

Wilson: The zodiac would check out people, and he'd just drive up, and bang bang and just shoot people. Kind of like the "Son of Sam" killer.

Stewart: I wish he were one that they would have caught. He's probably dead or in jail now.

Wilson: Yeah

Stewart: Is there any other details that you recall that you can share on murder victims or anything special that Kearney had said that attracted your attention?

Wilson: I was amazed when he located the marker at Angeles Crest. Stewart I know you had mentioned the area that had been buried under several feet of sand and Kearney somehow located this site.

Wilson: That was amazing! That was complete amazement! Mainly because when he was there with the body in the gully it was at night, was dark and he put the body in this ravine and then covered it with branches and stuff and then left it, never to go back again and we went up there it was like a moonscape. We were four feet above the highway.

Stewart: How did he find the area with so many changes in complete darkness at the time?

Wilson: His memory is such that he probably figured at average speed, and time, how far it would be. And I think he, when we turned on to Angeles Crest and turned up there he was calculating where he was going to take us, and when we went past it and turned around and he told us to stop, and he looked where the road should be and he starts digging down and we had a little GI shovel and a crow bar and dug down and he hits this aluminum marker. He hit that mile marker and dug it up, and Officer Marge Inquist takes off to St. John's car and got the murder book the Sheriff's department had given him on that case. One of the homicide detectives from the Sheriff's office had taken a photograph this mile marker where this gully was that the body wa found in.

Stewart: How close to the mile marker was the body found?

Wilson: It was within 15 to 20 feet from where the gully was. In other words when you took a picture of this mile marker and stood in the street and too the picture with the mile marker, it was within 20 feet.

Stewart: That is really amazing.

Wilson: Oh It was flabbergasting! If you go up there during the day it was a moonscape.

Stewart: When you look at Kearney, he doesn't look like a serial killer.

Wilson: What does a serial killer look like?

Stewart: As you talked, listened and observed Kearney was there anything indicating that this guy is a killer?

Wilson: No. He was very pleasant, he wasn't off the wall, although we though he was when he took us up there to the highway and when he proved to us, you know nobody else had that photo of that mule marker. It was 26.3 or something miles from the roadway and where the intersection of Angeles Crest and the Antelope valley freeway. He was probably looking over at the speedometer and figured it out.

Stewart: Do you think he had looked at his own Speedometer when he drove it?

Wilson: Probably, but I doubt it. The road way was very dark, and winding and you have to pay attention to where you are going. And I don't even think he looked at the mile markers.

Wilson responds - Kearney's Psychiatrist

Stewart: Kearney had made a comment to the psychiatrist that he felt he wasn't insane. He felt he wasn't mentally ill, and he knew the difference between right and wrong. Someone that would kill and cut up that as many people as he did, well, they have to be a little bit insane.

Wilson: Oh yeah, well some of the kids he picked up were going to be gay or were gay or were experimenting. A lot of them were marijuana smokers, with no kind of home life. One of them was just a no good kid. The parents didn't even file a missing report on him.

Stewart: One would think that any parent would file a report on their missing kids.

Wilson: Yeah, the kids been gone two years, you know they could care less.

Stewart: Kearney had mentioned that his family moved to a location where everyone around them spoke Spanish and they shouldn't have even been living there, because it was such a bad idea. Any idea where it location was?

Wilson: Probably the valley; yeah, the valley. He could have been somewhere over near San Fernando Valley, that's always been for years.

Stewart: I know you said the FBI wasn't involved ...I know he didn't cross any state lines, there were no Federal charges were there?

Wilson: No....he did not cross state lines, he took somebody for the purpose of killing them, yeah.

ACKNOWLEDGMENTS

It would be absolutely impossible to list everyone who has contributed to the writing of this manuscript. So if I have missed anyone, "Sincerely, I thank you!" Also, I want to personally send out my appreciation to the vast amount of people for your kind support and remembrance of victims and their families, who have suffered tragically over the years.

First and foremost, I'd like to thank my wife, Kim Stewart, for her constant support and constructive criticism. Also, I'd like to thank Bobbi Hardwick for her support and her kind contribution. I'd like to give a huge thanks to Top-notch *Historian,* Jim Mitchell, for his assistance in locating *Los Angeles County Detective*, Louis Danoff. Danoff was an extremely important source to this book; providing knowledge on the case, as well another vital connection with *Los Angeles County Sheriff's Department* Detective's Al Sett, and Roger Wilson, who were working with over 200 investigators in five counties. Wilson has bought several documented facts to the table, as well as his own personal "First hand" off the record account on serial killer Patrick Kearney. The wonderful and brilliant Marion Briggs, a *Forensic Document Examination* and *Handwriting Identification expert,* who has also added some fascinating facts to this murder case. Briggs' years of valuable assistance has opened a lot of doors of valuable research, and world-class forensic analysis.

There have been several viable resources that have offered assistance and support essential to this book, but the most imperative have been the families of victims. These special people include Marcia Born, sister of murder victim Robert "Billy" Benniefiel. Cameo Bell, the sister of five-year-old Ronald Dean Smith Jr., who was Kearney's youngest victim. Also Rachel Weldon of Colorado, the aunt of eight-year-old Merle "Hondo" Chance, and Neal Chance, the mother of the child. I want to give a special thanks to Elizabeth "Betty" McGhee, mother of victim Michael Craig McGhee, and his sister, Elizabeth McGhee. I know it has been difficult for all family members of victims, and I sincerely appreciate all of your continuous assistance.

I would like to express special gratitude to my son, Keith Stewart, *for* your continuous support, and expert knowledge on serial killers. To my musically talented brothers, Chris Stewart, and professional singer and songwriter Ron Stewart, survivors of the Trash Bag Murderer. Also special thanks to Sandy Henderson, for her help confirming essential facts presented in this book. I would also like to thank Bree Reynolds, relative of victim Oliver Peter Molitor and Karen Fryer sister of victim Larry Gene Walters.

Other supportive friends include the amazing and talented Georgia Durante, *Crime Writer*, *Stuntwoman, survivor,* and *Super model. Thank you* for your support and inspiration. It was Durante's amazing book, *The Company She Keeps* that motivated me, and led to this writing. Additional inspirations include Actors Joseph Gannascoli, and John Fiore – *Stars of the HBO series the Sopranos*, and the talented Actor Rick Wilson, of *Crime Wave – 18 months of Mayhem*, also my friend Michael Bell - *Highly acclaimed Celebrity Artist* and *BlogTalk Radio Host*. Also, to my friend, *Sensational Artist,* and designer of cover picture, Willie Smith. Renowned author and first-rate friend Dary Matera, thank you for your help with my proposal and professional advice. To retired mobster Henry Hill, another encouragement, whose life story became the basis for the Academy Award Winning film *Goodfellas* starring Robert DeNiro, Joe Pesci, and Ray Liotta. Thanks to Guy Sorensen and his father Robert C. Sorensen, a friend of Patrick Kearney's and his co-worker at Hughes Aircraft. I would also like to thank Cameron Bough for our many discussions and for giving me a new perceptive on serial killers.

My sincere thanks to *Investigative Research Specialist* Pat Pfremmer of Carmel, California for her outstanding efforts while uncovering crucial documents. *Also, to the County of Los Angeles Public Library, The Los Angeles Times, The Daily Breeze, Time Magazine and True Detective Magazine* for articles essential to this book. To *Records/Warrants Supervisor* Nancy Bandura, of *Riverside County Sheriff's Department,* Sheriff Leroy D. Baca, and Captain James Curtis of *Homicide Bureau*. Homicide Detective's Al Sett, John St. John, Marv Inquist, Roger Kao, Riverside Deputy D.A. Dan Bacalski, Judge E. Scott Dales, Deputy District Prosecutor Dino Fulgoni, Riverside Detective's Dan Wilson, Bob Cluchey, Jim Dougherty, Dale Henson, Riverside County Deputy Probation Officer Sue King, Banning Station Detective Larry Miller, Elsinore Station Detective R. McIver, Oxnard Police Investigators Rick Wallace, Leo Alvares, El Segundo Police Detective Roger Kahl, Imperial County Sheriff Lou Hettinger, Deputy Coroner Carl Smith, LA Coroner's Dr. Ron Taylor, Mark Taylor, Psychiatrist Dr. Seawright Anderson, Psychiatrist Carl Bert Steinbacher, Judge Howard M. Dabney, Los Angeles Municipal Court Judge Dickran Tevrizian Jr., Deputy District Attorney John Breault , U.S. Customs Officer Duke Reeves of Terminal Island, Hughes Aircraft Supervisor Bruce Hermanson in Culver City, Hughes Aircraft Inspector Frank Mac Duffee, Hughes Aircraft Foreman Gert Arnstein, Special Investigator Don Henry of March Air Force Base, X-ray Supervisor David Hadley - Loma Linda University Hospital, and the hundreds of other officers directly involved in the case.

REFERENCES & RESOURCES

Cover drawing was courtesy of artist Willie Smith. Check out his amazing online store at: http://www.zazzle.com/apparelconcepts http://www.greywolfgrafix.com

Apsche, J. (1993). Probing the mind of a serial killer. International information Associates.
http://www.uplink.com.au/lawlibrary/Documents/Docs/Doc5.html

Baca, Lee - Sheriff (2008) Los Angeles Sheriff's Department,
http://sheriff.lacounty.gov/wps/portal/lasd

Bandura, Nancy (2008) Records/Warrants Supervisor Riverside County Sheriff's Department, http://www.riversidesheriff.org/

Daily Breeze newspaper, Oct. 27, 1996 "Anguish and Anger" Staff writer (Page 118)
http://www.dailybreeze.com/

Death Penalty Information Center (2008) - Part I: History of the Death Penalty
http://www.deathpenaltyinfo.org/article.php?scid=15&did=410

Douglas, J., (1996). MindHunter. Mandarine Publishing
http://www.fantasticfiction.co.uk/d/john-e-douglas/mindhunter.htm

Durante, Georgia – Author/Stunt Woman (2008)
www.thecompanyshekeeps.com
www.performancetwo.com www.happymemorybooks.com

Eaton, Jim – (2004) http://ghoststudy.com/a_what_are_orbs.html

Elizabeth Engstrom is the author of nine books and over 250 short stories, articles and essays. Engstrom's interest in crime writing is not new; her critically acclaimed story about axe murderer Lizzie Borden remains a research tool for the never-ending speculation on that unsolved case.

Gannascoli, Joseph Actor -(2008) HBO Sopranos series
Http://www.josephrgannascoli.com/

Fiore, John (2008) Actor -HBO Sopranos series
http://www.myspace.com/johnnyslade

Fox, J.A., & Levin, J., (1994). OverKill - Mass Murder and Serial Killing Exposed. Plenum Press

Green, Melissa S. (02-May-2005). "History of the Death Penalty & Recent Developments." http://justice.uaa.alaska.edu/death/history.html

"History's Mysteries: Infamous Murders" David Hill (2001)-
http://www.imdb.com/name/nm1373948/

History of Capital Punishment in California © 2005 State of California
http://www.cdcr.ca.gov/ReportsResearch/historyCapital.html

History of California's Death Penalty -
http://www.deathpenalty.org/index.php?pid=history

Hughes, J.M. (Ed.).(1997). Oxford Concise Australian Dictionary (2nd ed.). Melbourne: Oxford University Press http://www.oup.com/us/corporate/worldwide/?view=usa
James Alan Fox and Jack Levin, "The Will to Kill" (Allyn & Bacon Books, 2001) Jan Brady, The Gates of Janus, (Los Angeles: Feral House, 2001)

Karyn Easton 2002, Paranormality.com   http://www.paranormality.com/zodiac.shtml
McDougal, Dennis -*Angel of Darkness* (1992) Warner- Books ISBN 07088 53420 Patrick Wayne Kearney

Peter Vronsky, "Serial Killers The Method and Madness of Monsters" (Berkley Books, 2004)

Pfremmer, Pat (2008) –Specializes: Adoption reunions, person location services. Resume includes: Detective business, Government Publications Unit of the University of California (Santa Cruz) Library and twenty-five years of service as of Santa Cruz County Law Librarian. Contact information - Ms. Pfremmer: forpat@gmail.com

Public Relations Quarterly: Serial Murder Public Relations Tactics, 2004
www.francesfarmersrevenge.com

The Arthur Leigh Allen File (2002) http://www.zodiackiller.com/AllenFile.html

The Los Angeles Times, July 2, 1977, "Suspects in Eight Slayings Surrender"

The Los Angeles Times, July 3, 1977, "Two Suspects May Be Connected to 43 Murders"

The Los Angeles Times, July 4, 1977, "Evidence Near Body Reportedly Led to Suspects"

The Los Angeles Times, July 6, 1977, "Pair Arraigned in 2 'Trash Bag' Murder Cases"

The Los Angeles Times, July 8, 1977, "Skeleton Dug Up"

The Los Angeles Times, July 15, 1977, "One Man Indicted"

The Los Angeles Times, December 22, 1977, "Admitted Killer of 15 Men, Boys"

The Los Angeles Times, December 23, 1977, "Man Sentenced in 'Trash Bag Murders'" The Los Angeles Times, January 7, 1978, "Confessed Trash Bag Killer Quizzed"

The Los Angeles Times, January 10,m 1978, "Trash Bag' Slayer Names 4 Victims"

The Los Angeles Times, February 16, 1978, "'Trash Bag Killer' Faces 17 More Counts"

The Los Angeles Times, February 18, 1978, "Apparent 13th Slaying by Hillside Killer"

The Los Angeles Times, February 18, 1978, "18th 'Trash Bag' Murder Count Filed"

The Los Angeles Times, February 22, 1978, "Trash Bag' Slayer Pleads Guilty"

The Los Angeles Times, July 2, 1977, "Suspects in Eight Slayings Surrender"

Suspects in Eight Slayings Surrender: Two Men Walk into Riverside County Sheriff's Office and Point to Photos Los Angeles Times (1886-Current File). Los Angeles, Calif.:Jul 2, 1977. p. a17 (1 pp.)

The Los Angeles Times, July 3, 1977, "Two Suspects May Be Connected to 43 Murders"

Two Suspects May Be Connected to 43 Murders: Pair, Held in Eight Sex Killings Dating to 1975, Cooperating in Hunt for Possible Additional Victims Nieson Himmel .

The Los Angeles Times (1886-Current File). Los Angeles, Calif.:Jul 3, 1977. p. 1 (2 pp.)

The Los Angeles Times, July 4, 1977, "Evidence Near Body Reportedly Led to Suspects"

The Los Angeles Times, July 6, 1977, "Pair Arraigned in 2 'Trash Bag' Murder Cases" Pair Arraigned in 2 'Trash Bag' Murder Cases

MYRNA OLIVER. Los Angeles Times (1886-Current File). Los Angeles, Calif.:Jul 6, 1977. p. b3 (2 pp.)

The Los Angeles Times, July 8, 1977, "Skeleton Dug Up" Skeleton Dug Up; Believed First 'Trash Bag' Death

The Los Angeles Times – Jerry Belcher. (1886-Current File). Los Angeles, Calif.:Jul 8, 1977. p. b3 (2 pp.)

The Los Angeles Times, July 15, 1977, "One Man Indicted

The Los Angeles Times, December 22, 1977, "Admitted Killer of 15 Men, Boys"

The Los Angeles Times, December 23, 1977, "Man Sentenced in 'Trash Bag Murders'"
The Los Angeles Times, January 7, 1978, "Confessed Trash Bag Killer Quizzed" Confessed Trash-Bag Killer Quizzed in Death of Boy, 8

BILL FARR. Los Angeles Times (1886-Current File). Los Angeles, Calif.:Jan 7, 1978. p. a32 (1 pp.)

The Los Angeles Times, January 10,m 1978, "Trash Bag' Slayer Names 4 Victims" 'Trash Bag' Slayer Names 4 Victims

The Los Angeles Times Bill Farr -(1886-Current File). Los Angeles, Calif. Jan 10, 1978. p. a19 (1 pp.)

The Los Angeles Times (1886-Current File). Farr, Bill - Los Angeles, Calif. Feb 16, 1978. p. d1 (2 pp.)

The Los Angeles Times, February 16, 1978, "'Trash Bag Killer' Faces 17 More Counts"

The Los Angeles Times, February 18, 1978, "Apparent 13th Slaying by Hillside Killer"

The Los Angeles Times, February 18, 1978, "18th 'Trash Bag' Murder Count Filed"

The Los Angeles Times, February 22, 1978, "'Trash Bag' Slayer Pleads Guilty"
Peter Vronsky, "Serial Killers The Method and Madness of Monsters" (Berkley Books, 2004)

Time Magazine, July 18, 1977 "Twenty-eight and Counting"

Time Magazine, July 12, 1993, "The Landscaper's Secrets"

'Trash Bag Killer' Faces 17 More Murder Counts: Homicide Complaint Against Patrick Kearney Is Largest Ever Filed in Los Angeles County 'Trash Bag Killer' Faces New Charges

Wilson, C., & Seamen, D., (1992). <u>The Serial Killer.</u> Carol Publishing's

Yochelsen, S. & Samenow, S. (1988). <u>The criminal personality.</u> New York Press

Writings by Kearney
The Frances Farmers Revenge Wen Portal
http://www.francesfarmersrevenge.com/stuff/serialkillers/kearney.htm

LETTERS FROM RELATIVES OF VICTIMS

Relatives of victims wanted the whole truth revealed on what this killer did to the victims to show what a monster he really is.

Tony, Neal called me this afternoon. She sounded better than she has for a long time. And she was so happy to get the book. She has been living for this book for a while. She will be forever grateful to you for writing the truth and caring enough to write the sweet words you said about Hondo, which she told you. She would be the last person in the world to want that man on the street and has attended some of the hearings when he was up for parole.
You are such a thoughtful person, thank you so much. Rachel Weldon (Hondo's aunt)

Tony, you don't know how much I appreciate your thoughtfulness for Neal (Hondo's mother). Today our Sunday school class prayed for her. She doesn't know what Kearney did that night. Thank you for everything. God bless you and your family. Rachel (Hondo's Aunt)

Thank you, Tony. Mike was not a bad boy but was a free spirit and could get in to things he shouldn't have, I haven't read the book yet but my daughter is in the process and she thinks you did a wonderful job and for that I thank you. Please keep in touch. Betty McGhee (Mother of victim Michael McGhee)

Hi Tony, I received your book thank you very much What a keepsake, my son John purchased one and would like for you to autograph it could you do this if their is a charged for this let me know Betty (Mother of victim Hondo Chance)

Hello Tony, Yes, my mom formed a group very popular to this day. I have some news clippings about it. It was called "Compassionate friends" It was exclusively for parents who had lost children. I can remember hearing the stories the parents would tell and the sobbing coming from the living room of our apartment when we were supposed to be asleep. The group started at our apartment and grew very strong and moved on. Ironically Billy's favorite thing to do was hunt for treasures in the trash. He would come home with some of the most amazing things and could not understand why they were tossed out. I often think the landfill must be like heaven for him. You are a truly blessed man to be alive today. Be grateful everyday you escaped his net. Take care, Marcia (Sister of victim Mike "Billy" Benniefiel)

Hi Tony, I received your book thank you very much. What a keepsake, my son purchased one and would like for you to autograph it. Betty (Mother of Mike McGhee)

Tony, I will ask her to call me when she gets the book and I believe God will help me comfort her. She has been living for this book for a while. She will be forever grateful to you for writing the truth and caring enough to write the sweet words you said about Hondo, which she told you. I remember he brought her a flower every day. I will let you know how things are going after she has had time to digest the book. She would be the last person in the world to want that man on the street and has attended some of the hearings when he was up for parole. You are such a thoughtful person, thank you so much. Rachel Weldon (Hondo's aunt)

The more that people that learn about his crimes, they will not forget, and hopefully the killer will stay longer behind bars. Kearney wants people to forget and NOT to show up at his hearings, so one day he may go free. It is my hope that the will never go free. This book is for Hondo and the others that senselessly lost their lives. Tony

I applaud Victim Robert Benniefiel's mother who has dedicated the trees in memory of the victims buried at the Palos Verdes Landfill. Robert's sister Marcia Born still goes up there to visit her brother who was killed by Kearney.

LATEST NEWS (FEBRUARY - 2012)

Marsy's Law – "Before 2008, when a prisoner was denied parole, the prisoner's next hearing would be deferred for one, two, three, four, or five years. After 2008, however, the prisoner's next hearing would be deferred for three, five, seven, ten, or fifteen years. In effect, the minimum deferral the Board can now give is two years longer than it could have been pre-Marsy's Law; the maximum deferral is ten years longer." *SUPREME COURT RULING*

The parole boards now the right to extent the prisoner's a parole hearing to five, ten, or fifteen years. For Patrick Kearney, they chose fifteen years. The justice department is finally starting to give murderers what they deserve.

UPDATE:

The killer has reported that he is not happy about this book. He wanted the truth about him to remain silent in hopes that all the victims will forget him so he can one day go free, which is not going to happen.

Years after Kearney refused to attend hearings so he would not have to face the relatives of victims, now he is angry, because this book has finally allowed the relatives a chance to speak out against the murderer for the whole world to read. However, prison officials refuse to allow the publication of *LA'S DEADLIEST SERIAL KILLER* in their prison; because they feel other prisoners will harm him when they learn he killed children. Even through there is two books in the prison library on Tex Watson, who also resides in the prison and is a murderer. The Justice system is still protecting this serial killer even while he is behind bars.

Recent letters from Patrick Kearney demonstrate how he is attempting to involve author (Tony Stewart) and discredit the printing of this book. It appears that the truth really hurts. Seems the angry killer; Patrick Kearney is now seeking revenge while attempting to include the author as an accomplice in his murders, which is complete nonsense. Kearney is actually trying to say that Author Tony Stewart *hand-delivered* all his murder victims to this killer. He is also denying the murders of victims that he once confessed to, stating that he was only protecting his lover David Hill and others.

This is a final attempt by Kearney to condemn the truth, but instead the book bought out the truth about Kearney's deep, dark, wicked, serial killer "Murderous" ways. Kearney was hoping that everyone forgot about his past, but we will never forget. If the truth from this book has angered Kearney in any way, shape or form than we have succeeded in giving the victims the last word. Remember the victims, not the killer.

The final word is that the killer Patrick Kearney is dying from *Fourth stage colon cancer.*

OTHER BOOKS BY TONY STEWART

http://www.lulu.com/spotlight/johnniedillinger

True Crime book reviews and news
By Emily Webb

When true crime author Tony Stewart contacted me to review his book *The Trash Bag Murderer* I was intrigued. Not only had I never heard of the "Trash Bag Killer" Patrick Kearney but there was also the added intrigue that the author was a survivor of this serial killer.

As a child and youth, Tony Stewart lived in the same Californian neighborhood as Kearney (he even did odd jobs for the serial killer) and he and his brother Ron separately had encounters with him that, unbelievably, did not end in their grisly deaths. (When you read the book you will discover the horrific manner in which Kearney killed his victims. In short, Kearney preyed on young men, teens and even children.).

"…Personally, I did not perceive any abnormal or peculiar characteristics in his persona; he appeared to be a calm, soft-spoken considerate man, but this compassion turned out to be pure deception to lure victims to their deaths. My brother and I were fortunate; we escaped…" author Tony Stewart, *The Trash Bag Murderer.*

Kearney, an engineer with an IQ of 180 (genius territory) turned himself in to authorities in 1977 (along with his lover and roommate David Hill) and confessed to the murders of over 32 males (the true number is thought to me up to 43). Hill was never convicted for lack of evidence. The details of Kearney's crimes are very tough to read but Stewart has been thorough in his detailing of the victims' lives and how they came to be killed. What I liked about this book is the personal element of Stewart's knowledge of Kearney and also the extensive research that the author has put into the story. As a working journalist I appreciated the research and determination Stewart has communicated in his work. A quest for the truth and also a respect for the victims and their families is at the heart of the book and Stewart has been dogged in chasing up case files and details of Kearney and the police investigation into his crimes that span the 1960s and 1970s in California and even Mexico.

There is plenty of extra content in this book beside the story – transcripts of interviews, a summary of Kearney's crimes and letters from relatives of the victims. There's also the extra-fascinating chapter where Stewart ponders whether Kearney could be the infamous Zodiac Killer who has never been found.

Verdict*: Definitely worth a read.*

Book Reviews

Tony Stewart not only brings this horror-movie-like true story to searing life, he has a chilling personal connection to the killer that adds an additional layer of tension and fear to an already terrifying tale. One wonders how many more Patrick Wayne Kearney's are roaming the streets today. – DARY MATERA, author of Stolen Masterpiece Tracker - The Dangerous Life of the FBI's Number 1 Art Sleuth

Tony Stewart's new book entitled, The Trash Bag Murderer is a sensational true story about a serial killer who murdered 43 people in cold blood. This is sincerely one of the most shocking crime stories of our century, nearly as inspiring and fascinating as my lifestyle portrayed in the movie Goodfellas - HENRY HILL, The Original Goodfella, (Academy Award winning film Goodfellas, based o n Hill's life), author of Gangsters and Goodfellas, Wise guys, Witness Protection, and Life on the Run

Tony Stewart survived to reveal this personal account on Patrick Kearney, a bizarre psychopathic killer with a severe personality disorder that manifested an aggressive behavior, which led to the deaths of over forty innocent people. Stewart has reopened the files to uncover gruesome truths and shed new light on the case. A fascinating true story! – JOSEPH R. GANNASCOLI – Vito --Star of the HBO Series: THE SOPRANOS, author of; A MEAL TO DIE FOR: A Culinary Novel of Crime

Tony Stewart's new book "The Trash Bag Murderer" is a bizarre true to life, suspenseful psychological thriller that so terrifying, it redefines the meaning of fear. A horrific account about confessed serial killer Patrick Kearney, who brutally butchered an estimated forty-three innocent people, dismembering and disposing the bodies in trash bags along the side of California highways. This narrative, as told personally by Stewart, the only survivor that lived to share this quivering, eyeopening story is a MUST to read! JOHN FIORE – Gigi Cestone -- Star of the HBO Series: THE SOPRANOS, Law and Order, NYPD Blue, and several other prominent films.

Tony Stewart, the survivor of a brutal serial killer, Patrick Wayne Kearney, reveals his own chilling encounter and escape from the most heinous executioner of the 70's. Stewart adds unveiling irrefutable new evidence that could change the course of the investigation and possibly re-open the case, leading to a final closure of one of the most gruesome killing sprees of all time. Fascinating reading. GEORGIA DURANTE - author of The Company She Keeps - www.thecompanyshekeeps.com

"Tony Stewart's TRASH BAG MURDERER is sure to be another sensational HIT! (Pardon the Pun!) It's exciting the way Tony paints us a picture with his words that is so intriguing and incredibly worth telling. His palette of subject matter is so mysteriously dark and compelling that it draws you in completely, and you can't put the book down! His palette is all too familiar to me, as an artist who has also painted some of history's most famous -- and infamous."-- MICHAEL BELL, Celebrity Artist http://mbellart.com

Tony Stewart delivers a bone-chilling account of survival in a situation that 99.99% of us assume could never happen to us. This story illustrates the reality that we do indeed live in a world where monsters are real and the boogey-man does exist despite what our parents told us. Tony's account gives us a glimpse inside the insanity and terror that surrounds a serial killer.
Rick Wilson - Actor "W.D. Jones" co-star - Crime Wave, The Boys of Summerville

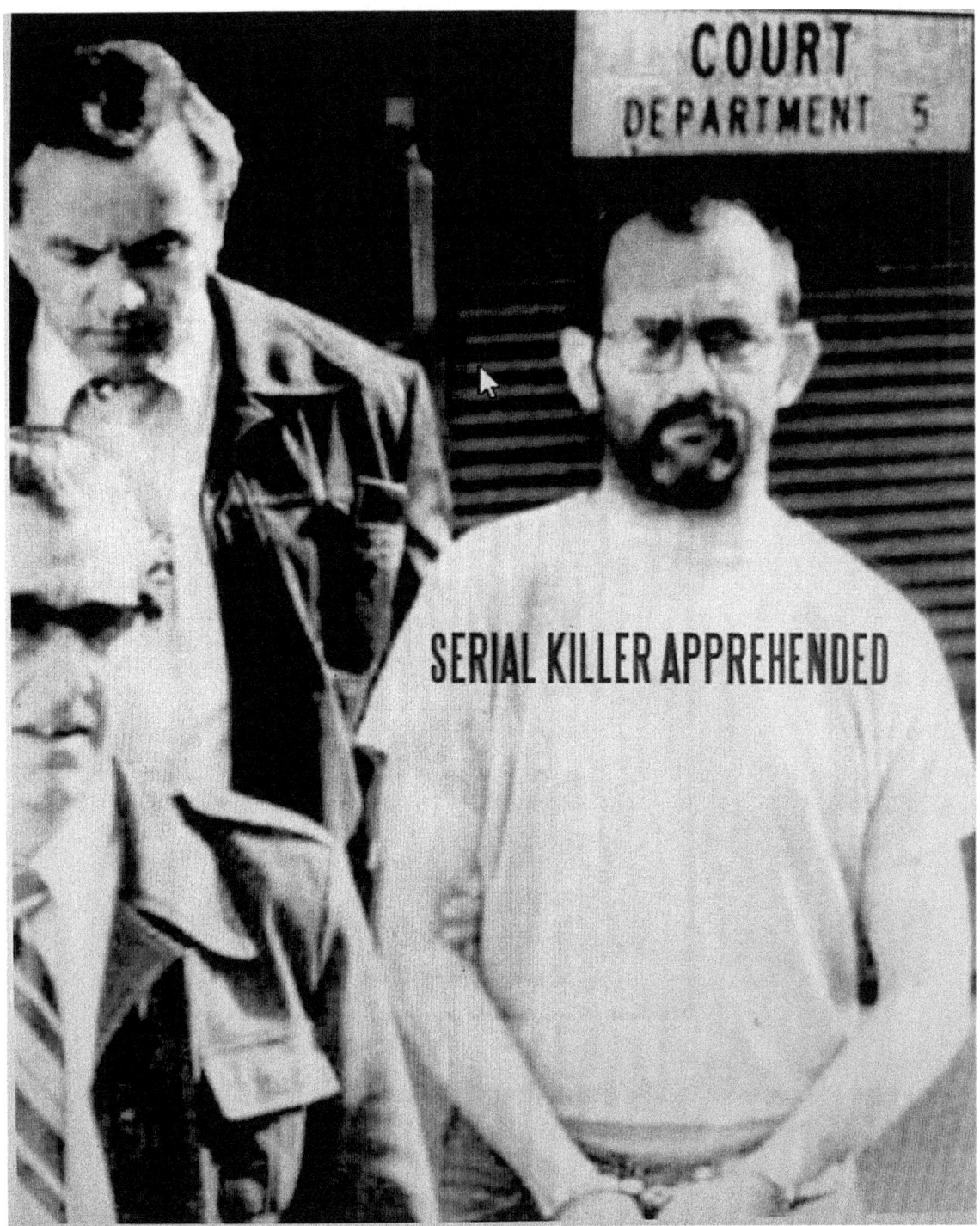

LA'S DEADLIEST SERIAL KILLER

By Tony Stewart (Survivor)

Serial Killer Patrick Kearney
The Trash Bag Murderer

Copyright © 2019 Tony Stewart
Email: Dillinger72234@aol.com

Lightning Source UK Ltd.
Milton Keynes UK
UKHW032312120819
347790UK00003B/267/P